ONE DAY AT
FENWAY

ONE DAY AT
FENWAY

A DAY IN THE LIFE
OF BASEBALL IN AMERICA

STEVE KETTMANN

ATRIA BOOKS

NEW YORK LONDON TORONTO SYDNEY

ATRIA BOOKS

1230 Avenue of the Americas
New York, NY 10020

Copyright © 2004 by Steve Kettmann

ISBN: 0-7434-8365-0

First Atria Books hardcover edition August 2004

10 9 8 7 6 5 4 3 2 1

ATRIA BOOKS is a trademark of Simon & Schuster, Inc.

Manufactured in the United States of America

For information regarding special discounts for bulk purchases,
please contact Simon & Schuster Special Sales at 1-800-456-6798 or
business@simonandschuster.com.

For Sarah

This book represents a group effort at capturing the flavor of a single baseball game between the Boston Red Sox and New York Yankees at Fenway Park on August 30, 2003. Jorge Arangure, Andres Cala, Pete Danko, Pedro Gomez, Tom Keegan, Brian Lee, Sean McCann, Brian McGrory, Amy K. Nelson, John Plotz, Samantha Power, Sarah Ringler, Gaku Tashiro, and Mitch Zuckoff were more coauthors than researchers. The author takes sole responsibility for all questions of interpretation and style, but dedicates the book to this All-Star team of reporters, who followed different people around for the day or contributed other important research.

CAST OF CHARACTERS
(IN ORDER OF APPEARANCE)

JOE TORRE, MANAGER, NEW YORK YANKEES: Torre was born in Brooklyn and batted .297 and hit 252 home runs over eighteen seasons in the big leagues, and had also managed the New York Mets, Atlanta Braves, and St. Louis Cardinals.

JOHN HENRY, OWNER, BOSTON RED SOX: A former soybean farmer in Arkansas and Illinois who never graduated from college, but did study philosophy at UCLA, UC Riverside, and Victor Valley Junior College in Victorville, California, Henry started out in the futures market. Known among his peers as the Bill James of currency traders, for his skill with mathematical modeling, Henry was a part owner of the New York Yankees and sole owner of the Florida Marlins before buying the Boston Red Sox.

LARRY LUCCHINO, CEO, RED SOX: Once an attorney, Lucchino was general counsel to both the Washington Redskins and Baltimore Orioles before spending more than five years as Orioles president, starting in 1988. He was president of the San Diego Padres from

1995 to 2001, and took over as president and CEO of the Red Sox in February 2002.

BRIAN CASHMAN, GENERAL MANAGER, YANKEES: The Yankees' longest-serving general manager since George Steinbrenner bought the team, Cashman grew up in Kentucky as a diehard Dodger fan ("Ron Cey was my hero, because he was short like me, but still he swung a big bat and did a lot of damage"). He worked as Yankee farm director and assistant general manager before taking over as GM after Bob Watson quit in February 1998.

DEBI LITTLE, WIFE OF RED SOX MANAGER GRADY LITTLE: She was active in charity work along with players' wives and was also working on a children's book about going to a game at Fenway Park.

GEORGE MITCHELL, RED SOX FAN: A former Democratic senator from Maine, Senate majority leader, and diplomat, Mitchell was a life-long Red Sox fan and owned a small piece of the team.

RAFAEL AVILA, RETIRED DODGERS EXECUTIVE: The father of Detroit Tigers assistant general manager Al Avila, Rafael Avila spent twenty-nine years working for the Los Angeles Dodgers, much of that time as director of the club's Dominican Republic academy, founded by Avila and Al Campanis in 1974.

RICH MALONEY, SCOREBOARD OPERATOR, FENWAY PARK: Since 1990, when he was a sophomore at Boston College, Maloney worked inside the Green Monster at Fenway Park, putting up scores by hand. He had a day job, too, working as a printing-services salesman.

PETER FARRELLY, RED SOX FAN: The writer and director (or codirector, with his brother Bobby Farrelly) of seven movies, including *Dumb & Dumber, There's Something About Mary,* and *Shallow Hal,* Farrelly grew up in Rhode Island as a Red Sox fan.

THEO GORDON, YANKEE FAN: A Navy lifer, born in Trinidad but raised in New York, and a committed Yankee fan.

JANE BAXTER, RED SOX FAN: An archeology professor at DePaul University and a Red Sox fan since she was a girl, she had a dorm room at Boston University with a view of the Fenway Park infield.

MARTY MARTIN, RED SOX FAN: The product of a broken home, he kicked around from foster home to foster home and never had time for sports, but finally made it to Fenway Park for the first time at age thirty-five, and was looking forward to a return visit.

SPIKE LEE, YANKEE FAN: Known as a New York Knicks fan given to jawing with opposing players, especially Reggie Miller, Lee grew up a baseball fan long before he turned to directing movies, breaking through with *She's Gotta Have It* in 1986 and directing seventeen more.

THEO EPSTEIN, GENERAL MANAGER, RED SOX: The son of a novelist and grandson of one of the cowriters of *Casablanca,* Epstein graduated from Yale and added a University of San Diego law degree. His first job in baseball was summer intern for the Baltimore Orioles, in 1992, and later he moved on to the San Diego Padres, working up to director of baseball operations. The Red Sox named him vice president and general manager in November 2002, one month before his twenty-ninth birthday.

ELEANOR ADAIR, RED SOX FAN: A highly regarded scientist with a Ph.D. in physics and physiology from the University of Wisconsin, she started attending Red Sox games in the late 1930s, and went on to build an international reputation as an expert on the physiological effects of microwave radiation.

BOB ADAIR, RED SOX FAN: Physics professor emeritus at Yale, where he started in 1960 and for years ran a large particle–physics group, Adair wrote *The Physics of Baseball* and consulted for Major League Baseball on the physics of bats, high-tech systems for training umpires, and other topics.

HIDEKI MATSUI, YANKEE OUTFIELDER: Called "Godzilla" back home in Japan, where he has the cult following of a rock star, Matsui was a Yomiuri Giants star for ten years, and hit fifty homers in 2002, his last season before signing with the Yankees for the 2003 season.

DAVID MELLOR, GROUNDSKEEPER, FENWAY PARK: Author of two books on grass, including *The Lawn Bible,* Mellor grew up a third-generation Red Sox fan, smashed up his knee in high school, ending any hopes of a playing career, and earned an agronomy degree at Ohio State University. He became director of grounds at Fenway Park in early 2001.

EUCLIDES ROJAS, BULLPEN COACH, RED SOX: Known as the Dennis Eckersley of Cuba for his record as that country's all-time saves leader, Rojas fled Cuba on a raft in August 1994, along with his wife and young son, and spent six months at Guantanamo Bay. He joined the Red Sox as pitching coach before the 2003 season.

BILL MUELLER, THIRD BASEMAN, RED SOX: A fifteenth-round pick (San Francisco Giants) after playing at Southwest Missouri State, Mueller went on to hit .290 or better for the Giants four straight seasons, playing third base, before injuries threatened his career. He joined the Red Sox in January 2003.

LOU MERLONI, SECOND BASEMAN, RED SOX: Born in Framingham, Massachusetts, Merloni grew up a Red Sox fan and played baseball at Framingham South High and Providence College, and was a tenth-round draft pick of the Red Sox in 1993.

MARIANO RIVERA, CLOSER, YANKEES: The Panamanian-born Rivera had been the Yankees' closer, or ninth-inning specialist, since 1997, when he took over after serving a brief apprenticeship as setup man to former closer John Wetteland.

MARK CARLSON, UMPIRE: A former United States Marine, Carlson was born in Joliet, Illinois, and was a catcher on the Parkland College baseball team. He graduated from the Brinkman-Froemming

Umpire School in 1993, and umpired in six different regional leagues before calling his first major-league game in June 1999.

GRADY LITTLE, MANAGER, RED SOX: The Red Sox manager since March 2002, Little was born in Abilene, Texas, and after a brief minor-league playing career, spent time as a cotton farmer, and then managed sixteen years in the minor leagues.

HEO SAE-HWAN, HIGH-SCHOOL COACH, SOUTH KOREA: As the coach at Kwangju Jeil High School in South Korea, he had been a major influence on the submarine pitcher Byung-Hyun Kim, and had also coached Hee Seop Choi and Jae Weong Seo.

SNAPSHOT: THE LAST OUT

The game had gotten to Joe Torre. He sat in the visitors' dugout at Fenway Park and watched Red Sox catcher Jason Varitek ground out to end the thing, then turned to hawkeyed pitching coach Mel Stottlemyre, because Torre always turned to Stottlemyre after a game and shook his hand.

"Should we sit here for a minute just to make sure the game *is* over?" Torre asked Stottlemyre.

Torre did not mention it to the reporters who asked afterward about Mariano Rivera almost self-destructing in the eighth inning, but the kind of exhaustion Torre felt that day in Boston reminded him of what it had been like four years earlier, going through his fight with prostate cancer.

"That eighth inning was probably the toughest I've ever had to endure," Torre confided the next morning. "We have the best closer in baseball. To see it starting to fall apart makes for a very uneasy feeling for me. Once I get Rivera in the game, there is no other strategic thing I can do. I have to sit and watch. It's like sitting at home waiting for the doctor to call and tell you you're all right."

Red Sox owner John Henry had written the game off in the top of the ninth, and his thoughts went to his counterpart, Yankee owner George Steinbrenner, who earlier that season had cried after the Yankees came out on top in another wild Yanks-Sox game.

"You think George will cry after this one?" Henry asked.

He directed the question to Red Sox CEO Larry Lucchino, sitting nearby in Henry's nearly empty luxury box behind home plate. Lucchino, notorious for his "Evil Empire" taunting of Steinbrenner and the Yankees the previous off-season, could only muster a tight smile.

Like Joe Torre, Henry and Lucchino were so depleted by the time Varitek grounded out to end the game, they did not know what to do with themselves. Lucchino squeezed an empty plastic water bottle so hard it cracked, and finally stood up slowly, as if he were testing his joints.

"This is the way the game ends," Henry said. "Not with a bang but a whimper."

Yankee general manager Brian Cashman got up from his seat behind home plate and let loose with a sound like air being released from a tire. His stomach felt hollow. He thought to himself that if he did not eat something soon, he might pass out. They would love that in Boston.

"Oh my God," he said.

The night before, he had left Fenway Park after the Red Sox soundly thrashed the Yankees and fielded a phone call from Steinbrenner. The owner wanted to know if his general manager was really at the game.

"I didn't see you," Steinbrenner said.

"Well, I was behind home plate," Cashman said.

That was not good enough for Steinbrenner. He wanted Cashman to sit right by the Yankee dugout so the players would be reminded every time they ran back in from the field that he was there keeping an eye on them.

"I want you where I can see you!" Steinbrenner said. "I want you by the dugout! You sit in my seats!"

But Cashman had not sat in Steinbrenner's seats. He had sat behind home plate, just as he had for Friday night's opener of the three-game series, and if the Yankees had lost the game, Cashman knew he would have had to listen to more shouts of "I didn't see you!" No wonder he felt relieved.

Down the first-base line, a few rows back from the field, Debi Little tried to avoid the obvious thoughts for any wife of a big-league manager, especially a Red Sox manager. Every win was one more day without worry, and every loss meant it was time to wonder where she and her husband would be next year. Her husband was more philosophical about the uncertainty than she was. He knew he would be second-guessed, disparaged, and dismissed. He knew that if his team did anything less than win the World Series, he would be to blame.

Grady had learned patience during the five years he spent driving a tractor through his cotton fields in Texas, cranking the country tunes and sometimes working right through the night. He knew better than to think the criticism a manager faced in Boston really said that much about him. Heck, Grady Little liked to tell people about how he could lay claim to being the first manager ever fired by George Steinbrenner, and that had been thirty years earlier. He knew how things went. One of his strengths as a manager was his lack of illusions, and that applied to himself and his own prospects, too.

For Debi, it was impossible to gain any distance. Sometimes she thought back to those first weeks after she and Grady started dating. He introduced her to his father, who had an immediate challenge for her.

"Hi, how are you?" he asked her. "Do you know what a triple is?"

Grady's father wanted Debi to know she would be marrying baseball, too.

"Yes, sir, I do!" she had told him.

Debi would not have it any other way, all these years later, but sometimes she did feel worn out by all the ups and downs. Mariano Rivera took the flip from Nick Johnson and stepped on first base and the game was over and Debi, too, sat and waited. It took so much out of her, putting all this emotion into a game. She needed a few minutes to catch her breath and put on a brave smile before she could walk up to the Family Room near the Red Sox clubhouse and try to set a good example for the other wives.

Senator George J. Mitchell was not a man who liked to hurry, but he was in a hurry now. His airline would call his name if he did not report to the gate for his flight to London and on to Belfast. So far he had checked half a dozen sets, and had no luck. Up ahead was a small lounge that was sure to have a TV. Mitchell, never sentimental except where baseball was concerned, allowed himself to hope for a break. But this TV, too, was tuned to a news channel.

Mitchell had been at Fenway until the sixth inning and pulled himself away for the drive to Logan. Post–September 11 security headaches forced even former Senate majority leaders to make adjustments in their schedules. The taxi ride from Fenway brought immediate disappointment: no radio. How could a taxi not have a radio? All Mitchell could do was ask the driver to hurry. He made it to Logan with time to spare, and changed cars and drove with his friends in giant circles through the maze of the Logan parking structure. They hunted for patches of good reception to follow as much of the eighth inning as possible. Now Mitchell was out of time. But before he handed over his ticket and took his seat, he called the Red Sox switchboard to ask what had happened.

"The Sox lost," he was told.

Once on the plane, Mitchell let his thoughts wander. Somewhere near Newfoundland he was finally able to tell himself, "Oh well, we'll get them tomorrow and next weekend in New York." And with that, the chief negotiator of the Good Friday Agreement in Northern Ireland drifted off to sleep.

One thousand, six hundred and forty-seven miles south of Boston, the game playing out at Fenway Park had come to feel a lot more distant to the people watching from the Champions Sports Bar in Santo Domingo, Dominican Republic. The sports bar had TV sets sprouting up in every nook and cranny, but none had shown Rafael Avila anything he wanted to see. He was the one who had first seen what Pedro Martinez was, and what he would be in baseball. Avila did not discover Pedro Martinez. No one discovered Pedro Martinez. Pedro just was.

Avila still smiled thinking of young Pedro, a skinny fourteen-year-old kid who was always tagging along with his older brother Ramon, another future big-leaguer. Pedro carried Ramon's bags, ran errands, anything at all, just so long as they let him hang around with the Dominican junior national team that Avila was managing. Young Pedro was always asking to play, so they would send him out to fill in at shortstop, or left field, or second base, anywhere and everywhere. He soaked up as much baseball as he could and listened closely to anything Avila said. Back then he was all promise. But now as Avila looked around at the kitsch on the walls of the Champions Sports Bar and nursed his Campari and ice, he knew that Martinez had started down the long, slow slide that sooner or later pulled all great athletes back toward ordinary.

★   ★   ★

Out in left field, inside the Green Monster, Rich Maloney was not taking it well. You had to be a fan to work in the empty space behind the left-field Wall game after game after game, putting up numbers by hand, and Maloney had been working out there thirteen years. He was not thrilled with Grady Little's managing choices that afternoon. He thought he had let Joe Torre dictate events. Maloney looked out through his small peekhole and saw two doves touch down on the warning track just outside. He hoped it was a sign. The doves glanced at each other quickly, and flew off.

As Joe Torre was not shaking Mel Stottlemyre's hand, and Larry Lucchino was crunching his spring-water bottle, and John Henry was staring silently out over the field, and Brian Cashman was exhaling, and Debi Little was collecting herself, and George Mitchell was hurrying around Logan Airport, and Rafael Avila was looking around the sports bar in Santo Domingo, Rich Maloney was reaching for a metal rectangle painted with that most inarguable of baseball figures, the zero. He was almost in a hurry to hold it up. Like many fans, he had a perverse desire to get on with it and accept the worst outcome as soon as possible. But instead of putting the figure up on the board for the bottom of the ninth inning, once Rivera touched first base, he turned to a visitor spending the game with him behind the scoreboard in left field.

"Want to do the honors?" he said with a sly smile, handing over the white zero. "Put a fork in it."

COUNTING THE DAYS: BUILDUP TO THE LAST SATURDAY IN AUGUST

To most of the country, September 28, 1960, was a date that carried no magic and no baggage. Presidential politics had lurched into the television era two nights earlier with the first Kennedy-Nixon debate. Cue up black-and-white images of young Jack, tanned and confident in his narrow-lapeled suit, squinting commandingly at haggard, dodgy-looking Nixon. Nikita Khrushchev, the round little Russian premier, was one day away from disrupting a U.N. session with one of his fist-pounding tantrums. Fred and Wilma and Dino would make their network debut on *The Flintstones* two nights later. But in New England, time might as well have stopped on September 28.

Time only worked right when it had somewhere to go. Ideally, the future got to be the future and the past knew its place. But to any New England baseball fan, which was to say, just about anyone in New England, the past long ago overflowed its banks. People believed, really believed, that the pain and disappointment they held as a kind of collective birthright offered a reliable foretaste of what came next. It all went back to losing Babe Ruth to the Yankees for a wad of cash back in 1920, of course, and lived on in countless late-season collapses and Game Seven reality checks, summed up with coded phrases like "Bill Buckner" or "Bucky Dent." The pain and disappointment were what people talked about most, but it might have been true that no single moment better summed up the mix of emotions that come with being a Red Sox fan than Ted Williams's last game.

Peter Farrelly was there that day in 1960. His dad, Doc Farrelly, would always remember the time his own father first brought him through the tunnel into Fenway Park, just as Ted Williams was batting, and the chills he felt all down his spine. Doc was actually a Braves fan—dating back to his boyhood love of the Boston Braves—but he was sure Williams's last game would be something special, and he had made a point of bringing Peter and his younger brother Bobby to the game.

The Farrellys sat down the first-base line, a few dozen rows deep, and the boys followed their father's lead. He had often told them how special Williams was, and what a graceful, fluid hitter he was. Every time Williams came up to the plate, the boys noticed the way their father watched Williams and they, too, could not take their eyes off him. Peter was almost four, Bobby barely two, and neither had any clear recollection of the game. But to say they did not remember would be wrong. Every real Red Sox fan remembers that day: the cold, dreary weather, the scattering of fans at Fenway, and of course the tremendous home run Williams hit in his last at-bat.

"Lo and behold, he didn't disappoint," Doc Farrelly said.

More than forty years later, the day stayed with Peter as one of the three or four most indelible of his life, almost up there with the time in first grade when he heard that JFK had been shot. He started to think about taking his own son, Bob, to his first game at Fenway. The boy had been to a game in Los Angeles, and another one in Miami, but never in Boston.

Unlike Bobby Farrelly, who somehow wound up as a Dodger fan (a *Dodger* fan!), Peter Farrelly had always been a Red Sox fan. He thrilled like a Red Sox fan, dreamed like a Red Sox fan, and cursed his own tormented faith like a Red Sox fan. Growing up in Rhode Island, his friends would call and say, "Let's go to the Fens." That was the destination of choice, like Wrigley Field in Chicago. Farrelly found that even into his thirties, as he threw himself into making movies for a living and scored successes with *Dumb & Dumber* and *There's Something About Mary,* his love for the Red Sox was somehow a constant. It still unleashed in him a thrillingly confused mix of emotions and still prompted him to strange outbursts.

Take the Fourth of July party at actor Jim Belushi's house on Martha's Vineyard, for example. One minute Farrelly was standing there blending into the crowd as much as a Farrelly brother ever blends into a crowd. The next thing you knew, he was across the room bear-hugging a thin, reserved man in his fifties who had no idea what was happening. It could not be helped. It was just something that had to be done.

"Man, I'm so grateful for what you've done!" Farrelly kept repeating.

The thin, reserved man was John Henry.

"I'm still sick about the Boston Garden being gone," the millionaire movie director told the billionaire baseball owner. "It makes me sad to think about the Fleet Center, which is a soulless place. The Red Sox always change. It's been twenty years since Yaz. But the one thing that has stayed the same is Fenway Park. That's what we go to see every year. You've saved this place."

Like many longtime fans, Farrelly worried when Henry and Tom Werner—the producer of *Cosby* and *Roseanne*—bought the team in early 2002 for a cool $700 million, the most ever paid for a baseball franchise, and put Lucchino in charge as CEO and president. Who were these guys? Could they be trusted? They could, it turned out. Henry and Lucchino came in with open minds and open hearts. They were smart enough to know when they had a winning hand to play, and Fenway was that. The trick was having the guts to make changes.

No one talked about it now, but when the new owners first said they were putting seats on top of the big green wall in left field, the famous Green Monster, a lot of people thought they were crazy. The Monster was what gave Fenway its character. All those pitchers twisting in bed at night, sweating out visions of medium-deep fly balls landing for homers, and all those crazy only-at-Fenway, line-shot-off-the-wall singles—you couldn't mess with something as special as that. Actually, you could. The new group put a few rows of seats on top of the Monster, and they were a huge hit. No one missed the netting that was there before.

To Farrelly, John Henry was a genius, and the Green Monster seats proved it. To Farrelly, the new seats and the other home-improvement projects under way at the old ballpark somehow made the place more like itself. They kept it how it was in all the important ways, only more so. They somehow made it seem a little more green, a little more compact and intimate, and a little more quirky and eccentric.

Every year, no matter what else had been going on in his life, the old buzz kicked in for Farrelly the first time he walked through the tunnel and back inside Fenway Park. The old ballpark was as much a part of the family tradition as tangerines in their Christmas stockings, and this year Farrelly would be taking Bob to his first game there. They would be catching a Saturday game in late August on what would have been Ted Williams's eighty-fifth birthday. The Yankees would be in town, facing Pedro Martinez. First place in the American League East might or might not be at stake, but Farrelly knew he would be giving his four-year-old son an unforgettable look at baseball as a happening, an event to breathe in and slowly exhale. Farrelly hoped that when it was all over, Bob would not be quite the same. Come to think of it, he hoped he wouldn't be, either.

Theo Gordon was tired of the lies. He had never told so many in his life, and it kept getting harder all the time—even if a lot of them were so trivial, it was almost a stretch to count them as lies.

Gordon kept track of all of them, to keep himself honest, if you could call it that, and so far he had told Jane forty-five. The more you told, the more you had to remember, and the greater chance you had of forgetting and tripping yourself up.

It was hard to believe Theo and Jane had met only five months earlier. That meeting had not exactly been storybook, or at least not storybook in the way one of his relatives back in Trinidad would have thought of it. They met playing dominoes online. Not that Theo was the kind of man who had trouble meeting women, but Navy life did come with certain realities. He was at the base in Virginia when Jane read his online profile and struck up a chat session with him. Now they were planning a future together. He had served sixteen years so far, and soon enough he would reach twenty and early retirement.

His thirty-sixth birthday was coming up in August, and he expected it to be quite a day. Jane had bought them a pair of tickets for a Red Sox–Yankees game at Fenway the last weekend of the month. Baseball was one of their common interests, or maybe obsession was the word, but they had to make certain allowances, considering their one big difference. Theo was born in Trinidad but moved to New York at age two and grew up a committed Yankee fan. Jane was a lifelong Red Sox fan.

An archeology professor at DePaul University in Chicago, Jane Baxter had been raised in the town of Lunenburg, Massachusetts, less than an hour's drive west-northwest from Fenway. Her father loved to take her and her friends to games, and had fun encouraging the kids to stay alert. He had a standing rule that he would buy a hot dog for the first kid to notice that someone hit the switch on the big orange triangle up on the famous CITGO sign.

Later, when Jane went to Boston University to study archeology, she had a room in Myles Standish Hall with a clear view of the infield. This was no accident, and no ordinary dorm. Originally a hotel, it was built in 1928 in the shape of a boat, and had rooms with names like the Captain's Cabin and Silver Lagoon. Babe Ruth himself used to fancy the place, and often stayed on the eighth floor. (Suite 818 was said to be his favorite.) He liked the view of the Charles River and, of course, Fenway Park. Jane couldn't quite swing a year in Suite 818, but she came close. She wandered the halls looking for what seemed like the best available view, and knocked on the door of 927 for a look from inside. The young women living there the year before her were not Sox fans.

"I knocked on the door and asked them if you could see the park," Jane recalled. "They said, 'Uh, maybe you can. Take a look. We have no idea.'"

She did, and you could, and she spent many happy afternoons in that room. She would keep the TV tuned to that day's game as a backup, and watch as much of the action as she could follow by looking out her window. To say that Fenway was in her blood was an understatement. The place was almost family, which was why she had been excited about surprising Theo Gordon with a visit to Fenway to celebrate his birthday, but he had found out weeks before. Now it was his turn to try to keep a secret. So far, at forty-five lies and counting, his luck had held out.

★   ★   ★

Fenway Park sits only 120 miles away from Bristol, Connecticut, where Marty Martin had spent most of his life, but he would never have seen the inside of the place if not for his neighbor. Martin was thirty-five when he visited Fenway for the first time. That had been one year earlier, during the summer of 2002, thanks to a group bus trip his neighbor Bob organized. Martin liked what he saw and heard and smelled. He liked the feeling of sitting in the crowded old ballpark surrounded by giddy fans. It almost made him feel like a kid again, which in Martin's case took some doing, since he never much felt like a kid when he was a kid.

His home life had been rough. His father drank and his parents fought often and loudly and Martin suffered from asthma. His parents divorced when he was twelve and he bounced from institution to institution, eventually becoming a ward of the state. Later he was in foster care, but again, nothing lasted for him and he was sent from one foster family to the next.

"I was out partying a lot," he said. "I was always out running away from the family problems, instead of learning how to deal with them."

His father had always been a Red Sox fan, and passed that along to Marty, but he had other things on his mind than sports.

"I was in friggin' hell," he said. "The institutions never let you watch TV unless you earned it."

The experience left Martin with an almost clinical detachment about what he had lost out on, and a certain durable cheerfulness about whatever came next in life. He had worked for American Medical Response since 1995 driving a wheelchair-equipped van painted red, white, and blue ("Red Sox colors," he said). He liked

his fear of making a mistake. His own father even thought so. But no, Epstein's poker face was there to keep the world from knowing how sure he was in his own abilities. He was making good decisions, and he knew it. He wanted to hide not his insecurity, but his security. Sometimes, in quiet moments, Epstein had to laugh about it.

"He's extremely talented and very bright and he's a huge Red Sox fan," Brian Cashman said. "Unfortunately, they've got a great one for themselves. My impression of him is right from the start he was someone who knew what he wanted to do. He was very comfortable that he could do the job. He's just a very smart, confident individual that has his eyes on the prize, which is a world championship, and I have no doubt he's going to have one at some point. I've told him I just don't want it to be on my watch."

Epstein was not cocky. He was far too open-eyed and canny to fall into that trap. Anyone whose mistakes were scrutinized by so many thousands of people learned soon enough that even triumphs came with trade-offs. Epstein knew what he had and what he did not have. He was baseball smart in a way many executives were not. He brought a fresh intelligence to the job, and far more experience than seemed possible for someone his age. He had already put in more than ten years of work for different teams, and learned from savvy decision-makers like Lucchino and San Diego general manger Kevin Towers. People who thought Epstein was uncertain at twenty-eight, when he became the youngest GM in baseball, just did not know him.

"What keeps me sane and honest is the routine of daily life," Epstein said. "I don't take myself too seriously. The whole job is such a joke. I mean, there are 162 games. If you take yourself too seriously, you'd be in huge trouble."

Balance was important to Epstein. He knew it would take years in his job to master all the details. He wanted everything right now, but he also had a curious kind of patience. His sister had bought him a guitar a few years earlier as a birthday present, and he did his best to play for an hour or two every day.

"If I get fired or win a World Series, whichever comes first, it has definitely crossed my mind to grow an Afro and become a roadie," he said.

You could even say guitar was Epstein's way of showing how confident he was in his Red Sox job. That time on stage with Eddie Vedder and the rest of Pearl Jam was fun, but it was more than that. The two had hit it off. Epstein was in awe of Vedder, and had a computer screen saver that showed him on stage with Pearl Jam. Vedder was intrigued by Epstein's combination of surface calm and poised intensity, which struck him as a refreshing contrast with record executives.

"He's got a lot of gears in there, and they all seem to be working together," Vedder said.

The Red Sox had played a series out in Seattle just two weekends before this three-game series at Fenway with the Yankees, and Vedder and his drummer stopped by the ballpark before a couple of the games. Epstein and Vedder converged on the infield and talked like old friends. They grinned when they first saw each other, and listened to each other the way you do when you can't think of anywhere else you'd rather be. Vedder was wearing long, baggy khaki shorts, a green L.L. Bean shirt, and rock-climbing boots, and it was easy to miss him, but no one did. Epstein strolled over to first baseman Kevin Millar and told him "Kev, Kev, when you're done hitting, Eddie wants to talk to you." Millar almost hopped up and down with excitement. Vedder had a dreamy intensity in conversation, and that day in Seattle, Epstein seemed to soak up some of his rock-star magnetism.

Eleanor Adair first started going to Fenway Park not long after new owner Tom Yawkey decided in 1934 to tear down the wooden grandstand and replace it with concrete and steel. The ballpark had been basically the same ever since. Eleanor's father would take her from nearby Arlington to see Ted Williams and Johnny Pesky and other Red Sox stars of the late 1930s and early 1940s. Other events mixed with her recollections of baseball back then. Lefty Grove ran off an amazing twenty-game home winning streak the same season that the Great Hurricane of 1938 hit Boston in September. Eleanor's father had just put up a big new neon sign at his Dodge dealership, and he was worried sick that it had been toppled by the high winds. He dragged Eleanor and her mother along for a wind-whipped walk down Massachusetts Avenue to check on the sign. Along the way they saw trees falling on both sides of the street, wires snapping, and a church steeple collapsing, but the neon sign survived the storm.

Sixty-five years later, it surprised Eleanor a little to realize how much she was looking ahead to another visit to Fenway Park, and how much she could still tap into that first girlish enthusiasm she had felt for the game sitting at her father's side at Fenway. Her life had been far too busy for baseball ever to crowd out her other interests and take over as an obsession. She earned her Ph.D. in physics and physiology at the University of Wisconsin and developed an international reputation through her work on the physiological effects of microwave radiation. Among her responsibilities over the years was a spot on the board of directors of the American Himalayan Foundation and her current post as chairman of the executive committee of the International Committee on Electromagnetic Safety. She had been a dedicated traveler for many decades, and when she and her husband, Bob, lost the youngest of their three children, James, in a 1978 climbing accident at Yosemite, she honored his memory by trekking great mountains all over the world. She had visited at least forty-three countries, including Nepal, where she trekked Annapurna. She had met the Dalai Lama several times and knew Sir Edmund Hillary.

"She calls him Ed," her husband said. "He calls her Ellie."

Bob Adair grew up in Depression-era Milwaukee, where his father worked in a factory as a stocking maker. He graduated from high school in 1941, finished three years at the University of Wisconsin, and in 1943 volunteered for the war, winding up serving under Patton's command in the 94th Infantry Division. He was leading a night patrol along the banks of the Rhine in March 1945 when heavy German machine-gun fire left him badly wounded. He spent the next year in hospitals, and came back to the United States determined to follow his passion for studying physics. He was teaching at Wisconsin when Eleanor transferred there as a graduate student. She had applied to Johns Hopkins, but was rejected with a letter that said, more or less, "We regret to inform

you that we do not accept women because they are a poor risk."
Their first date went well and Bob asked Eleanor if he could see
her again. She wasn't sure. She didn't want to be distracted from
her studies.

"Call me next spring," she said.

Bob persisted, and later they married and moved to Long Island, where he worked at the Brookhaven particle accelerator. Bob
had been planning to go to Chicago to work with the great Enrico
Fermi and his team of nuclear physics researchers, but a chance
meeting with the famous scientist changed his mind. Adair spotted Fermi all alone in an airport, reading *Catcher in the Rye,* and
dared to walk up and introduce himself. Fermi was brusque and
rude and brushed him off. That settled the issue for Bob Adair: He
went to work at Brookhaven instead.

Baseball had always been important to Bob. He was close to
his grandfather, who had played sandlot baseball in the 1890s.
Every time Bob visited his grandparents in Fort Wayne, his grandfather would buy them tickets to a semipro game for a dime apiece
and they would always sit behind third base, since Bob's grandfather had been a third baseman. Back then, minor-league salaries
were so low that many top players just could not afford to play in
the farm system. They could make a buck playing semipro instead,
and the baseball was at the level of Single-A or Double-A. Some of
the best games were against visiting Negro League teams, and Bob
would always remember the thrill of watching the Indianapolis
Clowns or the Cleveland Buckeyes. Bob would later write a famous little book called *The Physics of Baseball,* which explored
many riddles of the game, such as the question of whether a rising

fastball really rises. But as much fun as he had with the physics of the game, it could never touch those afternoons behind third base with his granddad.

All ballplayers had superstitions, and for Hideki Matsui and most Japanese players, there was no doubt that eating fried pork before a game brought good luck. The reason was simple enough: Through an accident of language, the Japanese word for fried pork was the same as the word meaning "to win." Eating *katsu* worked for Matsui that spring, his first playing ball in the United States, when he ate *katsu* and hit a home run in Tampa. That homer made a big impression on everyone and helped ease his transition. This weekend in Boston would be a good time for another home run. Matsui knew this three-game series was crucial. It was all new to him, so he had to go with his instincts and watch the faces of the people he trusted. He had noticed that his manager, Joe Torre, a good man who was strong and unafraid and had always shown Matsui respect, suddenly had a different way of walking. He was slower and almost hunched over. Matsui would have liked to relieve some of that pressure from his manager's shoulders.

The Friday night game in Boston had started well. Matsui came up against Derek Lowe in the first inning with Derek Jeter at third and Jason Giambi at second. Matsui made sure not to swing at any bad pitches, and once it was three balls and two strikes, he got a good pitch to hit and lined it to left field for a double that scored both runners and gave the Yankees a 2–0 lead. But the Boston hitters answered in the bottom of the inning with three runs of their own. Later, Matsui walked after Bernie Williams's leadoff double in the fourth and helped start a three-run Yankee rally that inning. But again, the Red Sox answered immediately, scoring four runs in the fourth, and led the rest of the way. Matsui grounded out his last two times up, and did not even get to step out into the on-deck circle in the ninth. Derek Jeter was the Yankees' last hope, and Scott Williamson struck him out. Matsui couldn't remember the last time Derek Jeter had struck out to end an important game. Come to think of it: How often did Jeter make the last out of *any* game?

Matsui was out of Fenway Park by 11:30 that night, and joined a couple of television reporters for a late meal at a Japanese restaurant. Matsui had sashimi, steamed green beans, soft shell crab, and, most important, the *katsu*. He was back at the team hotel by 1:50 a.m. and was glad to see there were no messages waiting for him. He liked this time of the early morning. If it was 2:00 a.m. in Boston, it was 4:00 p.m. in Tokyo, so he could catch up on his e-mails and send off replies before the end of the workday back in Japan.

He read a few articles online, and spent the most time on one about Phil Mickelson's pitching tryout that day with the Toledo Mud Hens, the Detroit Tigers' Triple-A farm team. The left-handed golfer offered three hundred dollars to anyone who homered off him, but none of the eighteen Mud Hens he faced could do that. Then again, most of them were pitchers. Matsui would have liked a chance to earn that three hundred.

Once he was through with his reading, he changed into the pajamas he always took on the road with him. It was important to feel comfortable and sleep well. That was why he brought his own pillow, too. He set the alarm clock for quarter to nine the next morning, just half an hour before the team bus would be arriving at Fenway, and turned out the light at 3:00 a.m. and drifted off into deep, dreamless sleep.

GAME DAY: MORNING RAIN

The first half-light of day found patches of blue just starting to clear high over Fenway Park. There were also sheets of pale gray clouds and a few fluffy white clusters, but the blue patches told head groundskeeper David Mellor to trust his hunch that they would be able to get in their game that day with no problems. Weather was like family. You did not always like everything it did, but only a fool would get mad at the weather. What you had to do was pay close attention, and follow every small development with the curiosity and alertness of someone who understood that he could always learn something new. You watched out for the weather the way you would a brother, and when it surprised you, you were glad, because that meant it had shown you something new and you could stash that away as one more piece of information and insight to help you try never to be surprised again.

Mellor had hobbled out of bed by 4:20 that morning, grabbed some breakfast, and looked over the morning papers. *The New York Times* had an article in its arts section about a baseball exhibition at the American Folk Art Museum in New York. The article mentioned Mellor's contribution as "one of the artists" in the show, and that made him feel good. Critic Michael Kimmelman cited Mellor's work in rolling the Fenway grass into the Red Sox logo, the American flag, and checkerboards and stripes, all in such a way that the patterns were invisible to players but visible from the stands or on television.

"Call it folk art for the masses, which is not the worst definition of baseball," Kimmelman concluded.

The Red Sox had brought Mellor in before the 2001 season because he worked hard at backing up his practical knowledge with science. He had written the book on grass. Actually, he had written two. His job was to keep the grass at Fenway just the right color and just the right texture, but not in that order. Healthy, luscious-looking green grass made a perfect canvas for a baseball game, but safety and playability always came first. Mellor's crew had more influence over the bounce of the ball than people knew. If a sinkerballer like Derek Lowe was pitching for the Red Sox, they would leave the infield grass unmowed for a day to help knock down all those grounders off the bats of opposing hitters. The ball would zig or zag more or less depending on which type of grass they used. None of it was quite as dramatic as moving the fences in between innings, like former Chicago White Sox owner

Bill Veeck, often called the P. T. Barnum of baseball, but it made Mellor and his crew part of the game in a direct way.

Mellor had a grandfather, Bill Mellor, who had played baseball at Brown and briefly with the Baltimore Orioles in 1902, the last season before that franchise moved to New York and became the Highlanders, later the Yankees. It took Mellor only a couple of minutes to dig through his subterranean office back behind the Fenway Park visitors' dugout to produce the actual letter inviting grandpa Bill to play in the 1939 Hall of Fame Game in Boston. Granddad did not attend, but what mattered was he might have. Mellor might have had a shot as a player, too, if not for all his knee trouble.

He'd had nineteen knee operations so far, but held on to a sense of humor about his mishaps and difficulties. He was almost proud of the time in 1995 when a deranged woman drove her car onto the field before a game at Milwaukee County Stadium and took a run at him. Even as he was doing his best to scamper away, Mellor addressed the woman as "Ma'am." Never a thin man, and six-foot-two, Mellor had to admit he presented a good target. His most recent mishap had come a month earlier during another Red Sox–Yankees series at Fenway. He rolled his ankle running up the dugout steps, broke three bones in his foot, and needed to have a pin inserted. Now he was on crutches and under doctor's orders not to work more than five hours a day. Fat chance of that.

The sun first showed itself over the right-field stands at 6:12 that morning. Somehow the place seemed even more quiet with shafts of light slowly working their way down toward field level. Out in center field, a couple dozen seagulls patrolled the bleachers looking for any scraps of food the clean-up crew had missed the night before. The infield was secure under its white tarp, made of ten-ounce vinyl, which looked more than anything like a giant puffy bandage. You could almost picture the manicured infield healing underneath. Mellor looked around a little before 6:30, checking to see if the crew of groundskeepers had assembled for the work of patching some rough spots in shallow right field.

"Sod just showed up, guys," Mellor said, more as a greeting than a news flash.

Euclides Rojas woke up at eight sharp, shut off his alarm, and smiled. He hadn't had the dream. Maybe it had been a good idea to watch that Western on cable late the night before. Rojas missed playing baseball, the way any former athlete did, only more so, and at first it was always a relief to be back on the mound. That part of the dream was great. Rojas would reach up and adjust his cap, and stare in at the catcher for the sign. Somehow, in the dream, the catcher always called the right pitch, and Rojas never had to shake him off. He would wind and throw and the hitters would go down swinging. Or maybe one would get a hit, and Rojas would get the next batter, and the next, and the next. But sooner or later, no matter how well Rojas pitched, the same thing happened: The game ended, and once it did, Rojas realized he was back in Cuba. That was when it hit him that he was going to have to escape all over again. That was when Rojas's dream became a nightmare.

The raft would never leave him, even if he had left the raft.

Rojas would not have minded dying there on the glass-flat Caribbean. At least he would be dying a free man, making his own choices. But Rojas was not alone. Late at night, especially that terrible day the drinking water ran out, he would take his turn paddling long past midnight, staring up at the stars and down at his wife, Marta, and little Euclides Jr., up at the stars and down at Marta and little Euky. They lucked out and spotted another boat full of people who had extra drinking water with them that they were willing to trade for food. Five days they drifted at sea before the U.S. Coast Guard found them and took them to Guantanamo.

Rojas knew a part of himself would always be adrift out there on the raft, waiting for fate to play its hand. The trick was not so much to let go of that, which was impossible, as to tune in to his new life in America. Rojas would consider himself lucky, the way things turned out, but he was just one person and he was not about to ignore all the people on the island who believed the lies the government fed them, and had no idea how much better life was across the Straits of Florida. Rojas knew the system would fall apart when death finally claimed the one who held it together. He did not like to say his name. No one did. It was enough to pull your fingers down the sides of your face, smoothing an imaginary beard, the way people did on the island.

They used to call Rojas the Cuban Dennis Eckersley. He was Cuba's all-time saves leader, and traveled the world with the national team pitching for Fidel. But the Cuban doctors who worked with the team told Rojas to keep pitching, even though his elbow was a mess. The pain was unbearable. Now he was lucky just throwing batting practice. An American doctor had gone in and fixed his elbow, and Rojas could straighten his arm. But he would never feel right inside until things changed back home. He wasn't a nut. He wasn't one to tell others how to think. But he knew what was right, and what was wrong, and no one could ask him to stop noticing the difference between the two.

He liked to focus on the work of being Red Sox bullpen coach. It kept him sane. It made Cuba seem farther away. He and his wife tried so hard to talk about other things than their family and friends back home in Cuba. He called Marta that Saturday morning before the game against the Yankees, as he always did, if she did not call him first. She and Euclides Jr. lived in Miami, where they had family. The boy's first day of school was coming up that Monday, and Rojas would miss it.

A friend called from Miami to wish him well for the game. Rojas had been surprised to find out just how many Cubans in Florida were Red Sox fans. Many had cheered Luis Tiant, the great Cuban pitcher who spent eight seasons with the Red Sox starting in 1971 and had three twenty-win seasons in Boston. There was no other way to picture Tiant than in a Red Sox uniform, turning his back to the batter just before he made his pitch. Now he had his own Cuban food stand on Yawkey Way just outside Fenway. Tiant had called Rojas the day before, asking him if he had any extra tickets for Saturday's game. That was how tough a ticket it was.

Rojas was at the ballpark by 8:40. His first task, as always, was to whip up a big batch of Cuban coffee. He kept his machine right there in the Red Sox clubhouse. Grady Little was one of the first to develop a taste for the strong, sweet coffee. Jerry Narron, the bench coach, liked it, too. Rojas drank a *cafesito* himself, and dropped off a few around the clubhouse. Later he would take the rest out to the bullpen.

During the Iran-Contra hearings, George Mitchell had told Oliver North that God did not take sides in American politics, but sometimes it did seem as if God took sides in baseball. Mitchell made no apologies for loving baseball, and for him that had always meant loving the Red Sox, hard as that sometimes was. "Every year of my life, I've been saying, 'This is the year,' " he said. "I'm still saying it."

Mitchell pulled out of his summer home in Seal Harbor, Maine, just before dawn, and drove past Frenchman Bay as the sun was coming up. He thought about the so-called Curse of the Bambino and how it was something for the fans, not the players. People were always citing history to make a point in politics, too, and it sounded good, but as a candidate running for office you were busy with the challenge at hand. History would not shake hands for you, or stake out a position for you, or raise money for you, and it would not swing the bat for you or make a pitch for you, either.

Mitchell's name had often been raised as a candidate for baseball commissioner, and there was no doubt he would be a good one. But it was questionable whether baseball's owners would accept someone like Mitchell, a man known to think for himself. One owner approached him in 1994 when he was Senate majority leader and warned him that if he became baseball commissioner, he would have to deal with twenty-eight big egos. Mitchell laughed.

"For me that's a seventy-two percent reduction," he said.

If being commissioner would have meant being less of a fan, Mitchell was glad he had never been offered the job. He would not have wanted to complicate his enthusiasm for the game that he and his brothers played so often as boys. George grew up in the town of Waterville in Kennebec County, Maine. He was the youngest of four sons, and the Mitchell boys were all athletic— the older three, that is. George's older brother John played basketball and was a local legend. People debated who was better, John Mitchell or Bob Cousy. Even now, if you looked up the prep listings for the New England Basketball Hall of Fame, there he was, four names below Patrick Ewing on the list: John Mitchell, Waterville High.

"I grew up in our hometown known as John Mitchell's kid brother, the one who wasn't any good," Mitchell remembered. "That was how I got into politics. I knew I couldn't exceed my brothers in sports, so I figured I would do something else to get better known than them."

Mitchell was born in 1933, Babe Ruth's last great year. Ruth was thirty-eight and hit .301 that year with thirty-four homers in his second-to-last season with the Yankees. Like all his brothers, Mitchell grew up hating the Yankees and loving the Red Sox. Young George knew the batting average of every Red Sox player long before he had any idea who Maine's governor was or who its senators were or anything at all about politics. He cut his teeth on the Joe Cronin–managed teams before and after the war, and the team that really grabbed his imagination was the 1946 club that ended up winning 104 games. Any kid could have told you that year what Ted was hitting, or Dom DiMaggio or Johnny Pesky or Bobby Doerr. George always had those numbers ready, and he could also have told you what Pinky Higgins or Catfish Metkovich was hitting, and what kind of numbers Mace Brown and Clem Dreisewerd were putting up on the mound.

That was the summer George turned thirteen and also the summer he attended his first Red Sox game. His oldest brother, Paul, was going to a Sox game with his wife, and they decided to bring George along. All three of them slept in the same bed at the hotel they found near Fenway. It was hard to tune in to clear memories of that day, but one that always jumped out at Mitchell was of Joe DiMaggio up to bat. He took one effortless-looking swing and ripped a line drive that landed harmlessly in the stands after just missing the foul pole down the right-field line, only 302 feet from home plate (it wasn't known as the Pesky Pole back then; light-hitting Johnny Pesky was just getting started poking weak fly balls to right field that struck the pole for the shortest homers in baseball). DiMaggio took another graceful swing and hit one right over the foul pole for a homer. Mitchell still shook his head thinking about it. He had always hated the Yankees, but he always respected them, too. To him, that combination of passion, respect, and history was what made the Red Sox–Yankees rivalry the best in sports.

Mitchell just wished he did not have to fly off to Belfast that evening. He hated the idea of leaving Fenway early. Who knew what he might miss? He was chancellor of the Queens University of Northern Ireland, and would be hosting a conference of the Commonwealth universities. It was a long trip to make for only a few days, but he knew it was important. There was still follow-up work to be done on the Good Friday Agreement, and he would be meeting with Gerry Adams at Belfast City Hall and with David Trimble, the leader of the Ulster Unionist party, and with Mark Durkan, leader of the Social Democratic and Labour party. He had put a lot of work into chairing the two years of negotiations leading up to the Good Friday Agreement, which ended a war that had gone on for a quarter-century. There had been many difficulties in implementing the agreement, and the bad news was that the parties had hit a stalemate and not been able to implement the agreement fully. But the good news was that there had been no return to conflict. Very few people were dying; only six people had died in sectarian conflict the year before, compared to the hundreds who were killed each year in the 1970s. It was important to prod the political leaders to continue to pursue implementation because there was always the risk that some act of violence would lead to retaliation and escalation.

The trip to Belfast also meant he would have to miss a Portland Chamber of Commerce dinner honoring Shepherd Lee, an old friend of his. That gave Mitchell one more thing to do that morning. First, he spoke at a fund-raising breakfast in Portland for the state Democratic party, and then he videotaped a message they could show at the dinner for Shepherd Lee. Once that was out of the way, he could get back to wondering whether Grady Little would start a right-handed-hitting lineup that day against the left-hander Andy Pettitte. Little could put Damian Jackson at second base, and Gabe Kapler in the outfield. A lot depended on whether Manny Ramirez could play, or whether that bout of strep throat was going to keep him out of action for a while. Mitchell joined friends for the three-hour drive down to the Fens. They helped the time pass by talking of what it would be like to see the Red Sox back in the World Series that year, instead of always looking to next year, next year, next year.

Seven-month-old Alexis's first wail of the morning sounded remote at first, like a train at the far end of a tunnel, but maybe that was because Bill Mueller was so deep asleep. He and his wife, Amy, had not gotten to bed until late the night before. The game ran three hours and ten minutes, and it was the kind of back-and-forth, take-nothing-for-granted thriller that vibrated inside you afterward, no matter how hard you tried to step away. Every game against the Yankees that year had a heft and gravity to it, as if it somehow mattered more and said more about the Red Sox as a team and about each of them as players.

The World Series was only seven weeks away, and these were games people would remember for a long time in New England. The question was whether you could turn them into games you were glad they remembered, or whether you would spend the rest of your days wishing they and you could forget. Mueller had homered the night before off Jose Contreras, the Cuban *caballo* whose fastball-forkball combination had lured the Yankees and the Red Sox into a clownishly overdrawn bidding war the previous offseason. This was payback as sweet as it came. The Red Sox rattled off fourteen hits, including three by Mueller, and the 10–5 win put Boston fans one-third of the way to what they were all craving, a three-game sweep of the Yankees, just as George Steinbrenner was gurgling and spluttering like a geyser about to blow.

Mueller's eyes were only half-open as he watched Amy slip out of bed and hurry off to get a bottle for Alexis. It was less than half an hour before sunrise, the calmest and most peaceful part of the night, and Mueller smiled dreamily as he stretched out and closed his eyes again. Amy came back a few minutes later, and saw that even though her husband was back asleep, he still had a smile on his face. God had his ways of helping a man keep his sense of perspective, and in Mueller's case, January 14, 2003, told him all he needed to know.

That was the day Mueller signed with the Red Sox, which was no small development in a baseball career that at that point could have gone either way, but to Mueller, the birth of his daughter that same day made baseball almost beside the point. Mueller still smiled to think about the timing of the two events. He was a ballplayer who was talented but not so gifted that he could do well without working as hard and putting as much into every game as anyone else, but when he left the ballpark he left the game. He filled so many hours thinking about baseball at Fenway Park or on the road, when it came time to go home to Amy and Alexis, it was all about them.

The challenge of staying focused through a long season took its toll, especially if you were leading the league in hitting late in August, when not even your wife or high-school coach would ever in a million years have predicted it. You had to work hard to lower expectations whenever and however you could. That was the most draining part, the emotional and mental side of preparing yourself, and it really hit you late in the summer. But the Mueller family puppy didn't care about any of that, and wasn't going to stop barking unless Mueller hopped out of bed for a minute to feed him.

Alexis Mueller was hungry again by nine, and this time there was nothing tentative about her crying. Amy brought her another bottle, and Mueller drifted back to sleep. Finally, half an hour later, he woke up and went in to see how his wife and baby girl were doing. It was easy to make Alexis laugh, and nothing made Mueller happier than seeing her giggle. He played "This little piggy went to market," tickling her under her arms, and they all laughed.

Mueller was still half-asleep when his ride arrived and took him into the ballpark by 10:30. Mueller did not feel really awake until Euclides Rojas, the Cuban bullpen coach, dropped off a small cup of sweet, strong Cuban coffee, just like Mueller's teammate Osvaldo Fernandez used to make for him when he was with the San Francisco Giants. Mueller was not so sure about it at first, but soon developed a taste for it. Not until Mueller drank Rojas's Cuban coffee that day, just before he headed out onto the field, did it fully kick in that he was at a major-league ballpark and his day job was facing ninety-five-mile-an-hour fastballs that just might hit you if you did not keep on your toes.

Spike Lee squinted out from the ferry pulling away from Martha's Vineyard, his six-year-old son Jackson at his side. They had woken up early to catch the 7:45 ferry and get on their way, and Lee had wondered about rain. The weather reports had been iffy, but looking out over the Sound, Lee was just sure there would be no rain-out that day. He was excited, and so was his son. This would be Jackson's first time at Fenway Park.

Lee was born in March 1957, which made him part of the last generation of boys who grew up with baseball as their first sport. He was born in Atlanta, Georgia, and when he was two the family moved to Brooklyn. His mother, Jacquelyn Lee, taught art and literature at a private school and got after all five of her children to read Langston Hughes and other great African-American writers. Spike (Shelton Jackson Lee), the oldest, was always an independent-minded boy, tough or stubborn depending on how you looked at it, and that was why his mother took to calling him Spike. His father, Bill Lee, wanted to be in New York to get more opportunities as a jazz bassist and composer, and working nights had some advantages. Father and son often played catch.

"I remember like it was yesterday playing catch with my father," Lee said. "That was the first sport a father taught his son in that era, and then you went on to football and basketball."

Now it was Lee's turn to play catch with his son. He and Jackson played catch all the time. (Jackson's older sister, Satchel, liked baseball, too, and with a name like that, she had better.) Jackson played basketball, roller hockey, tennis, even soccer. Spike and his friends growing up never played soccer, but it was one of Jackson's favorites, up there with baseball. Kids had so many options now.

Lee was always a baseball fan growing up, and as a kid in Brooklyn, he hated the Yankees and loved the Mets. Cleon Jones,

Tommie Agee, Jerry Koosman, Donn Clendenon—those were his favorites. He was twelve years old in 1969 and caught thirty or so regular-season games at Shea. He went to the championship series against the Braves, and to all the World Series games, too.

He would never forget the Bill Buckner game in 1986 when, incredibly, the Mets mounted that tenth-inning comeback in Game Six with three two-out singles and Mookie Wilson's ground ball through Buckner's legs. Spike looked up at the Shea Stadium scoreboard that night during the game and saw an amazing message up there: THE METS CONGRATULATE THE RED SOX!

"I've never heard of that before," Lee said. "Before the game was over?"

He went to public school in Brooklyn and then left New York for Morehouse College, the African-American liberal arts college in Atlanta. Growing up in Brooklyn, Lee had never heard of Martha's Vineyard. (Who was *Martha?*) But he and some friends at Morehouse took to visiting the Vineyard during the summer. Lee found out there had been a large African-American community on the island dating back centuries.

"I always loved it," Lee said. "I made a promise to myself: If I ever get any money, I'm going to buy myself a house on Martha's Vineyard."

It had been thirteen years since he bought the house, and ever since, summers on the Vineyard had been a big part of his life. His wife loved it. His kids loved it. They went to summer camp there and had a great time. Lee always enjoyed making sure everyone remembered that he was as New York as it got, especially when it came to his sports loyalties.

"I make sure I wear my Yankee shirt every day," he said, meaning, every day for two months.

"Any time people want to start talking shit I just say '1918' and they shut up," he said. "There's nothing they can say after that."

Now and then, he would run into Peter Farrelly or his brother, Bobby.

"Those guys are very funny," he said. "We talk Red Sox–Yankees."

Fans had a way of sitting back and watching the grounds crew wrestle with a tarp, hoping to see people slipping and falling and flopping all over the place—the more Abbott and Costello, the better. David Mellor did not give them much to enjoy. He played around in his head with tarp-removal mechanics the way some people daydreamed about Caribbean vacations or get-rich schemes. He had assembled eleven workers early that morning to take the tarp off the infield, fold it twice, and squeeze the air out of it by running the heavy metal roller over it. Once it was ready, they stashed it by the first-base line. Marriott had paid to have an ad placed on top of the tarp's covering, an arrangement with obvious difficulties. What if it rained? What if they thought it might rain? They would have to pull off the Marriott ad to get the tarp ready.

You needed anywhere from seven to forty-five minutes to take off the tarp, depending on how many people you had at your disposal and how much rain had fallen and needed to be cleared off onto a dump tarp. (They could roll it back out in a minute and a half, if they had the full crew of twenty-two out there.) Once the tarp was off, it was time to dress the infield. This was more complicated than it sounded. The pretty new ballparks that had popped up from coast-to-coast had state-of-the-art irrigation systems. Fenway Park did not. There were only eight watering heads on the whole field, which meant you did things the old-fashioned way and broke out the hoses to give the infield a good soaking, down through the layers of clay and sand and loam.

Next it was time for the kitty litter. That was not what they called it, but that was pretty much what it was. They needed a substance that would maintain a constant moisture level, even when water was poured on it, so they used something called Turface, a brick-red calcified clay. Up until two seasons earlier, they had used a different color, a pinkish gray. But John Henry wanted red to match the crushed brick they used for the warning track in the outfield.

Nomar Garciaparra, so meticulous about everything, was naturally very particular about the area of infield dirt he patrolled at shortstop: He wanted it nice and wet, so Mellor's people watered it more for him. Normally the infield grass would be trimmed down to a height of one inch, but two seasons earlier they made an exception. Garciaparra missed most of the 2001 season with injuries and played only twenty-one games. No one who filled in for him had his range, so they kept the infield grass long, sometimes as high as three and a half inches. The day he came back, they chopped it back down to one inch. All part of the game.

It took five tons of a special red clay they ordered from New Jersey to build the pitcher's mound, and still more of the same red clay for the right-handed batter's box. They would have used the New Jersey clay for the batter's box for left-handed hitters, too, but Trot Nixon had asked for firmer footing when he batted, so they used a different type of clay for the left-handed batter's box.

Mellor, ever alert to the weather, noticed the thickening cloud cover and called the weather service soon after 8:30 a.m.

"Hey, it's Dave from the Red Sox," he said. "It's certainly clouded up here. I just wanted to check."

He listened closely.

"Oh, really?"

He spotted Charles Burnetti, his top assistant.

"It's gonna pour in half an hour," he told him, deadpan.

Burnetti stared back blankly. Mellor tried to keep a straight face, but did not hold out long.

"Nah, I'm kidding," he said.

But an hour later, under a steady rain, Mellor gave the word to put the tarp back out there. This was not a popular decision. There were downsides to rolling the tarp back out. For one, it was a lot of work, and for another, it could leave the infield smudged and dirty. It might not look as good for the large television audience tuning in to that day's game. Mellor often said safety and playability came first for him, before appearance. He backed that up and put the tarp back out there, just to be sure. Half an hour later, the tarp was off again.

Joe Torre had the look of a sleepwalker as he strolled past the Red Sox clubhouse at 9:11 a.m., trailed by a column of Yankees. Torre was not the only one who looked bleary and guarded. The ancient-concrete underbelly of Fenway was not an inviting place. There was something oddly distracting about its time-honored charmlessness. Torre and his Yankee players could almost hear voices hissing out of the dark recesses of the warped and piecemeal concourse, calling on them to get out of there and go back to Yankee Stadium. Walking took a little extra work there, since right angles tended not to be right and the way past hot-dog vendors stacking buns and beer vendors rolling kegs into place always seemed to include an extra turn or two.

There were times, usually before a game, never in the thick of the action, when Torre felt himself drifting away. It wasn't that his concentration wavered. That was always intense, because it had to be. But in those occasional moments, he almost had the sense of looking at himself through an outsider's eyes. He would be sitting in the Yankee dugout before a game surrounded by more than fifty reporters, almost all of them staring at him, even if they made an effort to pretend they were not staring. Torre had spent time on the other side of the divide. Having made a living talking about the game for the television cameras, he understood how little the reporters wanted, and he was usually able to satisfy them with a moment of his attention and a genial attempt to respond to their questions.

But there were times when he felt it closing in on him, almost like that feeling of being enclosed in a tube of metal for a magnetic-resonance-imaging test. The only thing to do about that feeling of claustrophobia was to wait for it to go away. Torre was good at that. He was good at looking for the positive in questions or comments that would have set most managers off. But sometimes the other part got to him. Sometimes it made it hard to have fun. The way Torre looked at it, the only reason to keep putting on the uniform and heading out there was if he was still having fun.

Torre's knack for asserting his right to have fun and defusing a tense situation had always been one of his most important assets. There was that time in June 1996 when the Yankee pitching staff had been hit by injuries and the club went into Cleveland for a doubleheader and had to send out two rookie starters to deal with Albert Belle, Manny Ramirez, Jim Thome, and the rest of that loaded Indians lineup. Torre wasn't happy about it, but there wasn't much he could do ahead of time. He took advantage of a few free hours after they arrived in Ohio and got in a quick round of golf. He knew his cell phone would probably ring when he was out there. So what, let them call.

"What in the hell are we going to do?" Steinbrenner ranted over the phone to Bob Watson and Brian Cashman. "We're going into Cleveland and we've got these two peashooters throwing for us. Torre's playing fucking golf. Get him on the phone."

Cashman figured this was going to be one bad conference call.

"Well, I don't know what the hell we're doing," Steinbrenner said to Torre. "While you're out in the fucking woods, we're here trying to figure out how to fix this club."

There was a very brief pause.

"How the hell did you know my ball was in the woods?" Torre asked the Boss. "I can't keep the fucking thing in the fairway."

That made them all laugh and cut the tension. Torre did not have much of a golf round that day, but the Yankees and their pea-shooting pitchers took both games of that doubleheader and went on to sweep the four-game series.

If the fans knew half of what Torre had to take, they would understand if he walked away. He had stuck up for himself more this year than he had in the past. He had earned that right. He had accomplished enough as Yankee manager to speak his piece from time to time. It helped, too, but never for long. He knew that this three-game series in Boston could turn into a disaster. His team had taken a two-run lead in the first inning of the Friday night game, but the Red Sox came right back with three in the bottom of the first and barreled their way to a 10–5 victory that cut the Yankee lead in the American League East to three and a half games.

You hated to see a hot-hitting team like the Sox in full stride. This kid Ortiz was so strong and so happy all the time, and he had home runs in six straight games or something like that. There was just no way to feel comfortable playing a team like that, especially not at Fenway Park. The loss on Friday night just kicked up the pressure that much more for Saturday's game against Pedro Martinez. You could never try to explain away the pressure. That did you no good. The trick was to respect the pressure and to accept that you would always have to deal with it. People thought of Torre as kind and familiar Uncle Joe, but he was a realist. He knew some losses were more dangerous than others. Some had more power to rob your team of its most important resource—confidence.

People watching at home had the idea that confidence was an intangible, and a team or a player either had it or they didn't. But that was not how it felt if you were a manager or a player. Confidence was a commodity. You built it up, you watched over it, and you did not fool yourself when it was in danger of slipping away from you. This Saturday game at Fenway gave Torre an uncomfortable feeling in his gut. You could never know ahead of time, not for sure anyway, but he had an inkling that if his team lost this one, they just might get swept in the series and find their division lead dwindling down to almost nothing. The radio shows back in New York would go crazy, and so would the team owner. He would have the tabloid back covers to himself for days on end. Everyone would be talking about Steinbrenner's latest tantrum.

The first thing Theo Epstein did when he woke up at 8:30, five hours after he had gone to bed, was check his fingers. It had been that kind of night. He pulled out two Band-Aids, one for his thumb and one for his forefinger, and peeled both free so he could fix himself up a little before heading to the ballpark. Epstein had jammed with some friends late the night before and played guitar until his fingers bled.

Earlier, he had met up with some old college friends at the Tiki Bar on Landsdowne Street. Too many people recognized him there and wanted to shake his hand and talk Sox, so they moved on to the Bar Code, on Boylston. Epstein enjoyed knocking back a few as much as the next guy, especially when he was an undergrad, but he was responsible to a lot of people now. During the baseball season he limited himself to two or three drinks. His college friends wanted him to make an exception this one time, but he resisted.

If he wanted to catch a buzz, the best way was with his guitar.

He and some friends were playing "Pinball Wizard," and if you weren't going to play it like you meant it, why bother? So there was Epstein throwing his hand high in the air to play windmill guitar, Pete Townsend style. It left his hand raw and bloody, but it was worth it. If anyone kidded Epstein about getting too wild, he would quote Neil Young in "Hey, Hey, My, My," and talk about how rock and roll will never die and how once you're gone, you can't come back. He would say it with a half-smile, walls of irony in place, but he would mean it, too.

People had made a lot of Epstein's age when the Red Sox named him general manager, but if they wondered what his more private fears were, they might have been surprised. Everybody had anxiety dreams now and then, and in Epstein's case, they were guitar dreams, not baseball dreams. It was almost like the childhood dream of showing up at school and realizing there was an exam you knew nothing about, only this was the rock and roll version. Epstein found himself onstage in a club. Everyone was watching him, waiting to see what he was going to play. His guitar was tuned. His amp was plugged in. The sound check had shaken the whole building. But Epstein froze up and could not remember a single chord. He had no idea what to play. Everyone kept staring at him.

Epstein flipped on *ESPN News* without really thinking about it. He was always telling himself not to watch so many hours of highlights, including the same set over and over, but when you knew they would be rolling footage of a win, especially a home win against the Yankees, your fingers were on the remote almost before your head got involved. There would be more than enough days

where you dreaded watching ESPN. You left it on as an exercise in masochism, part of the training for answering to Red Sox Nation, and there again was your bullpen imploding. You left to run a few errands. You tried to get your mind off it. You came back later and flipped the TV back on and your bullpen was imploding all over again.

It took a conscious effort not to let a loss ruin your day, and sometimes it did anyway. The point was not how it felt to Epstein. The point was that he was responsible to a lot of people, and the welfare of the team could be affected if he took the losses too hard. The pressure was hard on his parents, too. The joke in the family was that his mother had started hitting the Valium right around Opening Day. At least he thought it was a joke.

"Early in the year people told me I sucked," he said. "I nodded and walked on. At times I agreed with them. That was hard."

The job of general manager demanded that Epstein develop the quality of not caring what people thought. That was an easy thing to say and a very hard thing to do. Epstein worked at it by telling himself that it was like someone in the business world who had a very important staff meeting every night after dinner and everything you did during the day built up to that meeting. Your day revolved around the meeting, but it was still only a staff meeting, no more and no less. That was what he told himself, but whether Epstein really believed a baseball game could be meaningfully compared to a staff meeting was not completely clear.

He worked a lot of late nights that first off-season after being named GM the previous November. There was a lot of catching up to do on player development. He flew down to Nicaragua to try

to sign Jose Contreras, and that was when the stories started about him trashing his hotel room and breaking windows and furniture.

"I thought it would take me years, if not decades, to earn a Led Zeppelin reputation for breaking things," he said.

Epstein could joke about it because he was sure he would never let his temper flare up again in a way that would make head-lines. He was so focused on self-control, he needed to get away from the ballpark before he could really relax, the way he had the night before with his college friends, confiding to them that he had a bad feeling about Saturday's game. The Red Sox did not hit Andy Pettitte well, Epstein knew, and Pedro was still recovering from that sore throat. His star pitcher had only been about 80 per-cent for his previous start, and there was no telling where he would be today. Epstein tried to steer himself to think of it more as an in-teresting question: Knowing what he knew, did he think his ace could manufacture a performance that day on the basis of blood, sweat, and guts?

About all that Epstein could find in his freezer that appealed to him for breakfast was some frozen waffles, and he popped a couple into the toaster. Once he finished that, he tossed in a load of wash and strummed his guitar while he waited. It was harder to play with the Band-Aids, but he found he liked the raw, exposed feeling of strumming with fingers that had so recently been bleeding. He took a quick shower, not bothering to shave, and slipped on a white T-shirt, still warm from the dryer, and khaki slacks and a green silk shirt.

Epstein hated having any kind of commute and lived in a brick building right across the street from Fenway. He walked downstairs and across the street to the ballpark and it was time to start worrying seriously about that day's game. Manny Ramirez's status was a key to the Red Sox's chances. He had sat out the game the night before with some kind of throat ailment, and it hadn't mattered. The Red Sox offense was so productive in his absence, it felt like getting a free pass. But given his misgivings about the game and his respect for Pettitte, Epstein expected the game to be a back-and-forth battle. Just having Ramirez available as a pinch-hitter could be important.

Epstein sought out trainer Jim Rowe just before 11:00 a.m. for an update on Ramirez, and heard he was expected at the ballpark any minute. Epstein's daily talk with his manager, Grady Little, was shorter than usual, since it was a day game after a night game. They discussed the lineup and also an issue with a player. It was important to huddle before either of them talked with the media, since even small differences in what they said could be fanned into a controversy that would drag on for days. Epstein headed out to the Red Sox dugout, stepping lightly on the old, cracked wood shifting under his scuffed leather shoes.

"When I first got here, I couldn't believe we had a $110-million payroll and we had floorboards that creaked," he said. "Some of the players complain, but some like to know they are walking on the same boards that Ted Williams walked on. It's a vestige of that time. In fact, it's *the* vestige of that time."

Epstein sat down and immediately his cell phone rang. It was one of his old college friends from the night before.

"Hey, buddy, you coming today?" Epstein said.

A pause.

"My fingers were all bloody," Epstein said, more animated than he ever was discussing baseball. "I've got Band-Aids on my fingers. See you later, dude."

Later, he headed up to the team's executive offices, and his cell phone rang again. It was small and black but had a display on the front, so he could see who was calling. This time it was Rowe, the trainer.

"What's up, Doc?" he said.

He paused to listen to Rowe's update on Ramirez.

"But can he pinch-hit today?"

Another pause.

"OK," he said. "OK, thanks."

Rowe and the team physician had said no, Ramirez was not available to pinch-hit. Epstein took that as a yes. They were concerned about swelling in the throat, but Epstein had a feeling that Ramirez would be there if they needed him as a pinch-hitter. After all, this was the Yankees, and one at-bat was one at-bat.

Brian Cashman wrestled constantly with the Steinbrenner Question. He asked himself again and again: Was the price too high? Did he put up with too much?

"Joe Torre says: 'If you're gonna take his money, you gotta take his shit,' " Cashman said. "He says that all the time."

Back in 1998 at his first press conference as Yankee general manager, Cashman had been asked what it would take to keep the Boss off his back.

"I think only going 162-0 would do that," he said.

That got a laugh, but it was true, too. The better you got to know Steinbrenner, the more you understood that nothing could ever ease his hatred of losing. The Yankees won four World Series in five years, starting in 1996, and almost won four in a row. You might think at some point that kind of success would lessen Steinbrenner's thirst to win, but no way. The man was not wired that way. He felt an endless need for fresh successes, and that need guaranteed he would never be satisfied with any general manager.

"I knew when I took the job that I'm not going to change him," Cashman said. "He's looking for someone he can tolerate. No one is good enough for him."

So how did Cashman deal with that?

"It's a combination of winning and being successful, to keep him somewhat satisfied, and then the periods where you're scuffling, how long do you have the will power to tolerate it?"

Spike Lee was around the Yankees enough to know how it was, and he was amazed Cashman could take what he had to take.

"He's got a rough job," Lee said. "I know he's on call 24/7, and when the Yankees lose, he's the one who catches holy hell, not Joe Torre. Not many have the mind-set or the thick skin for that job. I know Bob Watson. He said he couldn't take that shit. He said, 'I can't do it.' "

Watson had the general manager's job before Cashman, who was an assistant GM back then, but on Groundhog Day 1998, Watson kept poking his head into Cashman's office next door, obviously wanting to talk once Cashman finally got off the phone.

"Listen, I have to talk to you," Watson said.

Cashman hung up and Watson came in and sat down.

"Last night I quit," Watson said.

"What?" Cashman said.

"I met with Boss," Watson said. "I quit. I'm done. I can't take it anymore."

There was more.

"I've recommended you to replace me," Watson continued. "I think he's going to offer it to you today."

Cashman did not know what to say.

"You've got a lot to think about, buddy," Watson said.

An hour or two later, Steinbrenner summoned Cashman to come down to his hotel, the Regency, where he told his young assistant general manager that he had talked to Gene Michael and Mark Newman and a lot of people in the game whom he respected and leaned on.

"I can go out and recycle some other baseball guy who has done this job before and bring him in here to do this thing," Steinbrenner told Cashman. "But I'm told by these people that you can do it, and I want to know what you think."

Cashman had no idea. The general-managing part of the job was enough of a challenge without the working-for-George part. But some opportunities were too great to turn down.

"I'm your man!" Cashman told Steinbrenner, and recalling that day years later, he slipped into a squeaky cartoon voice like that of the littlest geek on the playground to convey just how not-up-to-the-task he felt at the time.

But Cashman made good moves right from the start. He asked for a one-year handshake deal, no long-term contract, so that, paradoxically, there would be no real temptation for Steinbrenner to fire him if the team hit a tough patch. Cashman also knew what he had on the field. That was the Yankee team that finished the regular season 92-70 and went on to win the World Series over the Atlanta Braves, winning four games in a row after dropping Game One and Game Two. The next season, the Yankees won ninety-six but finished two games behind Baltimore in the American League East and lost the American League Divisional Series to Cleveland. They won the World Series again in 1998, 1999, and 2000—and almost won again in 2001, losing to the Diamondbacks in the bottom of the ninth in Game Seven. Through all the successes, Cashman tried to remind himself often that when it came to dealing with the Boss, no number of wins or world championships would ever be enough.

"I don't have this ego where I was thinking, 'He's not going to do it to me,'" Cashman said. "It's almost like there has been a not-respect factor for the other people who walked through here. But George does it to everybody. He's an equal-opportunity tough boss."

Steinbrenner knew it, too. He made no bones about being a bad loser. As he put it one time, "I believe in what Ernest Hemingway said, 'The way you get to be a good loser is practice.' And I ain't gonna be practicing."

Cashman had never stopped respecting Steinbrenner for who he was and what he had done. He respected his willingness to put himself on the line, caring as much as anybody about every game his team played, and also his willingness to back up his big talk with cold, hard cash. Cashman tried to keep that in mind when things got tough, and they got tough often enough.

The great thing about Steinbrenner was that no matter how angry he got, no matter how pissed off he was about a given situation, he never seemed to let it fester with him. Cashman had often seen him tear into people about something, and the next day—whether he was right or wrong—it was as if nothing had happened.

"For the most part he'll get in your face," Cashman said. "He'll challenge his employees. It's all because he wants it done the way he wants it done. But after it's all said and done, if the employee weathers the storm, he turns the page on it. I've had the ability for the most part to turn the page, too, and understand that's just the way he is. You try not to take it personally, but at times you do."

Cashman had started with the Yankees as a summer intern during college, and being a Yankee lifer gave him certain advantages. He was not tainted by having come from somewhere else. He had not been conditioned by success elsewhere to develop an outsized ego, or deluded into thinking that Steinbrenner might share decision-making.

"This is his team," he said. "You try to put him in a position to be successful by giving him as many terrific recommendations as possible, but you gotta appreciate the fact that he's not gonna listen to all of them. And if you can't deal with that, this is the worst fucking place to be."

They had shouting matches all the time. Steinbrenner had hung up on Cashman. And Cashman had hung up on Steinbrenner.

"I've had a chance to leave here on a few contracts now," Cashman said. "I've had a chance to jump ship. Then you go back and think, 'You know what? Look what he's done for you. Look where you've been and who you are today.'

"Somebody asked me who had the biggest impact on my life. George might be a close second after my mom and dad. I've been working here since 1986 and it's because of an opportunity he gave. So I always get into this internal struggle about 'You owe him.' I know what he's done here, and at times what he's done to me, but I also know what he's done for me. You wrestle with that. So far I've come back with, 'You know what? If they want me back, it's hard for me to leave because of that, because I feel like I owe him.' "

Neither Theo Gordon nor Jane Baxter had slept very well. They had to catch an early train up from New Hampshire, her in her visiting Red Sox jersey, him in his home white Yankee jersey. They wanted to arrive in plenty of time to enjoy the scene out in front of Fenway Park before the game. Gordon could not imagine a better way to celebrate his thirty-sixth birthday. Later, they would catch a train back to New Hampshire to join Baxter's parents for dinner.

Gordon was still thinking about the forty-five lies he had told so far. He had kept track of each and every one, and planned to recite them to Baxter as soon as the time was right. He was nervous, but it did not bother him. Soon enough he would be reassigned from the base in Virginia to one in Iceland, and he would be there a year and a half. He wanted to enjoy everything about this day, and file away the memories to pull out later to pore over like an old scrapbook. But all he kept thinking about was the forty-five lies.

Baxter knew Gordon was planning something, but she did

not know when it was coming, so she figured she might as well not worry about it. She was excited about going back to Fenway. Maybe they would have time to stop by Myles Standish Hall and she could show Gordon the view from her old window in Suite 927.

The hardest part of moving out of their old house in Newton might have been leaving behind the mural on the playroom walls. It was a real beauty. Pooh and Tigger were there in the Fenway Park stands, and so was Elmo. The painted scoreboard looked exactly the way it did on June 10, 2001, the day their son, John Franco, was born, and if anyone knew how the scoreboard at Fenway looked, it was Rich Maloney, who had spent thirteen years putting up its scores by hand. The Maloney family mural jumped from wall to wall and made you feel as if you were right in the middle of a ballgame.

Marco was born five weeks earlier, and Rich and Stefania knew they needed more room, so they decided to buy Stefania's mother's white Cape Cod–style house. It was also in Newton, fifteen minutes west of Fenway, and on a cul-de-sac, which would be good for the boys when they got bigger and wanted to play ball out front.

"We just need seven more and a couple of backup pitchers and we'll have a team," Stefania said.

She had lived in the Cape Cod for ten years starting when she was fifteen and attending Newton North High, which was where she met Rich her freshman year. Stefania hoped he would ask her to the prom that year. He was a senior, and she liked his blue eyes and the way he cocked his head sometimes when he smiled. But she had to wait years for Rich to ask her out.

He moved on to Boston College, and during his sophomore year he took a public-relations course. One assignment was to set up an informational interview in a field where he might like to work. Rich knew just what field, too. He called up the Red Sox. They assumed he wanted an internship, since he was a college student and all, but actually, he was thinking he would like a job, something that would enable him to work up to Sox PR director. He wasn't having much luck with the Sox until someone figured out he was the son of Moe Maloney, Boston College's baseball coach. Soon he was inside the Green Monster, putting up scores by hand.

Stefania and Rich were married in 1998, and she taught preschool until John Franco came along to force a change in plans. She got a kick out of having a husband with such an unusual connection to the Sox and baseball.

"It's just really neat to know he's there," she said. "The novelty never wears off. There's no other person who gets a view like that."

She didn't mind that she could never go to a Sox game with her husband, or that he missed only one game when Marco was born, and that was the day of the actual delivery. Stefania was in the hospital four days, recovering from a C-section, and Rich would sit at her side most of the day and then hurry off to the park. Most of the time, though, his Fenway job worked out well. She liked knowing when her husband would be out of her hair.

"What're you doing?" he asked her one day when she was standing in front of the refrigerator, studying the Sox schedule to look for upcoming home games.

"Just looking for red dates," Stefania answered.

Rich was out of her hair by 11:00 that particular Saturday morning. Wearing a white polo shirt with an "O'Hara's Charity Golf Shirt" logo, a gift from a local bar, he climbed into the used Mercedes Benz 190 he had bought a couple of years earlier. He still had not figured out how to reprogram the security codes, so the radio did not work, but other than that, it did just fine for a car with 128,846 miles on the odometer.

"We're not good scorekeepers," he said as he drove.

He was talking about himself and his longtime partner behind the Monster, Chris Elias, and admitting that sometimes they succumbed to boredom during a slow game against a team like Tampa Bay or Detroit and fell behind on putting up numbers. The phone inside the Wall would ring, and someone in the control room upstairs would tell them to get with it.

No danger of that happening today, Maloney said, not with the Yankees in town and Pedro on the mound. He parked and worked his way through the pitted, quirky underbelly of Fenway and out onto the outfield grass in left. It was 11:30 by then, and the Yankees were on the field warming up. Roger Clemens was playing catch less than fifteen feet away, and gave Maloney a half-confused, half-angry look when he spotted him heading his way. Clemens seemed to be wondering why a short guy in a golf shirt got to be on the field with the Yankees. Maloney ignored him, glanced up at the NYY sign in place above the permanent BOSTON, and popped through the open door leading into the Wall.

"It smells like a zoo in here," Maloney said.

He greeted Chris Elias, who started working the scoreboard

the year after he did, and Garrett Tingle, their new assistant that year. Tingle, nephew of comedian Jimmy Tingle, played baseball at Emerson College, where Elias was one of his coaches. Seconds after Maloney stepped behind the Wall, one of the Red Sox hitters taking batting practice connected on a line drive that slammed into the other side of the scoreboard with a freakishly loud BANG! that kept echoing and vibrating far longer than seemed possible. The nerve-fraying racket defied description, but the sensation of hearing it explode in your head brought to mind a cartoon with the Roadrunner smashing a cymbal just behind the head of Wile E. Coyote, and his whole body vibrating as if he had been plugged into an electric socket.

"No matter how many times you hear that . . ." Maloney said, trailing off.

The room behind the scoreboard had the dimensions of an airplane fuselage and the look of a maximum-security prison. It was all cement and steel and exposed electrical wires. Only six feet wide and eight feet high, it stretched a good ninety feet long. The bare walls were unadorned except for a few scrawled signatures. Most were of nobodies, but here and there you could find a Jimmy Piersall or a Carlton Fisk or even a Mike Piazza. Oh, and Bernie Williams, that day's Yankee center fielder.

Marty Martin and his brother, Dean, made sure to arrive early at the Knights of Columbus Hall on King Street in Bristol. That would be just Martin's luck to show up a minute or two late, only to see the bus pulling out and leaving him behind. He could just see them all waving at him and laughing. He would have to live through a whole year of stories about what a great time his neighbor Bob and everyone else had at Fenway that day. Once again, Marty Martin would be the one left out of the fun, stuck on the outside, looking in. But there the bus was, and he and Dean took their seats and waited for the hour-and-a-half ride to begin.

They were hungry by the time they arrived at Fenway, and wandered around Yawkey Way, seeing Sox hats everywhere, bumping into people here and there, and smelling enough ballpark food to keep them occupied for hours. Martin loved it. If the new Red Sox owners were trying for a carnival atmosphere out there, they had succeeded beautifully. He was glad they were keeping Fenway Park, not tearing it down. That would be a tragic loss. The old parks had so much joy in them because of the history.

Martin and his brother decided against the Cuban food at El Tiante, even though it looked good and Martin had always liked Luis Tiant, the fiery Red Sox pitcher with the stylish leg kick and full twist. Instead, they went for the huge Italian sausages, which Martin washed down with a soda, not a beer. He didn't drink. Martin wanted to buy a David Ortiz shirt, too, or a Bill Mueller shirt, but he was concerned about time. It was not as if he knew the ballpark like the back of his hand. He considered walking from concession stand to concession stand looking for an Ortiz or Mueller shirt, and thought better of it. Better to go straight to the seats. He did not want to miss anything.

Hideki Matsui was surprised to find no one waiting for him when he arrived at Fenway Park that morning. Usually at least four or five Japanese media people would be standing there at the players' entrance before every game, just to ask him a quick question or two. He was that big a story back home in Japan. But the night before, the Japanese reporters had checked the board in the Yankee clubhouse, and seen "10:50" written there in black Magic Marker. They assumed that meant Matsui would be taking a bus from the hotel at 10:50 that morning, but 10:50 was the time for the bus back to the hotel the night before.

Matsui felt loose after a twenty-minute massage of his lower back, and had some time to relax before his batting practice group would hit—Aaron Boone, Karim Garcia, Bernie Williams, and him. Matsui always used a heavier bat for BP, his mascot bat. He took thirty-one swings during batting practice, but did not connect for a single home run. That was rare, but he was not going to see it as any kind of omen. The *katsu* was going to help him, after all.

He still did not like day games, and why should he? Back home in Japan, his team never played baseball games during the day, except during the preseason. To Matsui, playing at night under the lights was what felt natural. Most of his errors as a Yankee had come because of his trouble adjusting to playing under the sun and having to wear sunglasses and learning how to flip them down at the right time. He looked up that morning and saw the layer of clouds seeming to thicken over Fenway Park, and he felt lucky. Clouds were his friends.

Sometimes it still surprised Matsui when he caught a glimpse of himself on TV or in the mirror and saw that he was wearing the pinstripes. As proud as he was of Japanese baseball, no team in the world could compare with the New York Yankees. He had always felt like a fan when he watched them play. One of his favorite baseball memories was October 1999 when his team, the Yomiuri Giants, clinched the Central League early enough for Matsui to take a break and fly to New York and watch the Red Sox and Yankees in the second game of the American League Championship Series.

It was a cold night at Yankee Stadium, and a tense game. Matsui had seats just behind home plate, perfect for following the great battle between starting pitchers David Cone and Ramon Martinez, Pedro's older brother. The turning point of the game was when Paul O'Neill, playing with a fractured rib, singled in the seventh inning to bring home what turned out to be the game-winning run. O'Neill earned Matsui's respect that night, and so did the electric Yankee Stadium crowd. Back then, the idea of ever playing for the Yankees seemed to Matsui like nothing more than a dream. It was funny, he thought, getting ready to take the field. Somehow it still felt like a dream.

It was along about four in the morning when Larry Lucchino sat up in bed, gripped by a panic attack about that weekend's series with the Yankees and what it would say about the rest of the season. The bout with anxiety was all the more disturbing considering that only a few hours earlier, Lucchino had gone to bed feeling great, still enjoying the high of a good Red Sox victory over Jose

Contreras and the Yankees. But Lucchino's late-night panic attack quickly ran its course and soon he was back asleep.

His alarm went off at 7:30 and he held on for another fifteen minutes before getting up and calling his dog Natel, a black lab, and letting him outside and feeding him. Lucchino collected the *Boston Globe,* the *Boston Herald,* and *The New York Times* from his driveway and read them over as he ate a breakfast of Cheerios with strawberries, bananas, and blueberries. "I was particularly interested in reading *The New York Times* to see Tyler Kepner's perspective on the game last night, which was interesting," Lucchino said.

"The Yankees are playing another contending team and following their discouraging pattern," Kepner, the *Times*'s beat writer, had written. "When they play bad teams, the Yankees look flawless. But good teams expose their problems, and their fiercest rival did so tonight." That was the kind of thing Lucchino liked to read over his morning Cheerios. Too often during his long career in baseball, he had thrown the morning paper down in anger over what a reporter or columnist had written about him or his team.

There were always rumors circulating about Lucchino, and most of the time he liked it that way. A mystique was good to have and difficult to manufacture. Lucchino had a mystique. His hot-blooded younger days had helped build his reputation. He was enough of a free spirit to have flown to Paris with a friend in 1985, back when he was a young Washington Redskins executive, not yet forty, and rented Yamahas and spent ten days touring the French countryside. He and Jay Emmett had worked their way down to Saint-Jean-Cap-Ferrat on the Côte D'Azur, and made sure to stop at plenty of wineries along the way.

Lucchino was also enough of a hothead to have broken things on many occasions. He had an obsessive aversion to losing, and it showed. He hated unfairness, and was not above shouting now and then to express just how deeply that hatred ran. But Lucchino could be smooth, too. He grew up in a working-class Pittsburgh neighborhood, and always knew he was going to make something of himself. His mother would later tell stories about how, as a first-grader, Larry was intent on going to school even when three feet of snow had fallen outside. He went to a public high school, Taylor Allderdice, where he was a good second baseman but a better point guard, and later played on the Princeton team that made it to the 1965 Final Four.

After graduating from Yale Law School, Lucchino went to work at the Washington, D.C., firm Williams & Connolly, and soon made partner. The firm's founder, Edward Bennett Williams, was a friend of the Kennedy family, and Lucchino briefly dated Maria Shriver, the future NBC personality and California First Lady. Williams also owned a piece of the Washington Redskins, and in August 1979 he bought the Baltimore Orioles as well. Lucchino was general counsel to both teams, and in May 1988 Williams named him president of the Orioles, the opportunity that made Lucchino's career.

Not a year has gone by in recent decades without someone proclaiming that baseball needs saving, but the most important date in recent baseball history may well be April 6, 1992, when a new baseball stadium opened in Baltimore. Camden Yards wowed people. It had an intimate, old-time feel, but it was thrillingly new, too. Suddenly it dawned on owners all around baseball just how major a mistake had been made with the cookie-cutter concrete slabs of the 1970s. Soon throwback ballparks were popping up all over the place. Each was better than the last, culminating with an intimate new stadium on San Francisco Bay called Pac Bell Park. It was a baseball revolution, and as the man in many ways responsible for Camden Yards, Lucchino was one of its prime movers.

That was the background to Lucchino's arrival in Boston as the most baseball-savvy of the triumvirate of Henry, Lucchino, and Werner. There was a stop for Lucchino in San Diego along the way, but that did not deflect from the pleasing symmetry of a man known for Camden Yards showing up in Boston with the mission of trying to preserve the crumbling charm of a ballpark built back in 1912, five years after owner John Taylor changed the ballclub's name from the Pilgrims to the Red Sox.

The Henry-Lucchino group did not pay $700 million for the Red Sox so they could half-ass it as owners. These were men used to getting their way, and having their way work out just fine, thank you. They were not above devoting a large chunk of their time to PR. In fact, their philosophy of baseball ownership owed much to contemporary politics, where a Bill Clinton or George W. Bush constantly played the part of candidate running for office, even when no election was in sight, turning each day into an opportunity to sell himself through the media or win new votes through retail politics.

The new Red Sox ownership group knew that selling the community on their seriousness, their flair, and their skill was an essential part of organizing a concerted run at the World Series championship that fans in New England had been so desperately craving for generations. Prodded by ideas man Charles Steinberg, a former dentist and associate of Lucchino's in Baltimore, San Diego, and Boston, Henry and Lucchino decided to go to war. No one needed reminding about who the enemy was in this war. His name was George, and he lived in Florida.

The interesting part was defining this campaign as essentially a war of ideas. Just as Joe Torre knew that the confidence of his team was not an intangible, but something to be watched over carefully and nurtured, the new Red Sox ownership group saw selling their fan base on a new sense of promise and momentum as a necessary condition of winning that elusive World Series championship. Bringing in new statistical tools, and even number theorist Bill James, was part of the war of ideas, too. Other teams, most famously Billy Beane's Oakland A's, had found advantages in these tools; the Sox would do them one better by hiring the godfather of the movement. Best of all, James seldom visited Fenway, and no one knew just what he was doing behind the scenes to help the organization make moves and field a stronger team. James's calculations were of use to the Sox; so was his visionary aura, an added bonus among a New England following that included more Ph.D.s than that of any other two teams combined.

There were similar advantages in hiring a dashing young leading man like Theo Epstein, who had the virtues of being smart and shrewd and working well with Lucchino, and—do not discount this for a second—was also good-looking and fit and put a young, charismatic public face on the organization. The mere fact of shocking many in baseball by hiring a twenty-eight-year-old for so important a job, something that no team had ever done before—

that was a classic Lucchino move, bold and attention-getting and, yes, also risky. But it also signaled that these men were in this for the long haul; Lucchino knew that hiring Epstein would look better and better with each year, but he knew that even if the ownership group's plans were flawless, even if they all played their parts and worked to make it happen just the way they envisioned, they still might find themselves ending up as just another batch of Yankee roadkill. The only thing to do was fight back, and fight hard. That was where the "Evil Empire" thing started.

Reached by a *New York Times* reporter the previous December, shortly after the Yankees outbid the Red Sox and signed Jose Contreras to a four-year deal worth $32 million, Lucchino first said "No comment," then changed his mind. "No, I'll make a comment," he said. "The Evil Empire extends its tentacles even into Latin America."

The comment generated immediate heat. Lucchino was using the tools at his disposal to wage his war of ideas. Ronald Reagan had shocked American liberals in the 1980s with his talk of the Soviet Union as an "Evil Empire," and thrilled people from Tallinn to Tbilisi. Lucchino understood the strategic value of upping the ante. His statement soon became the second-most-talked-about use of the word "evil" that year, trailing only President George W. Bush's "Axis of Evil" State of the Union address in January.

"It was a semijocular reference to *Star Wars*—but only semijocular," Lucchino explained later.

Lost in all the controversy was the Red Sox's later realization that it might not have been so terrible that Contreras had ended up with the Yankees, at least based on the way they had knocked him around the night before in that 10–5 victory to open this important August 2003 series with the Yankees. Lucchino was the first to arrive in the team's executive offices that Saturday, and as usual he was the one who turned on the lights.

"I learned one of the important rules of baseball, which is: Come early!" he said. "It's a rule the fans should apply, too. If the game is at 7:05, you don't want to show up at 7:03, you want to come early and take off some of the stress and strain. Watch a little batting practice. Get the feel of the ballpark. And don't miss the start of the game. I always tell my friends and family: Remember Rule One—Come early."

Sam Kennedy, a young vice president of sales, greeted Lucchino that Saturday morning with a potential crowd-pleaser: life-sized head shots of two famous men, each mounted on a foot-long wooden stick. One: George Steinbrenner (Who else?), his face pulled back in something between a scowl and a sneer. The other? Need a hint? He was wearing army fatigues and a very familiar-looking beard. Right: Fidel Castro.

Lucchino said no to that one.

"I thought it was a little too Vaudeville," he said.

Lou Merloni had always enjoyed the old joke that if you wanted to make sure someone got lost in Boston, you gave them directions telling them: "Turn left at Dunkin' Donuts." Nationwide, the chain had 3,500 locations, but they were concentrated in Massachusetts, where there was one store for every seven thousand people. You could have your Krispy Kremes or whatever, but to a

Framingham kid like Merloni, waking up to Dunkin' Donuts again was a sure sign that he was back home.

Merloni set two alarms, just to make sure he would not oversleep. One time in A ball, he overslept and had to show up late. That gave him a terrible feeling that he never forgot, and ever since he always set two alarms. Out in the living room, his roommate Katie's five-year-old nephew Brett and seven-year-old niece Chandler had slept over and were watching Saturday morning cartoons. Merloni jumped in the shower and let himself enjoy the anticipation. He knew he would be back in the Red Sox starting lineup that day, and if that didn't get you excited, nothing would. His mother called while he was in the shower and left a message telling him that his grandmother would not be able to make it to the game, but she and his dad would be there, along with his oldest sister, Lisa, his second-oldest sister, Jill, her husband, Matt, and their three kids, Nick, Camryn, and Luke.

It was all such a blur. Merloni had known the Red Sox needed to add a backup infielder for the last month of the season. He heard they might go for Mike Bordick, the thirteen-year veteran from Maine who was always a favorite with managers. But it had been Merloni who got the call, just two days earlier. The Red Sox traded a minor-leaguer to San Diego and brought Merloni back to the organization where he spent the first nine years of his pro career after playing college ball at Providence. He had liked playing for the Padres, but coming home to New England just in time for the run-up to the playoffs was nothing short of mind-blowing. He had called up Nomar right away to give him the news, and Nomar hadn't believed him at first. He thought it was too good to be true.

Merloni spotted the morning edition of the *Boston Herald* as he sat at the Dunkin' Donuts in Framingham, drinking his coffee ("two and two—two creams, two sugars"), and waiting for his toasted sesame bagel with cream cheese. Right there on the inside of the back cover the *Herald* had an article on him. He started to read, then flipped the paper closed and tossed it back on the counter. Soon he was back in his black four-door Altima, polishing off his bagel in a hurry and holding his coffee in one hand and shifting with the other as he drove down the Mass Turnpike.

The closer he got to Fenway, the harder it was to stay calm. Earlier he had visualized Andy Pettitte out on the mound and pictured different pitches as they hung in the air and saw himself swinging and making clean contact and lining a single back up the middle. But now that he was on the way to the ballpark where he had seen so many games as a fan over the years, he felt the nervous energy kicking in, and also something else, too, something that hit him in the gut and was best not to think about too much.

Growing up in Framingham, he had been like every other kid and loved to spin out baseball scenarios in his head—two outs in the bottom of the ninth, bases loaded, the game tied, and now batting . . . *Lou Merloni.* But he never could have conjured this: arriving back in town only a day earlier, just in time to play against the Yankees, Pedro Martinez against Andy Pettitte. Merloni wanted to drive faster than seventy-five, so he could get there sooner and it could all start faster, but he held it to ten miles per hour over the speed limit.

A good reggae song came on the radio as he turned off Storrow Drive and passed over the Mass Pike with Fenway looming off to the right, and Merloni cranked up the volume. He rocked his shoulders to the music, and sang along, and kept his eyes moving, taking it all in. Just before he turned onto Yawkey Way, he turned the radio up one more notch and grinned, his car shaking with the bass.

"We love you, Lou, thank you!" some fans called to him from just beyond the players' parking lot, and he signed a few quick autographs before ducking into the clubhouse to think some more about how to get ready for Andy Pettitte.

Bob and Eleanor Adair hoped the traffic would not be too bad. The drive to Boston from their home in Connecticut was normally no problem, but who knew how crazy the roads would get as they approached Fenway Park? The Adairs lived in a rambling, low-slung craftsman-style cottage on a hill overlooking New Haven and, beyond, Long Island Sound. The place had been built back in 1929 by Thornton Wilder on the proceeds of *The Bridge of San Luis Rey*, his Pulitzer Prize–winning novel set in eighteenth-century Peru. The Adairs enjoyed having a house with a colorful history.

Bob liked to bring visitors upstairs for a look at the compact little guest bedroom where Sir Laurence Olivier was said to have been quite comfortable. Bob worked in Wilder's old study, a room dominated by a cathedral ceiling, a gothic carved-wood closet door, Bob's diverse collection of books, and, dangling from the ceiling, a pair of ballet slippers worn by Darci Kistler. Eleanor loved wine, and used to keep some of her collection in the bathtub; now the bottles were stored in a wine rack in the bathroom. She also collected antique oriental carpets and Buddhist religious paintings, called *thankas*. The couple kept their kitchen immaculate, and the only sign of clutter that Saturday morning was the splash of newsprint spread out on their small wooden kitchen table. They were reading the sports pages in preparation for the game.

Maybe it would have been different if the Great Hurricane of 1938 had taken out the big neon sign at Eleanor's father's Dodge dealership. As it was, Dodge was one of the fixed points of Eleanor's life; she never drove anything else. The Adairs had his and hers Dodge Caravans, and for the trip to Fenway, they opted to take hers. Eleanor firmly declined an offer of help with the driving duties.

"I'm the only one who drives my car," she said.

They were on the road by 10:20, and ran into their first traffic jam half an hour later. They had not even reached Hartford yet. Bob passed the time by talking about his work at Brookhaven from 1953 to 1960. He had his own particle-physics research group with a yearly budget of more than $1 million, and even when he left for Yale in 1960, he continued overseeing the group. Not until his sixtieth birthday did he turn it over to one of his students. Adair believed that scientists had to be both arrogant— "since you're boxing with God"—and humble, since you always had to be ready to be proven wrong. He brought both qualities to his now-classic book, *The Physics of Baseball.*

"The flight of balls, the liveliness of balls, the structure of bats, and the character of the collision of balls and bats are a natural province of physics and physicists," Adair wrote. "Baseball, albeit rich in anecdote, has not been subject to extensive quantitative studies of its mechanics—hence, models of baseball are not as well founded as they might be."

And:

"In all sports analyses, it is important for a scientist to avoid hubris and to pay careful attention to the athletes," he wrote. "Major league players are usually serious people, intelligent and knowledgeable about their craft. Specific, operational conclusions held by a consensus of players are seldom wrong. However, since baseball players are athletes, not engineers or physicists, their analyses and rationale may be imperfect. If players think they hit better after illegally drilling a hole in their bat and filling it with cork, they must be taken seriously, though the reasons they give for their 'improvement' may not be valid."

Adair's phone rang often that June with calls from reporters following up after Sammy Sosa's bat exploded to reveal a hollow, cork-filled center, earning the Cubs slugger a suspension. Adair patiently explained to anyone who called that corking your bat did not help you hit home runs. In fact, because a corked bat is lighter, it imparts less energy to a ball at the time of collision. Even accounting for the greater bat speed, Adair calculated that a standard fly ball to the outfield hit with a corked bat would actually travel three feet less than if it had been hit with an uncorked bat. Adair added that a player using a corked bat might make contact more often, given his improved bat speed and timing.

This was the sort of puzzle Adair enjoyed. If corking did not help hitters, why did they do it? The answer appeared to be some kind of placebo effect. He was interested in other areas where baseball player perception was at odds with the picture Adair could piece together through scientific models.

"You have to be a little careful because what they think they do isn't always what they do," Bob said as Eleanor battled traffic north of Hartford. "You have to get a feel for their rhetoric."

The best example was the rising fastball. It was possible to throw a true rising fastball, but only with something a lot lighter than a baseball. Just about anyone could throw a whiffle ball with sufficient backspin to make it rise. But baseballs were another story. The force of gravity ruled out imparting enough spin to a thrown baseball to make it rise in flight. The interesting question, then, was why so many ballplayers insisted they had seen a rising fastball. The answer was simple: They *had* seen it. That was because a baseball player's eyes were trained to follow the ball as it passed along a trajectory. So if it dropped less than their eyes were trained to expect, the fastball appeared to be rising.

The force of gravity dictated that a standard, ninety-mile-an-hour fastball dropped about three feet as it traveled the sixty-some feet from the pitcher's outstretched fingertips to home plate. So for a fastball to rise, it would have to have more than three feet of break. Who had ever seen a fastball break three feet in any direction? Even most slow curves did not do that. The trick to persuading players of this was understanding how they saw things.

"When I tell players that at the next opportunity they should watch the pitches from the on-deck circle and measure the path of the ball against the background of the stands, they instantly believe me," Adair said.

Eleanor turned on to the Massachusetts Turnpike shortly before noon, and with at least another hour and a half of driving ahead, Bob recalled his early interest in physics. Laughing, he admitted that the pulp-fiction magazines his father brought home in the 1930s were a major influence. As science fiction serials became more popular, pulp Western writers would just transfer old stories wholesale.

"I remember one science fiction hero who rode a space ship like a bronco and shot a ray gun like a pistol," he said. "I suspect I ended up with a romantic idea of science as a result."

If anyone wondered whether a billionaire currency trader ever got excited about a baseball game, as in, really excited, the way real people like you and your neighbor Dave and your aunt Jill did, John Henry could set their minds to rest. It was true he thought of baseball decisions much the way he did decisions about currency trading, but that was just the mental part. He was not in it for the mental part. He liked the raw emotions that came with being close to a baseball team and helping determine its fortunes. He loved baseball and loved winning, but mostly, he loved connecting with other people for a change.

All those years of painful shyness had left John Henry with a cloak of unapproachability. He would stand around in the infield before a game, looking like a man who had just taken home a barge full of money and was very politely thrilled not to have to worry about the things that concerned most people. Even so, he had a shrinking air about him, a vulnerable look. It was almost as if his compact frame might collapse in on itself if you nudged him in the ribs or talked too loudly in his presence. No one who met him would have any trouble at all believing that back when he was a kid in Forrest City, Arkansas, and all the neighborhood kids gathered at his house to play baseball because his family had the best yard on the block, young John was too shy to ask if he could take part in the game.

John Henry was so excited the night after the Red Sox man-handled Jose Contreras, he had not been able to sleep. He had watched a movie and not turned in until 3:30 a.m. His alarm woke him up at 10:00 a.m. that Saturday, which gave him plenty of time to get to the ballpark. His estate was cut off from city streets by two separate private roads and a winding driveway that cut through his wooded property. It felt remote, but was only an eight-minute drive to Fenway.

His wife, Peggy, whipped him up breakfast of a ham and non-fat cheese omelet, and he took his time at the table reading the morning paper. He wanted to enjoy every detail of the win the pre-vious night. The only sour note was the illness that had come over Manny Ramirez and caused him to miss the game. Henry was worried. Pedro Martinez had been hit by a sore throat two weeks earlier, and it had been tough to shake. What if Manny had the same thing? What if he was so weak he could do nothing but lie in bed and watch TV? What if other players picked up the bug from Manny and it spread from player to player?

Manny Ramirez was a riddle. He was so much like a big kid, people had trouble believing their eyes, and always wanted to imagine he was more complex than they thought. Actually, he wasn't. He stepped up to the plate every time with the same distracted half-smile and almost ridiculously low-key demeanor, as if it had truly never occurred to him to feel such a thing as pressure, and you know what? It hadn't. The more you talked to him, and saw him up close, the stronger the impression became that he was just being himself. Manny clowned around in the clubhouse like a man forever trapped in the mind-set of a five-year-old blowing out the candles on his birthday cake. And so what? It could be maddening, if you were his boss, but there was also something amazing, even awe-inspiring, about watching someone like that punish baseballs season after season after season.

It was almost quarter to twelve by the time Henry stepped into his Volvo Cross-Country station wagon, hit the remote to open one of the doors on his three-car garage, and pulled out onto his stone driveway. He flicked a switch on the car's sun visor and a gate at the far end of his private lane slid silently open. His drive to work took him up Brookline Avenue and past the Longwood Medical area, where Lucchino and pitcher Todd Jones were just then visiting with a sick patient. From there it was right on Boylston and left on Yawkey Way, where Henry would pull into the tiny players' parking lot squeezed into a corner of Fenway Park.

There was a problem. A uniformed Boston police officer stared at him coldly, and waved him off, dismissing him as some annoying fan trying to sneak past. Henry said nothing. Instead, he stared back at the cop and waited. It didn't take long before the cop realized his mistake and waved the team owner through a crowd of fans and into the lot. As Henry started to pull in, another Boston police officer cut him off. He had not recognized him, either. Once he had parked, Henry spotted Jim Rowe, the team's goateed trainer, who was standing outside to wait for Manny Ramirez. Everyone was eager to hear how sick Ramirez was.

"How's Manny?" Henry asked.

"He won't play today," Rowe told him. "It usually takes two to two-and-a-half days to get through. He might play tomorrow, but I doubt it."

Henry was not happy. He had more questions for Rowe, and the questions themselves were more important than any answers Rowe could provide. Was it running through the clubhouse? Was it the same thing as Pedro had? Was he past the infectious stage? Finally Henry moved on, adding as if talking to himself, "The main thing is we don't want it to spread."

One of the first things Mariano Rivera did after he woke up at 9:45 was to call his wife, Clara, the way he often did on the road. He still thanked God every day for looking after her back in November when she gave birth by C-section and six hours later began hemorrhaging. Her obstetrician had to hurry back from the recovery room to try to save her life. Mariano felt as helpless that day as he ever had in his life. They named the boy Jaziel, which meant "the strength of God," and now it would always remind them of the ordeal Clara went through the day he was born. Even months later, tears came to Mariano's eyes thinking about the events of that day.

"I prayed to God to take care of my wife and baby," he said. "You have to have the faith that He will."

That morning at the Ritz Carlton in Boston, Rivera asked his wife about Jaziel and their other two, little Mariano and Jafet. A quick shower later, he was in the elevator heading down to the lobby. Rivera always had the look of a man who worried less than others, and that was even more true before games. Life was different for a closer, especially a great closer. Rivera knew he would watch the early innings from the clubhouse, and if he did pitch, it would be almost three hours into the game. He was like the headlining act at a rock concert who knew he had to wait out an opening set or two. But Rivera had never let his cool unconcern lapse into cockiness. He believed in modesty, and believed in it deeply. If you were good, and knew you were good, what was the point of being showy about it? What did that get you? And what did vanity cost you? That would make a good topic for him to discuss if he followed up on his plans to become a full-time minister once his playing days were over.

Rivera had come too far to lose a sense of himself now. They called him the pride of Puerto Caimito de La Chorrera, a fishing village along the Caribbean coast of Panama, thirty miles west of Panama City, and that was fine with him. His father, also called Mariano, was a strong influence on him, and he had taught him early in life the importance of respect. The family was poor. They pulled a living out of the sea, and sometimes they would take the fishing boat out and spend the whole day out there, and the whole night, too, and still not catch a thing. There would be nothing to eat for young Mariano, his sister Delia, and his brothers Alvaro and Giraldo. Other times, they came back with a full load of sardines to sell. It was the kind of life that tested faith, and if people sitting in ballparks in the United States looked at Rivera and saw a rare depth in the poise and authority with which he stared out from the mound, it was safe to say they were seeing a little of Caimito and lessons learned on the Caribbean.

Young Mariano, like many other boys from Latin America, played baseball using a ball made of knotted-up fishing netting and a glove fashioned from a cardboard box. Even as an accomplished Yankee veteran, he was happy to show people how to make their own gloves from cardboard. You just punched out holes for your fingers, and you were good to go. Oh, and you could fold it up and put it in your back pocket, too.

The Ritz Carlton lobby was unusually quiet that morning. Wherever they went, all around the country, the Yankees were swarmed by autograph-seeking fans. Often, more fans wanted their signatures than wanted the autographs of the hometown team. But in Boston, the lobby was empty. Jerry Laveroni, the Yankees' head of security, stood just outside the hotel, guarding the front door, but there was nobody to guard. A light rain began to fall at quarter to ten, half an hour before the Yankee bus would leave the hotel for Fenway. Jason Giambi, wearing a black shirt and stone-washed jeans, was one of the players milling around the lobby. Karim Garcia took his family into the hotel restaurant for breakfast.

Rivera waited until he arrived in the visitors' clubhouse at Fenway to sit down with Derek Jeter, Enrique Wilson, Gabe White, and Antonio Osuna, and have a breakfast of bacon and eggs with potatoes. Wilson had on a beret, or he did until Luis Sojo walked by and plucked it off his head, drawing laughs from the other players. But no one did anything to disturb Andy Pettitte, who was wandering back and forth in the clubhouse in flip-flops. Everyone gave him plenty of room. No one said anything to Jose Contreras, either. He was sitting in front of his locker staring off into space, still trying to come to terms with his rocky outing the night before. Rivera left him there and went out onto the field to play catch with Osuna, another pitcher.

Even so many years into the salary explosion, baseball's appeal still depended in part on the sense fans had that many players had bodies a lot like theirs. Seeing someone as unglamorous as Karim Garcia gave people hope. He was putty-faced, short-armed, and round. He always looked like he had indigestion. If he could make millions and get to hang out in big-league ballparks, it almost felt like they could, too. But people also wanted to be awed. Rivera was the kind of athlete who awed people. Standing there on the outfield grass, lazily coiling and uncoiling his lithe, long-limbed body to toss the ball to Osuna, he looked half-asleep. The effort seemed to cost him nothing.

Rivera and Osuna decided to liven up the session a little and play a game of strikes. The rules were simple enough: The one who threw the most strikes was the winner. The loser had to pay up. Ruben Sierra, the muscular, switch-hitting slugger, stood talking to Jeter and Posada on the infield grass. Sierra tried to take a few grounders at short, a bold move for someone who had been known to turn playing the outfield into an adventure. Posada and Jeter laughed as Sierra clumsily fielded ground balls. The time came to head back off the field, and Rivera and Osuna ended their game of strikes with no money changing hands. Both men insisted the game ended in a tie.

★   ★   ★

Brian Cashman came down into the lobby at the Ritz Carlton a crisp five minutes before the team bus pulled out for the short ride to Fenway, and soon found he had a problem on his hands. George Steinbrenner had been very clear the night before about one thing: He wanted Cashman to sit in Steinbrenner's personal seats right next to the Yankee dugout.

"I want you to be where I can see you," Steinbrenner told him. "I want the *players* to see you as they come off the field if they're doing badly."

Cashman went and talked to David Szen, the Yankees' traveling secretary.

"George wants me to sit in the visiting owner's box right by the dugout," Cashman told him.

That was not good news to Szen.

"Well, George had me give those tickets to Spike Lee," he told Cashman. "This is going to be awkward. I'm going to have to get them back from Spike."

Cashman had a way of looking both worried and far too calm, all at once. He decided this was a time not to worry.

"Listen, forget it," he told Szen. "Let Spike have those tickets. I'm sitting where I want to sit. This is ridiculous."

Szen was still uneasy. What if Steinbrenner was ticked off about the seat thing?

"David, it's not your issue, it's my issue," Cashman said. "George wants me to sit there. I'm choosing to sit behind home plate, where I'm accustomed to sitting."

Cashman knew that if the Yankees won, Steinbrenner would not care if he sat up on top of the Green Monster and bungee-jumped down onto the left-field grass during the seventh-inning stretch. If the Yankees lost, he would get an earful, no matter where he sat.

One of the tricks to Cashman's success with Steinbrenner was an almost scholarly fascination he had with Steinbrenner's Stein-brennerness. The man was a headache, no question, but he was not a riddle.

Cashman still chuckled when he thought about a night years ago when he was an assistant general manager. He and Mary were not married yet, and Cashman lived on Ninety-second Street, near Third Avenue, with two roommates, Doug Smith and Tim Kaufman. One night the phone rang very late, around 1:30 a.m. The Yankees were playing in Anaheim, and Cashman was in his room with the lights off, watching the game on TV. He figured Doug or Tim was getting a call from a woman he was dating, and did not answer. A minute later, someone knocked on his door.

"Hey, Cash, some dude who says his name is George is on the phone," Doug called through the closed door.

"George?" Cashman called back.

"He says his name is Steinbrenner."

The roommate thought it had to be a gag. But the game was going badly. Jack McDowell was pitching for the Yanks against the Angels and the umpire behind home plate was screwing them. So Cashman hurried toward the phone, just in case.

"Aren't you watching this fucking game?" Steinbrenner complained loudly as soon as he picked up.

"Yeah, why?" Cashman said, and gave him the inning and the score and a few other details to prove he was watching.

"Well your roommate said you were fucking asleep!" Steinbrenner said.

"Well he's not in my room!" Cashman said. "I've got the lights out and I'm watching the game."

It was a good thing that Mary knew him back then when he was an assistant general manager. She knew from the time they first started dating what it was like to work for Steinbrenner, and that helped cushion it for her later when they had been married for years and he was the GM. She saw that everybody who worked for the Yankees was running the same rat race, no matter how tough it was for their families. Cashman had finally insisted in his last contract that he was going to take some of his vacation days. Before that, time off never seemed to happen.

"There would always be a fight whenever it came up," Cashman said. "There always seemed to be a crisis that needed to be addressed. Now I've gotten to the point where you know what, crisis or no crisis, I've got a wife and two kids now, and I'm taking the vacation. You can fight it, but I'm going."

Cashman hoped to be able to take eight days of vacation in 2003. More than that was unthinkable. It was the same general idea with his office, which was no-frills all the way. There was actually no decoration of any kind. One wall was stuffed with strategically arranged little plates, one for every available player in the National League. Another wall had the American League players.

"I don't have any pictures on the wall," Cashman said. "People ask me, 'Why don't you decorate your office?' I was told early on,

'Don't decorate your office, because that means you're getting too comfortable.' I've been conditioned because of him not to. If you kick back and relax and start surveying the landscape about what you may have accomplished, that's when your competition is getting a leg up on you. So we work Thanksgiving. I'm on the phone on Christmas and Christmas break. When everybody else is quiet, that's when he seems to turn up the heat on you.

"When you're giving your blood and guts every day—I feel like I go 24/7, 365 days a year—sometimes that type of intense expectations on a daily basis can wear on you. But you know what? At his age he can outrun anyone. He's a marathoner. I'm more of a sprinter. That's what causes the friction. It's not a place where most people can handle the work, I don't think. Coming here into New York with the fast pace, the nonstop, high-level demands, the failure-is-not-an-option-type attitude—I think that breaks most people. They can't keep up with the race. Eventually they get tagged out."

Every game against the Yankees had an added urgency, and Theo Epstein found himself doing things he did not do when the Sox played other teams, like pausing during the game, as early as the sixth inning, to count how many more outs they had in the game. He had grown up as a Red Sox fan, but that had changed when he went to work in baseball. He spent two summers working for the Baltimore Orioles, and back then he would root under his breath for the Red Sox. But later, when he moved to San Diego and took on more responsibilities with the Padres, he did his best to sever those emotional ties to the Red Sox. "I had no feelings for the club," he insisted.

He came back to be with his family for the 1999 American League Championship Series against the Yankees, and some of the old tingle was back. It made him think again, as he had often thought in the past, that it would be great to come back to Boston and work for the Red Sox. He thought maybe then he would let himself embrace those youthful feelings for the Red Sox again. But it had not quite happened like that. Now that he was the Red Sox general manager, he gave the team everything he had professionally, but he did not call on those old feelings he had as a kid. Or not so far, anyway.

One of Epstein's potentially annoying duties that Saturday reminded him of how he used to feel about the Red Sox when he was a boy. Joel Patterson, a businessman from Dallas, had made a five-thousand-dollar donation to charity for the honor of bringing his family to Fenway to watch the game with Epstein in his private box.

"Thank you for your donation to the Jimmy Fund," Epstein told Patterson warmly, saying hello to his wife, Lesley, and their thirteen-year-old twins, Tim and Chris. "We really appreciate it."

Epstein—who has a twin brother, Paul—stopped into the Red Sox cafeteria for some lunch and saw the Pattersons again. He asked if he could join them, and they all squeezed together at one small table.

"Do you guys have the same set of friends or a separate set?" he asked the twins.

"Separate," they said at the same time.

Lesley Patterson wanted to offer a fan's advice.

"We just can't imagine Pedro not a Red Sock and Nomar not a Red Sock," she said.

"Is that a hint?" Epstein said.

They all laughed.

"We should be able to work that out," he said.

Epstein's assistant asked Patterson how he survived as a Red Sox fan during all of the bullpen disasters in April and May.

"I drank a lot," he said.

"Me too!" Epstein shot right back.

Spike Lee had enjoyed the drive from Woods Hole. He checked out the New York papers, first the *Daily News* and then the *Post,* and caught some sports talk radio. Once they were in Boston, they stopped at McDonald's for breakfast. Jackson had McNuggets and Lee went for a McGriddle. But there was a holdup at Fenway Park. He went to pick up his tickets, dressed in his Derek Jeter jersey and his Yankee cap, and ended up having to wait in line for half an hour.

"Somebody hadn't got the seats done yet," he said. "So the Red Sox fans were getting on me already, but I didn't care. I think they took pity on me, because I had my son. If I didn't have my son—"

He broke off there and laughed. Anyone who had ever watched Lee's movies knew that he liked to challenge people. His friend Nelson George talked about the gleeful look that came into Lee's eyes when he was stirring it up, instigating, and the same gleeful look came into his eyes out in front of Fenway Park, watching to see what the Red Sox fans would throw his way.

He was on the field in his Jeter shirt by 11:45, but Red Sox security told him he had to go.

Rick Cerrone, the Yankees' veteran media relations director, shooed them away.

"He's with us," he told them.

Lee looked around, trying to find Derek Jeter.

"We need this one, baby!" he yelled out to him.

Jeter grabbed one of his bats and brought it over. He smiled at six-year-old Jackson, and handed him the bat.

"If you see any Red Sox fans, hit them," Jeter instructed Jackson with a straight face, only smiling after he started to walk away.

Nearby on the infield grass, Red Sox executive Charles Steinberg was huddling with one of his people. They had a problem on their hands. They had scheduled an aunt of popular former Red Sox pitcher Bill Lee (the Spaceman) to throw out the first pitch that day. The aunt had played in the All-American Girls Professional Baseball League, so she was a natural. But fifteen minutes before game time, Steinberg got the word that she would not be making it to the park that day after all. That was not good.

"Do you want to ask Spike?" Rick Subrizio suggested.

Subrizio was manager of ballpark entertainment.

"Yes," Steinberg said, warming to the idea instantly. "I do."

Lee was a little surprised a few minutes later to see Steinberg hurrying over to him.

"How ya doin'?" Lee said.

"Spike, I'm Charles Steinberg of the Red Sox," he said. "Can I speak to you for a minute?"

Lee said sure.

"Spike, we want you to throw out the first pitch today," he said.

Lee did a double take. He couldn't believe they were seriously asking him to throw out the first pitch. Had they looked at him? He was wearing a Derek Jeter jersey and a Yankee cap.

"You want me to do what?" Lee asked Steinberg. "Do you know who I am?"

"Yes," Steinberg said, smiling. "We know who you are."

"All right," Lee said.

"I can't guarantee you won't get booed," Steinberg added.

Lee laughed that off.

"I'm used to that," he said. "I've been booed in the playoff wars in Indiana and Chicago."

It did not get more intense than Red Sox–Yankees, Lee figured. This was the Hatfields and the McCoys. He would be shocked if they did not boo and boo loudly.

"I can't control the crowd," Steinberg repeated.

"Look," Lee said. "I'm not worried about a crowd."

No, he was not worried, just amazed. He could not imagine the Yankees or George Steinbrenner having Ben Affleck or Peter Farrelly or anyone associated with the Red Sox throw out the first pitch at Yankee Stadium. He wasn't sure what to think about the Red Sox. In a way they should be commended. But he didn't think it was smart. You didn't do things like that. It was screwy.

One of the first people Lee had talked to was Red Sox first-base coach Dallas Williams. He was from Brooklyn, too. Steinberg said Williams would escort Lee out to the mound. The idea was to have Williams take Lee's Yankee cap off and replace it with a Red Sox cap.

Once he had time to think about it, Lee was nervous. He didn't care about the boos. He cared about the throw. He had to represent himself well. He didn't want to go up there and let loose with some weak-ass baby toss. That was the worst. He was getting himself revved up when Brian Cashman came over to say hello, shaking his head and grinning at Lee's Yankee cap and Jeter jersey.

"Dude, you're awesome," he told Lee.

Cashman thought it was great to see a huge Yankee fan having the guts to show up at Fenway Park wearing his colors. It was the toughest place in the whole country to show up in Yankee gear, and there Lee was, practically taunting the fans to scream at him.

"I'm getting ready for some boos," Lee told Cashman lightly.

They discussed the seating situation. Lee suggested Cashman sit with them in Steinbrenner's seats.

"I can put my son in my lap," Lee told him.

"No, Spike," Cashman said. "You take all the seats. You sit with your son and I'll sit somewhere else."

Debi Little normally preferred to arrive at the ballpark just after the National Anthem. That was no knock on the singers, although, to be honest, some of them were not the best she had ever heard. No, Debi had spent a major portion of her life at baseball games, and she would rather squeeze out a little more time to do other things if she could. That morning she strolled through the big, sprawling mall connected to the Prudential Building that stared down at Fenway from a mile and a half away.

She was talking about her and Grady's son, Eric, who was born thirty-one years ago and had to wait a month before he ever saw his father. Grady was a player-coach in the Yankee organization that year and could not get away. Grady had a .207 batting average over six minor-league seasons, and after the 1973 season he finally gave up on playing. Debi was always painfully aware of what base-ball had cost her family. She found herself almost overcome one time when Eric called with their first grandson nearby, and Debi could hear the boy talking excitedly about the Red Sox.

They had moved so often when Eric was a boy. She and Grady always told him all that travel was a good experience. It would broaden him. But when he got older, they settled down for a few years, and now Eric lived with his wife in Charlotte, North Car-olina, doing his best to put down roots. He had a new baby boy, Luke, his second son, and Debi wanted to send a gift. She visited the Barnes & Noble in the mall to pick up a copy of *Fenway Park from A to Z,* a book the Red Sox Wives Organization had put to-gether.

Back at the apartment, she spent a few minutes packing the book and getting it ready to mail. She liked books. In fact, she was writing one. It would be a children's book all about a little boy going to a Red Sox game at Fenway Park. She remembered her and Grady taking Eric to games there when he was a boy. He would see the big CITGO sign, and know they were almost there. She caught a taxi and she, too, saw the big CITGO sign, and not much later she caught her first glimpse of the field that day. Debi had to admit that seeing the green grass of the ballfield always gave her a little thrill, even with so many thousands of games behind her. Grady felt it, too. Sometimes, late at night, she and Grady would come out and sit in the empty stadium, long after the game had ended and everyone had gone home, just so they could soak up the feel of the place. There were only a few workers here and there, picking up hot-dog wrappers or sweeping, and it felt like she and Grady were alone with Fenway Park and all its history and associations. They would just sit there quietly, turning to smile at each other and doing their best never to forget what it felt like to be there.

Any umpire who told you he didn't get up for a big game was trying to put one over on you. Mark Carlson was too honest for that. Was he more excited knowing he would be working home plate on a day when there was a great matchup of pitchers, Pedro Martinez against Andy Pettitte? You bet. That was true even though Carlson was still fighting off a sore throat. The last series he worked had been in Pittsburgh and a doctor there told him it was strep throat and prescribed antibiotics. Carlson was finding it hard to sleep. He had set his alarm for 8:45 that morning, but lay in bed until nine before calling his wife and hitting the gym for a full-hour workout. Carlson was big and bear-shaped, and took pride in looking fit. He believed in projecting a positive image as an umpire. People were going to curse you. Some were even going to think they hated you. But if you did your job well, you would earn respect for yourself and for everyone else who pulled on the black pads for a living.

Carlson enjoyed his work, but he was never one to overstate his own importance. His ideal game was one where the fans never thought about him one way or the other. If that happened, he knew he was doing his job. Even when he took his turn as home-plate umpire, calling balls and strikes, Carlson knew that no matter how tough his job got, he had it easier than the pitchers. They were the ones throwing the baseball. All he had to do was stand back there and say whether the ball crossed the plate or didn't cross the plate. He trusted in his judgment and professionalism and hoped for a good clean game.

The fans out on Yawkey Way seemed to have no idea that Mark Carlson, with his big, friendly face, alert blue eyes, and ready smile, was an umpire arriving at Fenway for a day of work. He squeezed up a narrow staircase near the Red Sox clubhouse entrance and into the umpires' room, and was glad to get one step closer to first pitch. He did not get nervous, but he always felt an urge to get going and have the game underway, especially a big game like this.

Carlson smiled when a hunched-over older man in glasses stepped into the umpires' room, helped along by a cane, and said hello to everyone. Carlson was unclear whether the old fellow, "Doc," was a friend of Ed Rapuano, the crew chief, or of Paul Nauert, who was working first base that day, or maybe of Rob Drake, who would be down at second. But what did it matter? They all greeted him warmly. Visitors were not that common, and they had a way of livening up the day.

"The most important thing to an umpire is his eyes," Doc told them all solemnly, reaching into a canvas bag and pulling out a small bottle of Visine for each of them. No one turned him down. That might have offended Rapuano. Or was it Nauert? Or Drake? Which one of them was it again who knew Doc?

All four sat down with Doc and listened to his stories of umpiring in the minor leagues. He had old photos, too, and wasted no time in pulling them out and passing them around. They all did their best to pay attention to him, even though he was shouting and it was often hard to follow what he was saying. Phones kept ringing with friends and acquaintances asking if the umpires had any tickets left out of the six they each received per game. They had all chipped in to help out Rapuano, who grew up in New Britain and had more family members and friends to take care of than the others.

The tension level hiked up a notch as the clock ticked past 12:30 and game time approached. A clubhouse attendant came in with a baseball, and Doc asked each of the umpires to sign it for him. Rapuano signed "To Doc, We call 'em like we see 'em." Once Doc was gone, the umpires looked around at one another, eyes wide, as if to ask: "Who in the heck was that?" They all laughed when it became clear that none of them had ever met this Doc character before.

Red Sox fans talked so much about whichever unlucky sap was momentarily entrusted with the job of managing the team, they tended to feel like they knew the person. But Red Sox fans did not know Grady Little. Part of that was by design. It was just not Little's style to give a lot away, no matter what people might expect of him. But part of it was about New England being a long way from Texas. Little came from somewhere else, and he used that distance as a shield. The thing you noticed when he spoke was something harder to pick up than just the Texas accent. It was something a layer or two deeper. He had a deep voice, but it was also nasal, and even when Grady Little was lowering his forehead and flashing one of his first-rate glares, he always had a little-boy sadness or resignation to his voice. He knew the deck was stacked against him, and he knew he had accomplished more than anyone had ever thought he would, just landing the job of Red Sox manager in the first place, but mostly he was tired of it all.

"What a lot of fans don't understand is everything we do is to try to win the game," he said. "I've been managing since 1980, in the minor leagues and the big leagues, and I can't ever remember making any move in a game to try to lose the game, ever. That's why I'm a winner. Sometimes it happens right. Sometimes you don't get good results. But you're doing it for a reason. These are human beings you're dealing with, and they're not perfect all the time."

Little's voice had an edge to it as he offered this self-justification. He was angry and he was bewildered, and this was still during the regular season. Like anyone who had spent most of a long life in baseball, Little had learned how much he did not know and had long since accepted that even if you gave it your best shot, the game would often find a way to outsmart you. What he could not stomach was the thousands of armchair experts at home who thought they had all the answers. Little knew better than to think anyone had all the answers.

It made him so angry, thinking about it, he often forced himself to turn to happier thoughts, like looking forward to seeing his grandchildren again.

"My grandson Braden called me," Little said. "He's four. He said, 'Pops, I have a baby brother and he peed all over himself.' "

It was hard to find time during the season to see his son and his family, and that ate at Little. He had given so much time to the game. "We enjoy every minute we can spend with them," he said.

If there was a manager who enjoyed talking with the press before each game, Little would like to meet him. He enjoyed it about as much as a hemorrhoid flare-up, and made sure the reporters knew it, too. Some of them were OK. Heck, he even liked some of them. But that didn't make the sessions any more bearable. They assembled in his office shortly before eleven, a dozen of them crowding into the cramped space, and Little looked as relaxed and carefree as a man waiting to get socked in the gut.

"He feels sick," Little said when asked about Manny Ramirez. "He's not well enough to play today. He's gonna go to the doctor."

They asked about Lou Merloni.

"He's had some success with Pettitte in the past," he said. "He'll have a chance to have success here today."

Little was giving the bare minimum, and everyone knew it. He sat behind his desk, face darkening, waiting for someone to ask something. The only thing worse than the damn questions was the silence when no one had the guts to speak up.

"Is what Manny has the same thing as what Pedro had?" a reporter finally asked.

"We don't have an indication that it's the same thing," Little said. "But it's taken him down."

Little looked back down and fidgeted even more than before. He interlocked his fingers, and then relaxed them. He rubbed one hand with the other. He looked up quickly, saying, basically: Now or never. The questions started up again, and he slogged his way through all of them until the reporters worked their way around to asking about Ramirez again.

"Manny's too sick to play today," he said, staring hard at one reporter. "Like you said yesterday, Dave, 'Good timing.' If he were well enough to play today, he sure as hell would be out there."

Little's anger had hopped up another level now, and was flashing in his eyes. The reporter at the other end of his stare was unnerved.

"I didn't say, 'Good timing,'" he said. "I said 'Bad timing.' There's a difference. Theo jumped on me yesterday, too."

"You said, 'Good timing,'" Little said.

The reporter could have produced a tape of the previous day's sessions, proving he had said "bad timing." He could have summoned several Supreme Court justices to hand over sworn affidavits testifying to their certainty that he had said "bad timing." None of it would have had the slightest impact on Grady Little. He was sure the reporter had said "good timing," and it didn't set well with him at all. The sarcastic little bastards. He wished he could whup one of them from time to time, just for kicks.

Larry Lucchino made a point of answering at least a few of the e-mails he received from fans every day. He did this because it fit with the philosophy he and John Henry were following, which was to show a high-powered politician's discipline for getting the little things right and taking advantage of every opportunity to get out your message and cultivate good will. But the reason he enjoyed the e-mail lay somewhere else. Lucchino was shrewd and experienced and good at anticipating both problems and potential solutions. But it could be boring to be thinking ahead so much of the time. Real glimpses of the outside world could be refreshing.

He slid into his chair, right next to a big plate-glass window overlooking Yawkey Way, and found he had 109 e-mails waiting for him to read. Most days, he had somewhere between fifty and a hundred. It was usually hard to establish much of a dialogue with fans he ran into making his rounds or out in public. The best contact Lucchino had with fans came right there, staring at his computer screen. Some asked questions. Others made comments or offered analysis.

"This is going to sound crazy, especially according to my wife," read one of the e-mails Lucchino opened that morning. "But I'm going to share this with you: I've been to eleven games this year and the team has won all eleven. Here's the crazy bit. I think there's some element of luck involved with the lucky pair of red shoes."

Lucchino laughed at that one. For all his savvy, he sometimes had a boyish quality. He had twice faced serious battles with cancer, and no one endured bone-marrow transplants without remembering, somewhere very deep and very private, just how painful and demoralizing the experience had been. Even so, Lucchino had a way of suddenly hopping at times, almost dancing. It made you wonder if beneath all the other layers, the real

Lucchino was the one smiling at the sheer fun of being at the center of the Red Sox universe, getting to live and breathe baseball and, every now and then, to cast George Steinbrenner as Darth Vader. Done with his e-mail session, he pushed back from his computer just after 11:00 and stood staring through his window at the throng of fans below.

"People are assembling," he said, lowering his voice to sound like a sportscaster setting a scene.

He made a quick call.

"How's the weather look?"

It looked fine.

"And tomorrow?"

It was going to be one of the most gorgeous days of the year.

"How about Springsteen? Are you willing to go that far?"

Lucchino was one of many in the Sox organization who had tickets to see the Boss at Fenway the following weekend, but that felt like a long way off. Lucchino had more immediate concerns, like a meet-and-greet coming up with a woman who had complained about being treated rudely by a waiter in the Hall of Fame Club, one of the so-called premium areas of the stadium. But still Lucchino stood by his window looking down at all the Red Sox fans milling around the open concourse, greeting each other and inspecting each other's Sox hats and shirts and signs, and grinning with anticipation. Lucchino wanted to go down and join them and absorb their enthusiasm and energy. Instead, he went with a marketing assistant to meet the complaining woman, her tongue-tied husband, and their plump young son.

"You might repeat the issues you had," Lucchino said to the

woman, easing into a silky voice he had probably used in his days as a litigator.

They had sat down at a table in the Hall of Fame Club and a waiter was hovering. Everyone ordered quickly, except for the plump young son, who wanted some kind of nonalcoholic piña colada.

"Did you say piña colada?" Lucchino asked him with mock shock, charming the son and the father.

The mother kept doggedly to her recitation of how rudely the waiter had treated her. She was short on details, and heavy on bland outrage. Lucchino nodded his head gravely, implicitly agreeing with everything she said.

"He's been reassigned," he told the woman. "He was probably playing out of position. Probably not suited to working with the public."

"That's why we were really upset," the woman said. "I don't think anyone should be treated that way."

Lucchino nodded gravely some more. He pretended not to notice that the woman kept repeating herself. He told her that, yes indeed, she could stay and enjoy the premium services of the Hall of Fame Club throughout that day. This seemed to be what she wanted. Lucchino repeated the line about the worker playing out of position. He thanked the woman and excused himself. He did not look relaxed again until he was down on Yawkey Way, talking to fans.

"If only you could capture this noise and buzz and feeling," he said.

The skies had cleared and the sunlight had that glittery brightness of just after light rain showers. The mustard being squirted on steaming hot dogs glowed a brighter yellow, and the ketchup took on a deeper red. Lucchino explained that the concept for the Yawkey Way concourse was based in part on Eutaw Street at Camden Yards and also on the Festival of San Gennaro in New York's Little Italy, which attracted more than a million people each September. (So far, though, there was no cannoli-eating contest on Yawkey Way.)

"You done good," a fan told Lucchino. "This is a great atmosphere."

Out beyond the outfield stands a few minutes later, Lucchino noticed red paint peeling off an ancient column. "A little paint wouldn't hurt, huh?" he told an assistant. He joked about Baseball Belly, a condition known to afflict both sportswriters and baseball executives, vowed to eat more salads, and waved his hand to indicate the new picnic area beyond the outfield seats.

"Last year we had Dumpsters in here, and TV trucks," Lucchino said. "This is a point of pride for all of us who worked on this. They actually cook in the concession stands now. Imagine that at Fenway. We brought it up to major-league standards."

To prove his point, he sampled several different food items, and offered them as well. They tasted pretty good. Much better than food cooked somewhere else and trucked in later, which was what Fenway fans had been sold in the past.

"Can you sign my ball, Mr. Lucchino?" a six-year-old asked him.

Seeing Lucchino talking to a fan, a man approached along with his seventeen-year-old son. The father, Alex Vispoli, was vice president of partner development at Gold Wire Technology, and his son, also Alex, was a junior at Phillips Academy in Andover.

"A year ago, he got Eagle Scout and you sent him a letter of congratulation," the father said, beaming in obvious gratitude. "Just wanted to thank you."

It was not a setup.

The kids had no idea what great seats Peter Farrelly had scored for the game, and he wanted to keep it that way. He and Bob had gotten up early to catch the 9:00 ferry for the forty-five-minute ride across Vineyard Sound to Woods Hole, where his brother-in-law John, married to his sister Beth, was waiting to drive them back to John and Beth's summer house in New Seabury, right next door to the house where the Farrelly parents lived year-round. Farrelly borrowed his parents' Mercedes and headed off with Bob and Tommy, John and Beth's fourteen-year-old son. They pulled off at the Mashpee Rotary and went into the Picnic Box to get some sandwiches for later in the day. The next stop was at another of Farrelly's sisters, Kathy, to pick up her thirteen-year-old son, Harrison. They had to hurry from there if they were going to make it in time for the start of the game.

Farrelly was excited. It was just so perfect. He had always despised the Yankees and New York teams in general. They were arrogant, he thought, and took way too much pleasure in rubbing it in when they won. But the Yankees were different under Joe Torre's leadership, Farrelly thought. All in all, he considered them the classiest Yankee teams ever. It all started with Jeter and Bernie

Williams and the tone they set. As a committed Yankee-hater of long standing it was hard for Farrelly to admit, but it had not hurt as much watching the Yankees win so often those last six years. He admired them. September 11 also left him with a soft spot for New Yorkers. He rooted for the Yankees to beat Arizona in the World Series. It was the first time in his life he had ever rooted for the Yankees, and it might turn out to be the last, too.

A Red Sox fan could tip his cap and admit that under Joe Torre and Brian Cashman, the Yankees had become almost likable, but as a committed Red Sox fan, Farrelly linked his identity as a sports fan to his status as a true connoisseur of heartbreak. Farrelly's Five Most Painful Sporting Events were drilled into his memory. He could recount them down to the last detail.

1. The playoffs, back in Little League. He was twelve years old, so it was his last of four years in the league. He played for a team called the Yankees and they were playing against a team called the Red Sox. About a week earlier, his team was beating the tar out of the other guys, but in the last inning one of the fathers started heckling a kid, and all the old men started fighting. The ump ended up with a bloody nose, and the game was called. (Thankfully, it was one of the few games Doc Farrelly did not attend, so he had no chance to deck any of the other fathers.) The league commissioner decided they had to play the game over, and their starting pitcher reached some kind of league-imposed maximum on the number of pitches he could throw in a week. The coach called

Farrelly over from shortstop to pitch the last inning with one out, nobody on base, and a one-run lead.

"So I walk over from short, not expecting to be on the mound all of a sudden, and I'm a little nervous," Farrelly said. "I walk five batters in a row, and the God's honest truth is, I'm not even that wild. I don't think I missed a strike by more than two inches on any pitch. The ump (not Bloody-Nose) was squeezing me big time. Thirty-something years later I still swear the league wanted us to lose, possibly because it was one of our dads who'd started the brawl and punched the umpire. Point is, I remember everything about that day—the ump's face, his teeth, his ears, the way my catcher kept firing the ball back at me harder than I was throwing to him, the pleas from the guys behind me to 'Just get it over!' my father's heart breaking for me, the other parents shooting me looks, the ride home with my brother and father, the sick feeling of letting everyone down."

2. The end of the 1972 season. The Red Sox lost the division by a half game when Luis Aparicio slipped rounding third on the next-to-last day. Farrelly was watching at home in the yellow vinyl chair that used to be green. It was a strike-shortened season, so the Red Sox played one game less than the division champs, who lost the same number of games but had one more win. He was sickened that the league allowed that inequity.

3. 1973, his Providence College Friars were in the Final Four. They had won nineteen in a row and were killing

Memphis State by double figures in the first half. It looked like a certain blowout. "I'm sitting on our family-room floor," he said. "Then our big man Marvin Barnes goes down with a knee injury. We lose. I bawl my eyes out."

4. 1976, the Patriots are the best team in the NFL, they're beating the feared Oakland Raiders in the last few seconds and have fourth and long. The Patriots stop them. Game over!!! Oh, but there's a whistle. Roughing the passer. Terrible call. Not even close. Worst call in NFL history. Raiders get a first down. "I throw something at the TV even though I'm at our neighbor's house," Farrelly said. "The Raiders score and go on to win the Super Bowl. I hate all refs for ten years."

5. 1986, Mets, Game Six. "I'm standing in my living room in L.A. with a shit-eating grin and a bottle of champagne in each hand while also linking fingers with my brother and five fellow Sox fans who are each hoisting their own champagne, and then . . . well, you know."

Like Larry Lucchino, John Henry had been checking his e-mails and making the rounds. He visited the .406 Club, an expanse of high-roller seating directly behind home plate, complete with bar and waitress service. Encased in thick glass that insulated them from most of the sounds of the ballgame, the six hundred seats in the club went for more than a hundred bucks apiece. The glass cut the area off from the rest of the stadium so dramatically, the Henry group had given some thought to smashing the glass and opening the area up to the elements, but they would have to give that one some more thought. Henry was on his way to meet Leo Mullen, Delta Airlines CEO, who had flown in from Atlanta to attend the game with his wife and six brothers, all from around Boston.

"You've done a great job," Mullen said, standing up from his lunch.

"So have you," Henry said.

"Isn't this a great baseball town?" Mullen's wife, Leah, said.

"It is *the* great baseball town," Henry said, smiling now.

One of Mullen's brothers thanked Henry for his investment in the Red Sox.

"It's the best thing I ever did," Henry told him. "It's a bargain."

"Will you keep Fenway Park?" another brother asked.

"It would be very hard to replicate Fenway Park," Henry said. "In the long term, I don't know if it's the answer. But in the short term it is. It's like the Eiffel Tower to Paris."

Henry smiled on the way out, and paused to stroke the golden hair on a little girl, almost the way a politician would. Handed a list of VIPs for the game a few minutes later, he was pleased to see that Senator George Mitchell was there.

"Oh, Peter Farrelly is here," Henry said. "He's such a great guy. He's as ardent a Red Sox fan as you'll ever meet."

The starting lineup was being announced as Henry walked through the grandstand. Fans pointed at him wherever he went.

"You ready for a World Series?" Henry called to one fan, a middle-aged man in a Red Sox shirt.

"We've been waiting our whole lives," the man said.

Two college students asked the owner if he would sign their Red Sox caps.

"Are you ready for a World Series?" Henry asked them, signing and moving on.

David Mellor came out to talk to crew chief Ed Rapuano before the game and had to sit in the dugout for a few minutes to wait for the right moment. Catcher Jason Varitek headed off to the bullpen at two minutes to 1:00, and Pedro Martinez followed him one minute later. Todd Walker and David Ortiz stopped by to talk with Mellor, but first they had to spend some time kidding each other.

"Man, with those glasses you look like a porn star," Ortiz told Walker.

"OK then," Walker shot back. "You and me, Ortiz. Let's do it. C'mon!"

Once Ortiz walked away, Walker turned back to tell Mellor that he had noticed a slight lip at the edge of the grass. Mellor gave him a thorough rundown on what they could and could not do with the dirt. During the National Anthem, Mellor kept talking to an assistant, since they had business to discuss, but even though he was on crutches, Mellor made sure to reach down and put his cap over his heart.

Even just before game time, the Champions Sports Bar in Santo Domingo was still almost deserted. Most Dominicans preferred to watch their baseball games in betting salons, called *bancas,* where the beer was cheap and plentiful. Rafael Avila opted for more comfortable surroundings. His heavy gold ring gleamed on his finger as he tilted back his Campari and ice.

Avila gave others credit for helping bring along Pedro Martinez after the Dodgers finally signed him in June 1988. No one as small as Pedro could pitch the way he did if he was not possessed. He burned inside with some kind of fanatical need to show his dominance. He had tempered that burning need over the years with a champion's pride and awareness of what he had already accomplished, but he had not changed so much.

Pedro Martinez grew up in Manoguayabo, half an hour away from Santo Domingo. When he and his older brothers needed a ball, they sometimes resorted to ripping the heads off their sisters' dolls and hitting those around the dusty road outside their simple house, where the six kids slept in three beds. Their father, Paolino, had been a baseball player in his day, and worked as caretaker at the school Pedro and his brothers and sisters attended. As a very young boy, Pedro often followed his father around. But later, he took to following big brother Ramon.

Pedrito yearned to play ball with his big brother and his friends, but when he was too small, his big brother said no, and Pedrito would cry. He was a sensitive boy, and his parents' long, loud arguments would wake him up and leave him shivering with fear. Their divorce marked him for life and left him with a nervous condition. Ramon became the center of the family and father figure. He signed with the Dodgers four years before Pedro, and the younger brother learned from his older brother's experiences. He took English courses back home in the Dominican Republic, and was ahead of his brother before he ever came to the United States.

Eliodoro Arias, the pitching coach at the Dodgers' academy in the D.R., taught both Martinez brothers to build up their strength through a rigorous program of running, weight lifting, and arm exercises. Pedro's fastball improved dramatically, and soon he was almost hitting ninety miles an hour. Avila, the director of that academy, was struck by the contrast between the two brothers. Ramon was much taller, but he had no blood. Pedro was always very emotional, and sometimes Avila was hard on him. Now and then, he had to pull his ears, as they say in Spanish. Raul Mondesi and Pedro would run around playing practical jokes on other players, sticking things on their backs and cooking up other mischief, and Avila always had to keep an eye on them. He made sure Pedro learned to be on time, no matter how long a bus ride he had, and taught him the importance of following instructions closely and always showing respect.

The screen at the Champions Sports Bar showed Martinez on the mound, warming up before the first pitch. Avila smiled, remembering how Pedro was always a character. He loved calling attention to himself, especially away from the field, but on the mound he was 100 percent concentration.

"Let's go, Pedro the Great!" bartender Rafael Gonzalez called out.

★　　★　　★

Debi Little saw no need to contain her excitement.

"That's Spike Lee!" she called out from her seats near the Red Sox dugout.

She was hoping for an autograph. It was just after 1:00. Her husband walked out of the dugout and stood with Lee for a picture.

"Why don't you wear a Red Sox hat?" Little asked Lee in that gruff Texas accent of his.

Lee didn't answer at first.

"I can't do that," he said. "Can't do that."

Debi stood and waved and tried hard to get Grady's attention. A Spike Lee autograph would be good for her charity work. But Grady did not see her, and she sat back down, disappointed.

The full house at Fenway was surprised when the announcement came. Throwing out that day's first pitch, they were told, was "filmmaker Spike Lee." Like Rich Maloney, out behind the scoreboard in left, many were wondering: *Spike Lee?* Why would they let *him* throw out the first pitch? And then there he was, Mars Blackmon glasses and cat-that-ate-the-canary smile in place, Jeter jersey on full display. The fans reacted the only way they could. They let loose with a hearty round of booing. They were a long way from late-inning form, but for so early in the day, their noise made an impression.

"Why is the audience booing?" said Debi Little.

Then she noticed Lee was in a Yankee jersey.

"Did he really have to?" she said.

Brian Cashman was in his seat behind home plate, shaking his head. He still could not believe it. How could they let him throw out the first pitch dressed that way? How could they? The question kept repeating itself in his head. That would never happen at Yankee Stadium. Never. If someone even tried, the marketing director would be fired.

The only way someone could pull that off in the Bronx would be to plan ahead. If somebody agreed to throw out the first pitch and walked out there in a sweatshirt and jeans and then, out there on the mound, suddenly pulled off the sweatshirt to reveal a Red Sox jersey on underneath—that would be the only way that would happen at Yankee Stadium. To other teams, that kind of thing might have seemed unimportant, but the Yankees took the sanctity of their field very seriously.

"Anna Kournikova showed up to throw out the first pitch at Yankee Stadium and she was half-naked and we made her put on clothes," Cashman said.

Lee had figured he would be tossing the ball to Jason Varitek, or possibly backup catcher Doug Mirabelli. He was not thinking Kasey Lindsey, a Red Sox ballgirl, but that was who they sent out to catch his pitch. Lee posed for pictures with Lindsey and the other ballgirls, and took the ball to go make his pitch.

The boos were great, Lee thought. He tried to soak them up.

"I don't care if this ball goes over the backstop," Lee told himself. "I'm going to throw this as hard as I can."

He walked out and stood on the mound in his Jeter jersey and Yankee cap, looking smaller than all those times courtside at Madison Square Garden. But he let fly with a pitch that had something on it and caught the corner of the plate for a strike. The crowd cheered. That was how it was with the fans in Boston. If you earned their respect, they let you know.

"I appreciated that," Lee said. "They saw I have some kind of skill. I play softball all the time. Every movie we do, we have a softball team. We play other movies and TV shows. We played *Manchurian Candidate* and beat them like 35–2. Denzel didn't play and neither did Jonathan Demme."

Kasey Lindsey, the ballgirl, was impressed. She got a better look at the pitch than anyone, and to her it looked like some pretty good heat and definitely a strike. She caught the ball and ran out to the mound to hand it to Lee for his collection.

"Congratulations, Mr. Lee, and nice shot!" Lindsey told him.

Lee headed back over to the Yankee dugout and most of the team was lined up in front to kid him or congratulate him or both. Lee Mazzilli held up his arm and flexed his biceps for Lee. Willie Randolph, a good friend, came over and congratulated him.

Jackson Lee had enjoyed the whole spectacle.

"Daddy, they were booing you," he said.

Lee told him it was all good, and Jackson decided it was fine with him if the Boston fans wanted to boo his daddy.

"He actually just threw a nice pitch," said Rich Maloney out in the Green Monster. "Had some gas on it."

A minute or two after Lee walked off the mound, hamming it up good-naturedly, Peter Farrelly brought his group through the concourse. His son Bob was playing it cool, but his nephews kept giving him looks as they walked lower and lower through the rows of stands. Farrelly did his best to walk slowly. He wanted to drag out the suspense as long as he could.

When they got to their seats, his nephews were amazed. They were in the front row, so close they could look right into the Boston dugout. The boys could not believe how good the seats were. Harrison was so excited to be looking at the Red Sox players from only a few feet away, he started shaking. His fingers would not stop trembling. Some of the players winked at him, and that only made Harrison shake more. It was almost as if he and his cousin Tommy were having out-of-body experiences.

"Isn't this incredible, Bob?" Farrelly asked his son. "These are the best seats in the house."

Bob thought it over.

"No, they aren't," he told his father.

"What do you mean?" Farrelly asked.

Bob twisted around so he could point one hundred feet behind them.

"Way back there," he said. "They're up higher, so they can see way better than us."

Farrelly stared at his son.

"You'll get it someday, Bob," he said.

TOP OF THE FIRST

	1	2	3	4	5	6	7	8	9	R
NYY										
BOSTON										

Derek Jeter set up on the edge of the batter's box, head down, and tugged at his batting helmet with his free right hand. He put both hands on the bat, flexing his wrists, and held it up near his eyes, like a man lifting a dusty old wine bottle to check the vintage. Later in the day, it would be a time-out signal to home-plate umpire Mark Carlson when Jeter held his right hand out to the side, palm down. So early, before the game had even started, it looked more like Jeter was flashing a quick hand signal to every corner of the packed-in crowd, telling them it was time to lean in and pay close attention because this show was starting.

Seven or eight heartbeats later, Trot Nixon was flat on his belly in right field. Pedro Martinez's first pitch of the game had floated

119

out over the plate, just where Jeter was looking for it, and he had done his impression of a tennis player, swinging inside-out at the ball just before it crossed the plate and drilling a line drive to right field. Nixon broke in quickly, but this looked like a double.

"Get that, get that," John Henry pleaded nervously from his owner's box.

Nixon ran in hard and made a headlong dive. He hit the out-field grass with his knees and slid forward on his belly, his red-stockinged legs kicking up behind him, but he managed to hold his glove out in front of him just long enough to make the catch as he tumbled forward. He flipped the ball toward the infield, found his sunglasses, and slipped them back into place over the layer of caked-on dirt that gave his Red Sox cap such a comical *Bad News Bears* look.

"Look at that hat," John Henry said, shaking his head and smiling.

Marty Martin was just glad he had not missed anything. He and his brother Dean had found their seats in right field and set-tled in before the first pitch. Martin was determined to make the most of the day, and started clapping even before the game started. He wanted to yell for every Red Sox player that came up, and against every Yankee. He watched Jeter swing, and it almost seemed like the ball was flying out toward Martin and his brother before Pedro Martinez had thrown the first pitch. It all happened so fast, Martin had trouble processing what he saw. He thought Nixon had no chance at all to get to the ball.

"That was amazing," Martin told his brother, Dean.

Even after Nixon's catch, the packed Fenway crowd had a tense feel to it. Later in the game, a spectacular play like that would have released built-up tension and generated real emotion. It was too soon for that. The fans, like the people sitting in the dugouts, seemed to be bracing for a long, exhausting afternoon.

Theo Epstein said nothing. He stood in the general manager's box, arms folded, and watched Nixon dive and make the catch. Epstein hated the view from his box. You didn't see as much, and he could never see enough. The more he saw, the more he understood, and the more he understood, the more he knew. Knowledge was power.

"There's no advantage whatsoever to watching from here," he grumbled. "It's horrible."

But he tried not to complain too loudly. He was there to spend time with the Patterson family, and the twins were sitting right next to him, along with their father.

Asked if he ever cheered, Epstein misheard the question.

"Four times in college," he said.

"Not 'chew.' 'Cheer.' "

"Oh, 'cheer,' " he said, blushing. "No, I never cheer."

Some general managers might have scolded their leadoff hitter for swinging at the first pitch, but not Brian Cashman. He cared about plate discipline and liked Yankee batters to work a count. But he knew what it was like to be a hitter ready to take a rip at the first pitch of the game. That had been his style. He played second base and led off back at Catholic University in Washington, and he always had the same thing in mind.

"I wasn't a walk guy," Cashman said. "I was the type that I swung at the first pitch of the game. It drove my coach nuts. To me

121

the best pitch of the game was always the first pitch. You usually get a fastball, and I loved hitting fastballs. So if it was a fastball in my zone, I wanted to hammer it. That was my aggressive attitude. My coach would give me speech after speech. He backed off in the second year and just said, 'You know what? Forget it. You always seem to put the ball in play and get on base with it.' "

Theo Epstein was eager to get a read on what they could expect from Pedro that day. His previous outing, Martinez had been a sick man, drained and weak. Even now there was a puffiness around Martinez's eyes that alerted anyone paying attention to his many recent days of bed rest.

Nick Johnson would offer a good test. Jorge Posada was the best player on the Yankees, Epstein said, but Nick Johnson was the toughest out. Martinez started him out with a low slider that caught the inside corner for strike one. He left his second pitch just off the plate and Johnson reached out and poked it back up the middle for a single.

"If anything, Pedro looks a little too strong," Epstein said. "He looks much healthier."

Epstein pulled out his cell phone to call an assistant sitting behind home plate with a speed gun.

"Was that ninety-four?" he asked. "Yeah, he's conserving. He looks strong. He's holding back."

Jason Giambi stepped up to the plate and earned a hearty round of boos from the Fenway crowd. That might have been more of a tribute than he deserved, given the season he was having. Probably it was the fans' way of venting their displeasure over his last name. Jason's kid brother, Jeremy Giambi, was a big disappointment with the Red Sox that year. He was a singles hitter, not a slugger like his brother, and even at his best he was not going to carry a team. But usually Jeremy got on base a lot. Not this year. He tried playing through an injury and ended up with miserable numbers.

Jason came into the game third in the league with thirty-five homers, but he too had struggled. An eye infection of all things had plagued him, along with various nagging injuries, and he was batting only a few points higher than .200 as late as June. Giambi had climbed back up to .258, but for a player making more than $11 million a year, he had been enough of a bust that Steinbrenner had started mumbling to an ever-wider circle of confidants about his buyer's remorse. Everyone in the game knew that Mark McGwire had taught Giambi tricks about how to get bigger and stronger back when they were teammates in Oakland. It was a lot easier to look the other way when the big muscles produced big numbers, which was why the clock was ticking loudly for Giambi: He was running out of time to prove he really was a Yankee.

Martinez showed Giambi respect, starting him out with two balls, missing in once and then down. Next he dropped in a knee-high curve for a strike, and then served up a fastball right down the middle, but all Giambi could do was foul it down the first-base line. The ball squirted between first baseman Kevin Millar and Yankee first-base coach Lee Mazzilli and rolled down to the tarp cover David Mellor's crew had so recently unrolled and rerolled. It bounced off the MARRIOTT lettering and kicked over to ballgirl Kasey Lindsey, who was playing it perfectly.

Lindsey waited near the foul line, glove ready, and scooped the

ball up and ran over to hand it to a young boy in a bright red
T-shirt, keeping an eye out to make sure Giambi did not rip another foul ball while she was distracted. Lindsey, a softball player at
Tufts until she was injured halfway through her senior year, had
good hands and so far had not flubbed any plays in her time as a
Red Sox ballgirl. She even snagged a hard line drive once. That
earned her a nice hand from the crowd. Her one firm rule was that
if she got the ball, she always gave it to a kid.

"It's definitely the most fun thing I've done in my life," she
said. "What makes it most rewarding is getting to see the fans' reactions to getting a ball or just anything that happens during the
game. That's what I'm out there for."

Martinez killed some time by staring in at catcher Jason
Varitek for the sign and tossing over to Kevin Millar at first base,
even though Nick Johnson was not exactly a threat to run. Martinez's 2-2 pitch was a cut fastball high and inside. Giambi popped
it straight up, and Varitek only had to take six steps back from
home plate to glove it for the out.

"His pitches are too high," Ralph Avila said in the Champions
Sports Bar in Santo Domingo, which was still empty.

"Don't put them that high!" he shouted at the version of Pedro
Martinez he saw up on the bar's large-screen TV.

Brian Cashman, watching from his seat behind home plate,
did not much care whether Martinez was leaving pitches up high
or whether he was still feeling the effects of his sore throat. Martinez was always dangerous. Cashman had so much respect for
him and what he could do to you. He had that rare combination of
a great competitive nature and great natural ability, and his funky

little throwing motion allowed him to get more movement on his pitches than anybody else. His arm was more elastic than arms were meant to be.

"He's like Gumby," Cashman said. "He can do things with his arm and his shoulder that other pitchers physically cannot do. He's got this elasticity that allows him to have that whiplike power arm but still be able to locate at the same time. His power is down, but it doesn't matter. He's still effective."

People tended not to remember it now that recent front-office battles between the Yankees and Red Sox had generated so much offseason talk, but the Yankees and Red Sox had competed for Pedro Martinez back in 1997 when Martinez was just twenty-five, coming off a 17-8 season, his fourth year in Montreal. The Red Sox had a trade in place. They would give the Expos Carl Pavano and Tony Armas, Jr., in exchange for Martinez. Montreal went back to the Yankees to see if they wanted to make a better offer.

"The only way we could top it is if we offered them Mariano Rivera, Ramiro Mendoza, Eric Milton, and Homer Bush or Jorge Posada," Cashman said. "We said no, and he joined the Red Sox and he has kicked butt up there ever since. But we made the right decision for us, because we had some champions there. Mariano and Posada have been huge additions for us. Ramiro got some big outs for us. Three of those guys have four rings on their fingers. We made the right choice, despite losing out on one of our era's greatest pitchers."

Epstein's optimism a few minutes earlier had seemed questionable. Martinez had thrown three pitches and the Yankees had already hit two balls hard. But as Martinez pitched to Bernie

Williams, the Yankees' lanky cleanup hitter, it looked like the young general manager was seeing things a few steps ahead. Martinez worked the outside corner relentlessly, and when Mark Carlson refused to ring Williams up on a 1-2 pitch that Martinez was sure caught the outside corner, he did not let it bother him. He came right back with the same pitch, only this time he placed it maybe one inch farther outside. Williams waved weakly at it for the strikeout. Martinez turned away and started his walk toward the dugout almost as soon as he released the pitch.

Out in the Green Monster, Rich Maloney snaked his arm upward to put out a white zero for the Yankees' first frame.

"That deserves a toast," he said, popping a Heineken as the *Cheers* theme kicked in on the ballpark loudspeakers.

BOTTOM OF THE FIRST

	1	2	3	4	5	6	7	8	9	R
NYY	0									
BOSTON										

Andy Pettitte did not look like a pitching star. Nothing wrong with the face. Who could knock the face? Actually, it was not a face, it was a mug. The word had been retired decades ago, cashing it in along with *swell* and *dame,* but for Andy Pettitte you needed to bring it back. He had a mug. He had the hound-dog cheeks, the schnoz, the mouth like on a guy named Nick or Vinnie who talked too much and too loud. But Pettitte also had a bruised look. It took little effort to see him as some sad-eyed former high-school quarterback who knew he had played out the run on his talent long ago.

Only the thing was, Pettitte never saw it that way. He was convinced he was a champion. He believed he would find a way to win. He was somewhere between stubborn and dumb as a post when it came to believing that no matter what happened around him during a game, everything would work out fine in the end. This stubbornness or pride was what made him a winner. It was what gave Joe Torre the feeling that the more pressure there was, the more he liked having Andy Pettitte out on the mound.

"He only had to win one game to prove to me that he could win big games, and that was Game Five of the World Series in 1996, which he won 1–0 in Atlanta," Torre said.

Out on the mound, Pettitte did his best to disappear. Johnny Damon wagged his bat in the air behind him and stared out from the batter's box and saw the pitching equivalent of the headless horseman. Pettitte wore his Yankee cap pulled down as far as he could get it, so the visor was just above his eyes, and held his glove right in front of his face, so it almost touched his nose. That left only a narrow slit. There was nothing else to see.

Watching Pettitte work to Damon offered some insight into why he tried not to give too much away. Pettitte had followed Roger Clemens's example in recent years and become a workout fiend. His legs were stronger and his arms and shoulders were bigger. That made him a better pitcher. The added bulk and improved fitness also gave him more of a physical presence, which became noticeable especially when he struggled, the way he did to Damon, and started showing off some nervous tics.

Pettitte missed inside with his first pitch, and caught Posada's throw back to the mound awkwardly, as if he was too preoccupied to concentrate on it. He missed low with the second pitch, and took an extra hop forward. He came back with a strike, and then missed low again to make it 3-1 and took an extra step toward home after he threw it, kicking his front foot forward to vent a little frustration the way a golfer might after letting a short putt lip out. Pettitte got the ball back from Posada, grabbed it with his pitching hand and threw it back into his glove to let out a little more frustration. He dropped in another fastball for a strike, but Damon fouled off a tough pitch and then singled back up the middle, bouncing the ball just over Pettitte's outstretched glove. Pettitte leaped, but not high enough. Once the ball was past him, he jumped up and down in an abbreviated version of a classic toddler tantrum.

Too much could be made of body language as a tool for understanding a baseball game, and sometimes too much was made. But there was no question that every player in the Red Sox dugout took notice that Pettitte was having a hard time out there. He seemed to calm down a little with Damon on first base. Pettitte had a great pickoff move, maybe the best in baseball, and immediately made use of it. Damon obediently danced back to first base.

Bill Mueller, batting from the right side against the left-handed Pettitte, kept stepping out of the box to stare down at third-base coach Mike Cubbage. He wanted to see if the hit-and-run was on. It was not. Damon stayed put at first until Mueller bounced sharply back to the pitcher's mound. This was the break Pettitte had been waiting for: a perfect double-play ball. He snagged the ball quickly, spun around to face second base and planted his feet, knees bent, just the way they teach you during pitcher infield drills. But he hesitated for one beat, not sure who would cover the bag, Derek Jeter or Enrique Wilson, who was getting a start that day in place of slumping Alfonso Soriano.

"He threw it away," Theo Epstein said even before the ball left Pettitte's hand.

The throw was high and wide. Wilson came off the bag to try to catch it, but it bounced away and rolled into shallow center field. Pettitte punched his glove angrily and stared far past the outfield, not wanting to look at the baserunners on first and second with nobody out.

Marty Martin and his brother Dean jumped up out of their seats and hopped up and down like gleeful little kids.

"This is where you've got to make it hurt," Rich Maloney said out in the Green Monster.

John Henry had chosen that inning to go for a little walk. Senator George Mitchell had arrived just as Trot Nixon was making his diving catch in right to start the game, and now Mitchell was sitting in L-1, the box one over from Henry's, near Larry Lucchino and his wife, Stacey. Henry stepped inside L-1 and the chef, Joe Pitta, moved in to cut him off.

"Mr. Henry, fish tacos today!" he announced.

Henry did not look thrilled.

"It does smell fishy," he said.

Pettitte's throwing error caused a flurry of excitement. Henry, hearing enough to guess at what had happened, pumped his fist and ran toward the glass at the front of the suite to see for himself. He and Senator Mitchell said hello as quickly as possible, since neither man wanted to miss anything.

Bob and Eleanor Adair were not so lucky. The directions they had been given had not been the best, and they were lost. They realized they were heading in the wrong direction down Commonwealth Avenue boulevard, and Eleanor pulled a U-turn to send them back toward Fenway. The stop-and-go traffic punished them for having made the wrong turn. It gave them plenty of time to do a little calculation about how much of the game they might miss. They decided not to compound their error with more aimlessness, so they asked a cab driver for directions. He turned out to be very obnoxious.

Spike Lee was settling in to watch the game with Jackson, and wondering if the kid was going to be eating all day long, when an attendant came over with a question.

"Gabe Kapler would like you to sign a bat for him," the attendant said. "Would that be all right?"

Lee gave it a poker face.

"OK," he said after a brief pause. "But get me a ball signed by Pedro."

The attendant did not know if Lee was kidding.

"I don't know if I can do that," he said.

Lee signed the bat.

Next up was Nomar Garciaparra. Pettitte threw two quick strikes but then distracted himself by making a weak pickoff attempt at second base. Damon had a short lead and he was back to the bag in plenty of time, making the whole exercise pointless, except that the throw was low and Wilson had to bend down to catch it. All Pettitte had succeeded in doing was to demonstrate that he still had a case of the yips when it came to throwing down to second.

"We've done a great job of driving the pitch count up in the first inning," Theo Epstein said.

"He's going to hit it off the wall," Senator Mitchell predicted.

Pettitte's next pitch was a cut fastball that Posada wanted low and inside. It missed. The ball came in thigh-high and tailed out over the fat part of the plate, and Garciaparra sent it flying over Bernie Williams's head in center.

Bill Mueller could watch the flight of the ball as he ran down to second base and had a pretty good idea it would sail over Williams's head. That was a situation where you could gamble. If it did fall, you were that much ahead. If Williams somehow caught it, you knew you had a lot of time to get back to first base, especially with Williams's weak throwing arm. If you did not gamble, you never knew where you might end up. Once you saw the outfielder on the dead run, back to the infield, you knew it was not much of a gamble anyway.

Damon was in a different position. He did not have as good an angle to judge the flight of the ball, and he had to stay put near second base so he could tag up and run to third if Williams somehow made the catch. But that did not happen. The ball hit the STOP & SHOP sign painted on the metal roll gate out in the deep part of center field and kicked around. Mueller rounded second at full speed and wound up only a few paces behind Damon. If Mueller had passed Damon, he would have been out, but there was no chance of that actually happening. Damon was too fast, and Mueller too smart. But the much slower Mueller could have a little fun and kid the speedster Damon.

"Go! Go! Go! Go!" Mueller yelled as loud as he could as he rounded third just behind Damon.

Both scored easily on Garciaparra's triple. That gave the Red Sox a 2–0 lead with nobody out and big David Ortiz coming up next. He tried to go the other way and poke a single through the left side of the infield, not a bad idea at all, but third baseman Aaron Boone handled it easily. That brought up Kevin Millar, and Joe Torre made the decision to bring in his infielders so that Garciaparra would not be able to score from third on a ground ball.

"That's a sign of respect for Pedro," Theo Epstein said.

Millar chopped at an inside pitch and fisted it into shallow center for a base hit.

"That's a run," George Mitchell said.

Out in right field, Marty Martin had been cheering for every Red Sox player who came up to bat, and yelling "Let's Go Red Sox" along with the crowd as loud as he could. Now he and Dean were up on their feet again, high-fiving and smiling at everyone around them.

Soon, the "Let's Go Red Sox" chants turned into cries of "Yankees Suck"—and Theo Epstein grimaced. He was chewing gum, his arms still folded, and shook his head sadly.

"It makes the Red Sox fans look weak," he said. "It's also, as my mom would say, vulgar."

Spike Lee was telling Jackson about what it was like when the Red Sox and Yankees played in the Bronx.

"There are fights," Lee told him.

"There are fights?" Jackson asked.

"Not between the players," Lee said. "Between the fans."

"I want to go," Jackson said. "I want to see those fights."

Hideki Matsui kept sneaking glances into the crowd. He did not like the long, sticky grass and had to concentrate hard, but whenever he got a chance, he looked around at the fans. He was surprised to see so many police officers stationed at different places inside the stadium. He thought he even saw some fights out in the outfield. To him this game had a very special atmosphere. The intensity level seemed to be even higher than during the Yankees' last two series in Boston.

Catcher Jason Varitek was up next for the Red Sox.

"He's a tough out, but he hits into a lot of double plays," George Mitchell said. "You see he's got a good hole to hit to on the right side with Nick Johnson holding on the runner at first and playing him to pull. They'll probably pitch him inside."

Brian Cashman was trying to stay calm. He was not about to yell out to the mound, but he had a way of talking almost to himself. He watched Pettitte fidget on the mound, tug at his hat and pull on his nose, then come in with a low fastball over the outside corner for called strike one and another one, in the same spot, that Varitek fouled back to the screen.

"Come on, Andy," Cashman said as Pettitte looked in for the sign. "Make your pitch. Come on, ground-ball double play right here. We need this."

Pettitte missed low with a curve and then came back with another one, this time in the zone, and Varitek chopped it right back to the mound. Pettitte could not have asked for a better gift. Another double-play ball, and this time, he had a catcher lumbering down the first-base line.

"That should be two," Theo Epstein said.

Pettitte spun around, reenacting the earlier play, and again something went wrong.

"I think after making the bad throw the first time, he tried to steer it," George Mitchell observed.

That was how it looked to Joe Torre, too. He thought Pettitte made an adjustment after the earlier bad throw and tried to aim this one. But that was not how Pettitte saw it. Out on the mound, he watched his throw sail to the left of the bag and wondered why Derek Jeter did not swoop in to catch it. Instead, Wilson came over to take the throw, even though he had to hurry back over after first breaking in to try to field the ground ball. The Yankees got one out, but had no shot at Varitek at first. Pettitte raised both his hands high in the air in an unmistakable "What was *that?*" gesture. He pumped his fist angrily, punched the air quickly, and looked down and shouted.

"My fault," Enrique Wilson mouthed to Pettitte.

"That was a good throw, actually," Cashman said.

The throw was right over the bag on the shortstop side, and Pettitte was wondering who was covering. Cashman made a mental note to ask about the play later, if the Red Sox won. If the Yankees won, he could forget about it. That was one thing you learned if you were a general manager. It was your job to ask questions, but sometimes you did your job best by *not* asking. That went for managing choices, too. Cashman and the Boss did not always see eye to eye on what to say to Joe Torre.

"You find out why he did this," Steinbrenner would tell him.

Cashman would find out—sometimes. Other times he said no.

"I'm not going to ask," he would tell Steinbrenner. "I don't need to ask. It didn't work. He knows it didn't work."

Or Cashman might be asked by ownership to go down and talk to a player who was struggling, but he knew he didn't need to talk to him. The press took care of that. If a guy was struggling, he had been on the back page of the tabloids. He had been booed by the fans. The player did not need Brian Cashman to remind him that he was struggling or to confront him about why that was. Instead, that was a time to back off and put your arm around someone.

"But there are times where I do ask Joe, 'Hey, what was your thought process on this?' " he said.

Pitching coach Mel Stottlemyre hustled out to the mound, pumping his arms as he ran, gave Pettitte one of his quick, pointed pep talks, and hustled back to the dugout, pumping his arms as he ran again. Hulking Gabe Kapler, filling in that day for Manny Ramirez, came up next and punched a single through the right side of the infield to give Stottlemyre and Joe Torre more to worry about.

Bob and Eleanor Adair had finally made it inside. They had heard enough cheering from outside to know something good must be happening, and hurried inside to find Trot Nixon up to bat, just after the Gabe Kapler single. Pettitte had already thrown him three balls. Nixon, like many left-handed hitters, had trouble against left-handed pitchers.

"He really worked on that in the offseason," Theo Epstein said. "He bought a pitching machine with a video simulator."

Epstein liked numbers, and he made no apologies for that. He played with Nixon's numbers against lefties, looking to see if there was a breakout point, depending on the number of at-bats, but had not come up with anything conclusive. Numbers to him were just one more way to try to see more of a baseball game.

"It's a tool," he said. "I'm not dogmatic about it. You have traditional scouting. That's one lens. You have a statistical picture. That's another lens. We try to look at both. We use all available information. Trot will get a hundred at-bats this year against lefties. He's such a complete player, you want him out there, but you don't want to lose two hundred at-bats."

Bob and Eleanor Adair hurried down toward field level and discovered that their seats were right smack in the middle of a knot of Yankee fans congregated near the visitors' dugout. The Adairs sat down in time to watch Nixon hit Pettitte's 3-1 pitch sharply back up the middle for the third comebacker of the inning. Pettitte jumped to his side and grabbed the ball and was relieved to realize that he only had to throw to first base to end the inning.

"That's amazing," Senator Mitchell said. "Try getting three runs with three balls that were hit back to the pitcher. You don't see that too often."

Bob Adair finally had a chance to sit and enjoy the game, but he was not so sure his great-grandchildren would have the same opportunity.

"I think baseball will last my lifetime, but not that much longer," he said. "Kids don't play it. When was the last time you saw a bunch of kids without adults playing baseball? The sociology of baseball when I was a kid was wonderful. There were no adults involved at all. Did we do it beautifully and wonderfully and elegantly? No, of course not. But we did it. It was great training for citizenship, and everything else."

TOP OF THE SECOND

	1	2	3	4	5	6	7	8	9	R
NYY	0									0
BOSTON	3									3

Hideki Matsui came out to lead off the top of the second and no one in the Fenway Park crowd would have guessed the Red Sox had jumped out to a 3–0 lead. Maybe it had to do with the sun coming out and beating down with an after-the-rain brightness that had a way of making people blink and yawn. Or maybe there had already been too many wild Sox-Yanks games that year and no one wanted to do any assuming. But for the time being at least, the Saturday crowd was subdued.

"How are you doing?" Matsui asked home-plate umpire Mark Carlson from his spot in the batter's box. "Nice to meet you."

Matsui believed in being friendly and polite. Everywhere he went during his rookie year in the major leagues, he introduced himself to people he had not met before. He had been doing it since spring training in Florida and would do it as long as the season lasted.

Matsui admired Pedro Martinez. He ranked him right up there with Roy Halladay of Toronto and Tim Hudson, Mark Mulder, and Barry Zito of the Oakland A's as the best pitchers in the league. Matsui could not detect any differences in Martinez's throwing motion from pitch to pitch. He had no clues to help him guess whether he would see a breaking ball or a fastball or a changeup. That made it difficult to get a hit.

Martinez, like most multiple Cy Young winners, considered it a point of honor to feed on an early three-run lead. He still had an edgy look out there, but mostly he wanted to get on with things. He kept Matsui guessing and was ahead 0-2 when he threw a pitch that looked like it caught the outside of the plate. Mark Carlson did not see it that way. Martinez's next pitch was inside, but looked like it might have tailed back over the inside of the plate. Carlson called that a ball, too. Martinez hit the outside corner on his next pitch, almost in the exact spot as two pitches earlier. Called strike three. Matsui could not even swing. The pitch was perfect, he thought. Nothing to do but fall forward theatrically, poking his bat down into the hard-packed clay to steady himself, and walk back to the dugout.

"He's throwing to the corner," Ralph Avila said in Santo Domingo. "That's the great thing about Pedro as a pitcher. There are four basic pitches in baseball, but Pedro has many variations. He can throw the ball wherever and however he wants it."

Senator George Mitchell was thinking aloud about how he

and his brothers grew up on baseball and how, sixty years later, baseball was still so important to them.

"Whenever I talk to one of my brothers in the summer, the first questions are, 'How did the Sox do last night?' and, 'Were you at the game?' and, 'Who did well?' and, 'Who didn't do well?' " Mitchell said.

"Sports are an important part of life," he continued. "I have kids. I have a young son now. He's only five. We go out and play a little baseball every day. He loves it, and I love it. It's a great way for family and dads and kids to have a bond."

Martinez went to work against Jorge Posada, and set about making a statement. He started Posada off with a little lollipop of a changeup that dropped in over the outside corner of the plate, just low, hitting all of seventy-three miles per hour on the speed gun. Martinez came back with the same pitch, again seventy-three miles per hour, only this time he put it on the inside corner, and Posada swung and missed. A cut fastball off the inside part of the plate made it 1-2, and Martinez threw a high fastball out of the zone that was a clear challenge. Posada did not swing. Martinez came right back with a belt-high fastball that tailed over the inside edge of the plate, and Posada swung and missed. Martinez had made him look bad. He had as much as taunted him.

"Pedro is clicking on all cylinders," Senator Mitchell said.

Walking slowly back to the Yankee dugout, Posada stared out at Martinez for a few steps, glanced down briefly, and stared out again, this time longer than before. He strapped on his catcher's gear in a kind of daze, paying no attention at all to the movements of his fingers, and watched Martinez's string of three straight strikeouts end when third baseman Aaron Boone lifted a lazy fly ball down the left-field line. Gabe Kapler ran it down in fair territory to end the inning.

Spike Lee watched Kapler make the catch and looked down at the ball in his hand. If Kapler had not wanted Lee to sign a bat, he would never have asked for the autographed ball, and to his surprise, the Red Sox employee had come through for him. Lee and his son each spent a few minutes handling the ball and looking at Martinez's signature.

"He's a great pitcher," Lee said. "I think he has a lot of idiosyncrasies. He's a warrior, though."

BOTTOM OF THE SECOND

	1	2	3	4	5	6	7	8	9	R
NYY	0	*0*								0
BOSTON	3									3

It was funny. The way Joe Torre saw it, any time you fell behind 3–0 to Pedro Martinez, you had an enormous problem on your hands. It took a lot of work and skill and luck to dig out from a *two-run* deficit against someone as good and as fiery as Martinez. Giving him a three-run lead to work with made coming back borderline unthinkable. But it was almost as if the Red Sox had scored too quickly. You went into the game saying, "We have to stay close with Pedro, we have to stay close with Pedro." All of a sudden you looked up and saw you were already three runs down. But you still had eight innings to go. That was a lot of time. You were not about to start telling yourself you could not find a way to win. Torre just had to make sure all his players stayed in the game and did not let the Pedro Martinez mystique go to their heads.

If Andy Pettitte could settle down long enough to let the offense narrow the gap, they could at least try to make the game interesting. It helped having Manny Ramirez out of the lineup with that throat thing. Torre did not know where Ramirez was. He could be sitting in the clubhouse, watching the game on TV and waiting to come out and pinch-hit. Torre had no idea. But he *hoped* he would have to worry about Ramirez. That would mean it had become a closer game.

Lou Merloni came out to start off the Boston half of the inning, and tried to control his emotions. He was sorry that his grandmother was not there in the stands, but it brought back great memories of other days at Fenway knowing his parents and his sisters Lisa and Jill and Jill's husband, Matt, and the three kids were all there, along with old friends he had not even had a chance to talk to in the blur of recent days. His phone would be ringing for days to come with people wanting to celebrate his return to New England.

Merloni was glad he was leading off the inning, so he could stand there with a great view of Pettitte's warmup tosses to Posada. That gave Merloni a chance to go through his visualization exercises again, as calmly as possible, the way he had that morning in the shower. Finally it was time to step in against Pettitte, and Merloni watched a fastball land just outside.

Senator Mitchell clapped once, glad to see the local kid getting ahead in the count, and then leaned back and took a good-natured crack at putting baseball into a larger context.

"What are the things that are most important in life? What are the things that people feel passionately about?" he wondered aloud. "Religion. Nation. Family. Two of the three represent a human need for causes of some kind."

Mitchell paused to wait for another loud round of *Loooo!* Two more Pettitte fastballs had also missed outside, and then Merloni fouled off two outside pitches.

"You have to believe in something and feel strongly about something to feel fully committed and fully alive," Mitchell continued. "For some people, sports teams take on some of the aura of causes that you believe in and become part of your life. One of the things that makes the Red Sox so unique is that this sense of being part of a cause exists over a wide area, all over New England."

Lou Merloni knew they were working him outside, outside, outside, and his only chance was to go with the pitch and hit it to right. He gave that a try and flied out to right fielder Karim Garcia.

"One of the paradoxical aspects of it is the longer you lose, the more committed and passionate and wait-till-next-year people are," Mitchell said, wrapping up the thought. "I don't think that would be the case if they finished in the cellar all the time. The fact they're always challenging makes it really interesting and something that you feel strongly about and you latch onto it in your life."

Next up was the leadoff hitter, Johnny Damon. Pettitte again missed with three straight pitches. His fourth pitch to Damon was a letter-high breaking ball that could have been called either way. Carlson called it a strike. One curve later, Damon bounced to the right side of the infield and Nick Johnson fielded the ball and flipped it to Pettitte as he ran over to first. Pettitte had a little trouble with his footwork, but got his toe on the bag just before Damon could do the same.

Senator Mitchell smiled, mulling over a familiar question: If what made being a Red Sox fan so special was the unique pain of falling just short year after year and decade after decade, what would it be like if the Red Sox finally won the World Series? Would it rob Sox fans of some special identity?

Mitchell was ready to find out.

"It would be great!" he said. "I'd be prepared to wait another eighty years. I won't be around, but a victory would be great."

Pettitte wasted a couple of pitches to Bill Mueller, too, missing low with two breaking balls. Behind 2-0 to the league's leading hitter, Pettitte caught the outside corner with a well-placed fastball, and then did it again. Mueller fought off the 2-2 pitch, a breaking ball in on his hands, and fouled it straight down off the instep of his left foot.

"Ow!" Theo Epstein said sharply, flinching almost as if it had been his foot where the ball hit.

Mueller walked off the pain, chewing his gum fiercely, and finally stepped back in and tried to drive a high pitch in on his hands, but popped up to Aaron Boone at third base. Pettitte now had a one-two-three inning to try to build on. But as he headed back in toward the dugout, he was not about to congratulate himself. He pulled his cap off with his left hand and reached his right arm up so he could bury his face in the shoulder of his road gray uniform top, wiping the side of his face and grimacing. Pettitte knew it had taken him far too much effort to get through that inning. His pitch count was way too high already. Falling behind hitter after hitter was just not going to cut it.

Theo Epstein decided it was time to make his escape. As soon as the inning ended, he turned to the Patterson twins.

"Do you guys wanna come down to my seats for a few innings?" he asked. "They're really good."

The boys looked at their mother, and she nodded her approval. The boys were excited, but not half as excited as Epstein. He walked out of the box in a hurry, forcing the twins to run to catch up. Fans pointed out the young general manager as he rushed past them, identifying him the way you would a tourist attraction.

"That was Theo," one would say to another.

"Theo got his hair cut," one woman noted.

Epstein kept right on hurrying. He was still doing his best to keep his poker face together, but the closer he got to his seats just behind home plate, the easier it became to catch glimpses of the little-boy baseball fan he tried to keep bottled up inside.

Joe Torre did not like to say much to his players during a game. It just was not his style. There was no point in talking about the importance of the game until after it was over. If he had called a team meeting that morning to say, "We lost last night, this game is really important," that would only raise questions about him. Torre knew what it was like to have pressure added for no good reason from higher up in an organization.

It was important for a manager to keep his role in perspective.

The players were the ones who decided a game. They made the pitches and the plays and got the hits and ran the bases. Torre liked to stay out of their way as much as he could, and only once in a while did he make a point of saying something during a game to try to give the team a shot in the arm. This was one of those times. Torre saw the frustration kicking in and knew it could start to snowball. The players trotted back into the dugout after Aaron Boone gloved Mueller's pop-up, and Torre sat in the dugout waiting for them to assemble.

"Guys, we need to get the fight back," Torre told his players. "Let's go. Just because we're three runs down to Pedro doesn't mean the game is over. We need to keep battling. If he beats us, he beats us, but we have to make him earn it."

Brian Cashman was not the type of general manger to tell you that people exaggerated the importance of managers. He just might be the last person on earth to tell you that, in fact. More than anyone, he knew what Joe Torre meant to the Yankees and their run of success.

"The manager's main job is to manage people, and I think the guy we have is the best at that," he said. "Part of that is to make sure that there is a separation between the general manager's office and the manager's office. Don't get me wrong. The front office has to have a strong presence, but if you have the right individual that you trust, and I trust our guy implicitly, I'll take some bullets so he can always be the good guy and maintain the relationships that he has with the players. Joe has a great personality. He's got a tremendous warmth about him.

"I think having a strong manager of people is even more important over the course of a year in a big market than having a strong chess maneuverer, for instance, on the field. Ultimately I think the players will decide the outcomes of games more so than not, regardless of who is in the dugout. But I think it's important to have the honesty and the integrity and somebody, a former player most likely, that guys know has been through the wars and knows what they're going through and has that gentle touch, especially in our market. I've had situations where I've been the bad guy. I don't mind, because I understand that you want these guys to go to war for their manager more so than for their organization."

Cashman and Torre make their relationship work by trying not to surprise each other. It takes frequent communication to stay in sync.

"Joe and I wind up talking three, four, five times a day," Cashman said. "He'll call me after a home game as we're each driving home. We talk all the time, and I can't believe that some general managers go a week without talking to their manager. I don't know how you do your job that way. One manager told me he called his GM and it took him three days to call back. I can't imagine that."

TOP OF THE THIRD

	1	2	3	4	5	6	7	8	9	R
NYY	0	0								0
BOSTON	3	0								3

A phone rang at a large house in Cincinnati, Ohio, as the Red Sox took the field at Fenway to start the third inning. The man who answered no longer played baseball. He batted .267 during the 2001 season, his lowest average in nine seasons, and decided it was time to retire and wrap up his seventeen-year big-league career. But people still remembered him. They still talked about the way he played.

"Hey, Paulie," said the voice on the other end of the line, calling from Fenway Park. "They're still selling 'O'Neill Sucks' shirts here."

Paul O'Neill was the kind of player who would listen to a short Joe Torre pep talk and go out and immediately pull a ball into the right-field corner for a leadoff double. Or he would work the count and get in a lot of good glaring and make Pedro Martinez work. Karim Garcia was not that kind of hitter. He watched one Martinez fastball ride in toward his shins, just off the plate, stepped out long enough to tap both shoes with his bat, and then reached out to try to drive a high and outside pitch. The result was a lazy fly ball to left that gave Gabe Kapler no trouble. That brought up Enrique Wilson.

"You own him, Enrique," a Yankee fan sitting near the Adairs bellowed. "You own him, like a pair of shoes, like a pair of shooooooes."

Wilson took a different approach than Karim Garcia. He watched a couple of breaking balls away, one for a strike, one just off the plate, and then took an easy swing and flipped another low and outside breaking ball into left for a single. It was neither pretty nor impressive, but it got him to first base. Martinez, working from the stretch now, looked in control against Derek Jeter and had him 0-2, but two pitches later, Jeter got a fat curve and lined it to left to give the Yankees back-to-back singles. Martinez, watching the ball shoot between Mueller and Garciaparra for a base hit, jerked his right hand across the RED SOX logo on his chest, angry with himself for putting the ball in a place where Jeter was so likely to drill it.

Grady Little watched from the dugout and thought again that Martinez was still sapped from his battle with the sore throat. You could tell right away when an individual was still sick or not feeling at his best physically. Martinez was still rebounding from the medication he had taken for the sore throat. It was understandable he would still be weakened, but he just had to fight through that somehow. Pedro at 80 percent was still better than a whole lot of pitchers at 100 percent.

Nick Johnson already had one sharp single under his belt when he stepped up next. Brian Cashman, watching behind home plate, still felt almost a paternal feeling where Johnson was concerned. He was their pride and joy. They had worked so hard, hoping to see him end up as a spectacular Yankee. His first year as GM, Cashman was close to wrapping up a deal with Seattle that would have brought Randy Johnson to the Bronx. Just imagine the Big Unit in pinstripes. But the Mariners had insisted they include Nick Johnson, and for the Yankees, that was a deal-breaker. That was how highly they thought of Johnson, then and now, but you could not ignore the nagging injuries. They were fluke things, like falling on his wrist diving for a ball in foul territory, and then he would be down forever and the tests would show nothing other than a bruise. Johnson was just a slow healer. But he was a very patient hitter with one of the best eyes in baseball. He was going to be a superstar one day if he could stay healthy.

Martinez started Johnson out with his signature pitch for the day: It was a fastball low and inside that Martinez wanted to break back over the inside edge of the plate. But this one missed, and Mark Carlson said so. Martinez caught the outside corner with his next pitch, a belt-high fastball, to even it up at 1-1, and then another fastball missed up.

"Too high!" Ralph Avila shouted in Santo Domingo, sounding almost disgusted.

"Where is Pedro's velocity?" George Mitchell asked. "He needs a hard ground ball to the second baseman."

Spike Lee was thinking that it was almost unfair how noticeable it was to everyone when age or injuries took their toll on a pitcher.

"You can kind of camouflage stuff at other positions, but that radar gun don't lie," Lee said. "If you regularly throw mid-nineties and now you drop numerous miles off your fastball . . ."

Martinez came back with the same pitch he had thrown to start out Johnson: the low and inside fastball tailing back over the plate, only he moved this one over a little. Johnson was fooled, and checked his swing, and this time it was a called strike. Martinez tried the same pitch again, more or less, only this time it drifted out over the plate, much as his breaking ball to Jeter had. Johnson lined it to the right-field corner and it took one hop, just past the Pesky Pole, and landed in the seats for a ground-rule double that scored Wilson and sent Jeter to third base. If the ball had been hit less well, it would have bounced lower and Trot Nixon would have had to run it down, and the Yankees would have scored another run.

Jason Giambi was due up next and as he stepped up to the plate, Brian Cashman thought that all in all, he had been a good acquisition. They had signed Giambi as a free agent the previous off-season after Oakland owner Steve Schott decided he did not want to pay to keep him. Giambi got off to a bad start his first season with the Yankees, but came around and finished with good numbers, hitting .314 with 41 homers and 122 RBIs.

"I thought he was our best player his first year," Cashman said.

Giambi had cleaned up his image when he joined the Yankees, but Joe Torre still had to get after him now and then.

"Joe tells him, 'You've got to shave,' " Cashman said.

There was a perception in New York that Giambi had not delivered, but for Cashman, he was a clear asset.

"In terms of the production he's brought at that position, it's not even close," he said. "The measured increase is phenomenal. His effect on our offense has been everything we had hoped. I don't think George is happy because we haven't won a world championship in a while. Unless we do that, I don't think he's happy with anybody."

Pedro Martinez took the same approach toward Giambi as he had before, starting him off with two inside fastballs. One missed, and Giambi swung through the other. But Martinez's third pitch was another fastball that missed inside by only a few inches. That was all it took to hit Giambi, who liked to crowd the plate, even if it meant often getting hit by pitches.

"That's unavoidable," Theo Epstein said as Giambi trotted down to first base. "You have to pitch him inside and he did that and just came in too far. He established the inside part of the zone, then he'll go away. Also, it sets up the double play."

"Now he really needs a hard grounder to second," George Mitchell said. "Even more than Nick."

Eleanor Adair, sitting in the midst of so many Yankee fans, was surprised at how much they were heckling Martinez. Almost every time he looked in after a pitch, someone would yell, "Ask him where it went, Pedro!" or, "Was it high?" or, "Was it low?" or, "What was it?" She was glad to see that not much had changed at Fenway since she went there as a girl, but she did miss some things.

"We always used to say *'Whoooooooop'* as a foul ball rolled across the net behind home plate," she said. "They don't do that anymore."

Joe Torre was encouraged. He was glad to have a run on the board and glad to have the bases loaded for Bernie Williams, his cleanup hitter. But mostly Torre was encouraged at the way his hitters were reacting to Martinez. He could see they were not fooled, and were not having much difficulty picking up his pitches. That was a good sign. Even if they did not get a hit, they came back to the dugout feeling that they easily could have. A great pitcher like Pedro Martinez was often in such control, locating so many of his pitches, that when you finally did get a good one to hit, you missed anyway. But Torre could see from the dugout that Martinez was giving his batters a lot of chances. Torre knew that could change in a hurry. Martinez might find himself again and be unhittable. But Torre could see opportunity.

Bernie Williams gave it his trademark deep knee bend, back straight and head held high. He looked like a man trying to balance something on his head as he squatted down to pick something up off the ground.

"I'd almost rather face Giambi than Bernie Williams," said Rich Maloney, peering out from his peekhole in the Green Monster. "Bernie's digging in."

Martinez came in with a low, tailing fastball away and Williams drilled it toward the Green Monster in left-center. Johnny Damon thought at first that the ball would bounce off the wall, and raced back and to his right. Gabe Kapler raced back and to his left. Since Damon was left-handed, and wore his glove on his right hand, they looked like mirror opposites approaching each other. The ball, the center fielder, and the left fielder all arrived at the same place at the same time.

Damon held his glove up, ready to make the grab, and Kapler came cutting across from the other direction. He lifted his mitt up high to make the catch, and was able to snag the ball, but his outstretched glove hit Damon flush in the face an instant later and sent him tumbling toward the nearby Green Monster. Damon smacked right into the out-of-town scoreboard section of the wall, his cap flew off his head, and he crumpled to the ground.

"What happened?" Debi Little wondered aloud, speaking for everyone in the crowd trying to sort out the confusing scene.

"That's the problem with Kapler," said a scout sitting behind Brian Cashman. "He just runs at full bore. He's the type who gets people hurt out there. He runs full speed and he's dangerous to the other outfielders."

The sound inside the Green Monster when Damon hit the Wall was sickening. It was not as loud as when the line drive smacked into the outside of the scoreboard during batting practice, but almost, and this was much, much worse. The outside of the Wall was studded with protrusions of metal that could seriously hurt someone slamming into it.

"Whoa," Maloney said, straining to follow the action just outside his peekhole. "Johnny hit the Wall pretty hard."

As soon as he had made the catch, Kapler spun around and threw the ball back into the infield, and then quickly hurried over to help Damon up. (Jeter tagged up at third and scored to make it a one-run game.)

"Are you all right?" Kapler asked Damon, leaning over.

"My calf cramped up on me," Damon told him, staying put where he had gone down.

Everyone waited for a sign that he was all right. John Henry, still watching from just behind George Mitchell, thought he had heard Damon hit.

"That scoreboard is dangerous," he said.

"He's lucky he hit him with a glove," Mitchell said. "It could easily have been an elbow."

Mark Carlson took the opportunity to step out from behind home plate and walk out to the mound for a short conversation with Martinez.

"Pedro, if you want to throw some while we're waiting, go ahead," Carlson told him.

Carlson was going to turn away and remembered something else he wanted to say.

"Hey, are you still feeling sick?" he asked.

"Yeah, I'm a little bit drained still," Martinez told him. "I was pretty sick last week."

Carlson nodded.

"You know what?" he told Martinez. "I've got the same thing. This past week I was diagnosed with strep throat."

They talked about that briefly as Little, Mueller, Nixon, Garciaparra, and assistant trainer Chris Correnti all converged on Damon to see how he was doing.

"Thank you," Martinez told Carlson, ending their conversation. "I don't need to take any extra pitches."

The group around Damon talked back and forth for a few

minutes, and then Damon took to his feet. He looked wobbly, but not as wobbly as might have been expected.

The Fenway crowd cheered wildly, relieved that Damon was staying in the game. He rounded up his cap and sunglasses and put himself back together.

"Wrong guy to bump into," Damon joked after the game. "Wrong Wall to bump into."

"Did I switch the '1'?" Maloney asked, not sure if he had after all the excitement over Damon.

Theo Epstein had watched the whole sequence without betraying a hint of emotion. He said he was not worried about Damon or Kapler, who were both tough, sturdy characters. Even when everyone stood up to cheer, Epstein remained impassive. Which begged the question: Were there ever times when he clapped?

"Occasionally I do a single sitting clap behind the radar," he said, demonstrating with his hands held down where no one would be looking.

"Cashman would nev—" he started, and then thought better of it.

"When I'm at a game and I look over and I see another GM clapping or cheerleading, I don't find it appropriate," Epstein said after thinking over what he wanted to say. "It's a pretty humbling game, so if you're going to cheer when things are going well, then you may show emotion when things don't go well and that would show up our guys. It's better to keep on an even keel. I feel it inside, but I don't have to show it."

The crowd still had an odd buzz to it when Hideki Matsui came up next and the game got going again. Matsui saw nothing but low fastballs, falling behind 1-2, and fouled off two more fastballs before finally seeing something else, a high slider. He popped it up to Bill Mueller at third to end the inning.

"I'm glad Johnny doesn't have to bat this inning," John Henry said as Damon trotted in from center field looking like he was not entirely sure which dugout was his.

BOTTOM OF THE THIRD

	1	2	3	4	5	6	7	8	9	R
NYY	0	0	*2*							2
BOSTON	3	0								3

Center fielder Bernie Williams was not about to let Garciaparra triple over his head the way he did in the first inning. Williams cheated in a little whenever he could. It was one of the allowances he had to make for having a subpar throwing arm. But now he moved a few steps back before Garciaparra came up to lead off the bottom of the third. One pitch later, he was running back to the uneven corner that made Fenway's center field so difficult to play. The triple had come down on the STOP & SHOP sign. This ball came down almost the same distance from home plate, but a few feet to the right, and Williams had no trouble catching up with it to make the catch.

Andy Pettitte looked unsteady pitching to David Ortiz. He

missed away with a curve, not a bad pitch, and then tried sneaking a cut fastball over the inside corner. It missed for ball two, and when Pettitte took Posada's throw back to the mound, he practiced throwing once without the ball, quickly, as if thinking aloud about something he was doing wrong. Ortiz fouled the third pitch straight down onto his foot, and cried out in pain and hopped around for a while until he thought he felt better. Pettitte missed inside for ball three, and Mark Carlson pointed down to Ed Rapuano at third to make sure Ortiz had not gone around. He had not. It was 3-1.

"That's a hitter's count," Bob Adair noted.

Pettitte tried sneaking a sinker over the inside corner again and immediately wished he hadn't. Ortiz crushed the ball to right for a no-doubt-about-it homer. It was his sixth homer in his last seven games.

"Off a lefty!" Maloney yelled from inside the Green Monster. "That was like the one he hit last night, and thirty rows deeper."

Everyone around Theo Epstein jumped up to cheer and clap and watch the ball land in the right-field stands. Epstein sat in place without moving or speaking. He did, however, reach down for his Poland Springs bottle and take a sip.

"I knew it was gone," he explained. "When all the fans stand up, I can see between them."

Senator Mitchell stood and clapped, interrupting himself in the middle of a talk on why it would have made sense for the United States to push for United Nations backing in Iraq.

"He can really hit!" he said happily.

Brian Cashman, sitting behind home plate, was thinking you

had to expect that when you fell behind 3-1. The hitter knew you had to throw a strike, and you just hoped you could put it in the zone but not in a spot where he would crush it. Ortiz had been a great pickup for the Red Sox. He had been big in their clubhouse and he continued to destroy Yankee pitching. They didn't seem to be able to find a way to get him out.

Cashman was sure he would be hearing again from the Boss about Ortiz, a sore subject with him. Steinbrenner had not been happy in January when the Red Sox signed Ortiz to a one-year contract. It did not matter to him that the Yankees already had Jason Giambi and Nick Johnson to play first base and DH.

"Why didn't we get him?" Steinbrenner had asked Cashman that January.

"Because we have Nick and Giambi," Cashman told him.

"Well, I still wanted him," Steinbrenner said.

"Where are you going to play him?" Cashman said. "You can't have them all."

Now Ortiz was having a hell of a year, especially against the Yankees. Steinbrenner was not the kind of person who let go of these things. His philosophy was you could always find a spot for another good hitter, and it ate at him not to have Ortiz in pinstripes. All year, every time Ortiz did well, Steinbrenner reminded Cashman that so far as he was concerned, he had been right about Ortiz all along and his baseball people had been wrong.

Marty Martin thought at first that he might have a chance to catch the Ortiz home-run ball. Watching games on TV was easy, but Martin was finding out that in the stands it was a lot more difficult to follow the ball. He watched it land a few rows forward and over to his left, twenty feet away. Even before it landed, people started hopping up and down and shrieking. Martin had never seen anything like it before.

Ortiz rounded the bases in a hurry and touched home, kissed his hands, and then gestured skyward, the way he always did. He trotted back toward the dugout, and raised a hand to give hitting coach Ron Jackson a high-five, then gave Harrison, Peter Farrelly's nephew, a high-five, and gave Tommy, Farrelly's other nephew, a high-five, too. Ortiz pulled his batting helmet off and then went down a row of Red Sox giving more high-fives. Assistant trainer Chris Correnti came over to ask where that one pitch had hit him, and Ortiz leaned over to point to the spot.

"Right here," Ortiz told him. "That hurts. But it's all good. I'm a big boy."

Farrelly stared at Bob, wondering why he looked disappointed.

"That's a home run!" Farrelly told him.

"But you said when it's a home run, he gets a point," Bob said.

"That's right," his father said.

"Then why does he have to run around the bases? Why can't he just run to the dugout?"

"Good question, Bob," Farrelly said.

Bob had another question.

"Where are the fireworks, Dad?" he asked.

The last game they went to had been in Florida, and down there, they blasted off fireworks after a Marlins homer.

"Look, when you're at Fenway, you don't need fireworks," Farrelly told him. "That's a gimmick."

Bob Adair was explaining another misconception among baseball players. Ask any player about the effect of humidity in the air on a ball's path and they would all tell you it slowed it down. In fact, that was wrong. Humidity had no noticeable effect on the flight of a ball. But Adair was curious. Usually when players believed something, there was a reason. Eventually he surmised that players only tended to notice humidity on calm days. But even a slight breeze could make a major difference in the flight of a ball.

Ortiz's ball would have been out no matter what, though. For the moment, at least, the flags were hanging straight down.

"There's no wind at all," Adair said.

John Henry had left his box and was walking through the concourse past fans toting beers and hot dogs when the crowd roared. He hurried to the nearest TV set to watch a replay of the Ortiz homer, and then ducked through a steel door to head into the Red Sox clubhouse to see how Johnny Damon was doing.

"I always like to check on players who are hurt," he said.

Kevin Millar, up next, worked the count to 2-1 and then hit a hard grounder up the middle that Wilson smothered, moving to his right.

John Henry emerged from the clubhouse.

"Damon is going to stay in the game," he announced.

Jason Varitek was having some trouble finding his timing from the right side of the plate. He wanted to work the count to see more pitches and did that. But once it was 2-2, Pettitte threw a low and outside cut fastball that was almost in the dirt. Varitek swung and missed to end the inning.

★   ★   ★

Theo Gordon fought back a wince. He and Jane Baxter had been enjoying the game. They liked their seats, which were down the third-base line and twenty-five rows up, giving them a good view of the pitcher's mound and really of the whole field. But now it was time for Theo Gordon to tell Lie Number 46. Someone with the Red Sox was going to stop by, and Gordon had to convince Baxter that it was all on the up-and-up. It did not help that the Red Sox representative was Colleen Reilly, better known as Maggie-the-Base-Girl, who ran out onto the field after the fifth inning in a *League of Their Own* uniform and used a broom to dust off the bases. Reilly showed up at Gordon and Baxter's seats, as planned, and gave them a big smile. Maybe a little too big.

Baxter was suspicious. It wasn't so much the story Gordon had told about how he knew someone who worked for the Red Sox and he had it arranged for them to go up on the Green Monster to check out the new seats up there. That sounded fun. It was Reilly—she was a little too perky. She was young and sexy and had a way of smiling, as if she was about to pinch you or say something funny to catch you off balance, like some bawdy Dublin barmaid who always had three or four blokes following her around and flirting with her but was never flustered or bothered. Baxter had trouble imagining her and Gordon as friends, and if she wasn't his friend, well, then, what was she?

TOP OF THE FOURTH

	1	2	3	4	5	6	7	8	9	R
NYY	0	0	2							2
BOSTON	3	0	1							4

John Henry liked to catch at least part of every game in the stands, sitting with the fans to get a feel for their mood, so he headed down to his personal seats next to the Red Sox dugout. He sat down in the second row, right behind Peter Farrelly and the three boys: Bob could not wait to show him a baseball that Papa Jack—Red Sox hitting coach Ron Jackson—had given him. Farrelly explained that Bob was only four and that this was his first time at Fenway.

"Look at that wind," Henry told Farrelly and the boys, pointing to a flag showing a breeze out toward right. "It's the David Ortiz breeze!"

The boys all looked out at the flag, and then back at John Henry.

"It's like the park is handed down from generation to generation from father to son," Farrelly said. "It's three hours where you spend quality time with your dad—no work, no TV, no nothing. You're at the ballpark and you have three hours of conversation."

Farrelly looked ready to continue on this theme for half an inning or so, but Bob interrupted him.

"I have to go pee-pee," he announced.

Farrelly excused himself and escorted Bob to the men's room.

Jorge Posada was up first for the Yankees in the fourth. Martinez started him off with a low breaking ball that missed outside, and then tried to put a slider past him low and inside, much as Andy Pettitte had tried to beat Ortiz with a sinker low and inside. The result was the same. Posada creamed it to right for a homer. The instant he made contact, Posada had no doubt it was gone. The Yankees had hammered Pedro Martinez to answer for the Ortiz homer: This was frontier justice, baseball style.

"Wow, he crushed it," Theo Epstein said.

"He repeated the pitch of the first inning, but it didn't work this time," Ralph Avila said in Santo Domingo. "His fastball isn't moving and his curveballs are high."

Marty Martin watched the ball unhappily. He had been so excited about that Ortiz homer, and now this. The ball was hit so high, it hung up in the air a long time, and Martin watched it with a kind of detached fascination. He had the feeling it was going to come right to him, but he had been having that feeling all day long. He thought at first that Derek Jeter's drive to right on the first pitch of the game was hit toward him. It wasn't even close. He was just sure Ortiz's ball would come right to him. He had been off then, too. Now this Posada ball was playing with his head. He was having a hard time figuring out how it could land anywhere other than right on top of him.

Martin finally decided he had better lift up his hands, just in case. How hard could it be to catch a baseball? Everyone was standing, ready to grab the ball, but it came right to Martin. He reached up and the next thing he knew, his hands were burning and the ball was down on the concrete below him.

"I dropped it because it hurt like hell," he said.

But he recovered and scrambled for the ball, picked it up quickly, and held it high for everyone to see. He was so caught up in the moment, he had no idea what the crowd wanted. They were roaring all around him. The noise was amazing. They seemed to want him to do something. He thought maybe they just wanted him to raise his arms, so he did that. But that was obviously not what they were after. Their deafening shouts slowly dissolved into a clear chant.

"THROW IT BACK! THROW IT BACK!"

The Red Sox fans wanted to make a show of contempt for the visiting Yankees. Martin got the idea. This was a once-in-a-lifetime deal. He had an opportunity to be part of something, and to be a hero of the day. Who was he to say no to them?

Martin tossed the ball back onto the field, and the crowd cheered wildly, almost savagely. The rowdy fans out in right field near Martin reacted first, hopping up and down and high-fiving each other, and the reaction spread from section to section like electrical current. Trot Nixon scooped up the ball and turned and tossed it back toward the infield, where it ended up in the hands of Kasey Lindsey, the ballgirl, who in turn gave it to a fan sitting near the Red Sox dugout.

"For a kid in the stands, just getting a ball is important," Lindsey said. "An adult might care if it came from Jorge Posada, but a kid wouldn't."

But up in the owners' box, Red Sox CEO Larry Lucchino was outraged.

"Charles, the gesture is nullified by the girl handing it to the fan," he complained to his right-hand man, Charles Steinberg.

Theo Epstein had no reaction at all. He sat calmly, and turned his neck and saw Marty Martin toss the ball back onto the field and then turned back to face the mound, lost in his own thoughts, buried behind his expressionless exterior.

But that was not the end of it. Out in the right-field stands, a security detail moved in and escorted Marty Martin to the exit. He was getting kicked out of the place for doing what every Sox fan wanted him to do. That was team policy: Fans who threw things onto the field, even baseballs, were ejected. They took Martin out Gate B and asked him to wait outside while they figured out what to do with him.

A Boston police officer who helped escort him out told Martin he could expect to be treated as a hero.

"They will probably let you back in," the cop told him.

But that did not happen. Martin and his brother were booted out of the game, and that was that. Martin was too caught up in enjoying his sudden hero status to work up much outrage.

"Everybody kept coming up to me when I was standing at Gate B," he said. "They kept shaking my hand. One guy bought me a beer. I said I don't drink, so he went back and got me a soda."

Back near the Red Sox dugout, Peter Farrelly had more explaining to do. He was glad to see Marty Martin throw the home-run ball back. He had not seen that done much at Fenway, the way it often was at Wrigley Field in Chicago, for example, but he was all for making a new tradition.

"What's going on?" Bob asked him.

"It's a Yankee home run," Farrelly said. "We don't want those. We throw it back on the field."

Posada was still running the bases when Red Sox baseball operations assistant Jed Hoyer started making faces at Theo Epstein to get his attention. He had seen enough of Pedro Martinez that day.

"Warm someone up!" Hoyer mouthed to Epstein. "He's got *nothing*."

Epstein took this in.

"You want to warm someone up *now*?" he mouthed back.

Hoyer nodded emphatically. Epstein shook his head.

"He's young and reactionary," he said. "You can't warm someone up in the fourth when the ace of your staff is on the mound."

Martinez's first pitch to Aaron Boone, up next, missed outside. He missed inside with another pitch and low with another and worked the count full.

"His command is way off and he is putting balls over the plate," Epstein said.

Boone fouled off the next two pitches, both toward the outside corner, and then Martinez let one go that was an obvious mistake: belt high, and right down the middle. Boone hit a deep fly to left that hit high up on the Green Monster, missing a home run by only two feet. He coasted into second base with a standup double.

"Sometimes youth is served," Epstein said. "Sometimes Jed is right."

If Martinez needed a break, Karim Garcia looked ready to offer one. Up next, he could have forced Martinez to throw strikes, but instead took a wild swing at a low, outside breaking ball that was not close to being in the strike zone, and missed. Martinez gave Boone a quick look at second, and then came back with a well-placed cut fastball, low and in, that Garcia fouled down the first-base line. He frowned and shook his head, doing his best impression of a man who believed he should hit a tape-measure home run every time up. Ahead 0-2, Martinez came back with a pitch not that different from the one Boone had drilled to left. Garcia lined a clean single to center that moved Boone to third.

Martinez staggered back toward the mound, looking lost. He reached a hand up to swipe at his forehead, and then called Jason Varitek out for a quick conference. Varitek did his best to calm him down. Martinez drifted back out to the mound, sighing noticeably. Enrique Wilson already had one single, giving him seven hits in seventeen career at-bats against Martinez, and the Yankee fans sitting around Bob and Eleanor Adair made sure everyone heard about it.

"Pair of shooooooes," the one Yankee fan bellowed again. "Pair of shooooooooooes."

Wilson could not help but crack a quick smile at that as he walked out to the batter's box. Martinez started him off with another breaking ball that drifted up in the zone, and Wilson wasted no time. He singled to right, bringing in one run to tie the game and sending Garcia over to third base.

"They're smacking him around," Rich Maloney said behind the Green Monster. "They've got eight hits."

More seemed imminent, the way Martinez was pitching. Everyone knew Derek Jeter would be ready to pounce on the first pitch Martinez threw him, the way he had in the first inning, and sure enough, Martinez came in with a breaking ball away and Jeter swung. But instead of giving it his picture-perfect inside-out swing, he tried to pull the ball, and chopped a bouncer to the left side of the infield. Third baseman Bill Mueller moved to his left and fielded it cleanly, even though it took a bad hop, and made a good throw to second. The Red Sox did not have much of a chance at a double play anyway with Jeter getting down to first base in a hurry, but Enrique Wilson did a good job of making sure Lou Merloni had no shot at throwing to first. Karim Garcia held at third base.

Theo Epstein sat with his arms folded and braced himself. He had told his friends the night before that he had a bad feeling about this game, and he had told himself that morning that Nick Johnson was the toughest out on the Yankees. Johnson already had a single and a double, and now he came up with a chance to give the Yankees the lead. Epstein glanced out to the Red Sox bullpen and saw that Jed Hoyer was getting his wish. A young Boston pitcher named Bronson Arroyo was limbering up and throwing his first warmup tosses to bullpen catcher Dana LaVangie.

Nick Johnson watched a pitch dart low for ball one and then

watched a breaking ball for a strike. It was right down the middle, another mistake pitch, but Johnson was looking for something else and let it go. Martinez came back with a good tailing fastball that started out inside and moved back toward the plate as it came in on Johnson. He watched it go by, and Mark Carlson called it a ball. The fans behind home plate often made noise about calls they did not like, and often they were just being fans, wanting desperately to see the world through a fan's eyes. This time, though, there was a deeper, edgier sound to their complaint, as if they were truly indignant.

Martinez was not happy. His breaking ball was not doing what he wanted it to do, and he needed that low, inside pitch. He was a three-time Cy Young winner, and three-time Cy Young winners got that call. That was how the game worked. It might as well have been written in stone. But for some reason, Mark Carlson did not give him the call. Martinez put his head down and told himself it didn't matter. He would get the next call. It always worked that way. A close call went against you, and the next close call went your way, and you were not exactly satisfied or happy, but you could live with it.

Martinez came back with the same pitch, and he put it just where he wanted. Again, Carlson called it a ball. Martinez was infuriated. Had they forgotten who he was? Was he no longer Pedro Martinez? He took the throw back from Varitek and stood off the rubber, staring in at Carlson. Finally he raised his outstretched palms in the air, asking "What's going on?" Martinez waited another ten seconds before making his next pitch, his best changeup in some time. Johnson fouled it into the dirt to make it 3-2. Jeter was running on the pitch and had to trot back to first base and get ready to run again, since it was a given that he would be breaking on the pitch with the count full.

Martinez's first 3-2 pitch to Johnson was a fastball above the knees with a decent amount of movement on it, and Johnson fouled it back. The attention level in each dugout rose one more notch. Fans and sportscasters made a habit of looking at a game from the outside after it was over, focusing on whichever detail jumped out as most important. Sometimes those details really were the crux of the event. Often, though, the course of a game was determined at moments that might not have been as obvious. There were small stress points in the narrative of a game, and the biggest difference between great players and ordinary players was their visceral awareness of these key moments.

Derek Jeter did not trot back to first this time, he walked, and took his time about it, too. He reached a hand up to adjust his belt buckle as he walked, and then reached up again to adjust his helmet. For the great players, a sense of calm kicked in when the game felt about to pivot. This sense of calm sprang first of all from the satisfaction of knowing the game was getting more interesting, and second from the need to stay a little extra cool. Jeter was a case study in nonchalance as he headed back to first, ready to run down to second again.

Martinez's second 3-2 pitch to Johnson was a fastball on the outside corner that Johnson fouled off. It was a good pitch, but not a great one. If it had been lower, it might have been a great pitch. Martinez got the ball back and sighed, collecting himself. He knew that even when he was having a bad day, he could often find a way to make one or two great pitches and get out of a jam and find a way to win the game. He knew that if he could do that, his struggles could be forgotten. This game was tied. The Red Sox had hit Pettitte hard and Martinez knew they would find a way to score more runs. If he could just get Johnson, he was sure he would win the game.

Back when he was younger, Martinez used to throw a lot harder. His fastballs were often in the mid-nineties and with good movement, too. That was back before he tore his rotator cuff in 2001. It was only a slight tear, but still, any injury to the sensitive part of his throwing shoulder was bad news. Now he had to conserve more, but he usually kept a little in reserve so that when the game was on the line, he could put a little more on his pitches. He had done that so far to Johnson, but not in a commanding way. Varitek came out to the mound to talk, and he and Martinez huddled until Mark Carlson trotted over to break it up.

Martinez's third 3-2 pitch to Johnson looked like a setup pitch. It was up and away, tailing from Johnson. He fouled this one off, too, giving Jeter the chance to do some more running. Johnson stepped out of the box, as he had after every pitch, and lifted his gloved hands up so he could spit on them and rub them together. Then he stepped back in lazily, showing the confidence of a hitter who knew he was swinging well and knew he had a pitcher in a tough spot. Martinez stepped off and threw over to first base to keep Jeter close, then turned back toward home and stared at Johnson.

"This guy is hanging, hanging, hanging," Rich Maloney said out in the Green Monster. "Fucking get him out!"

Martinez finally came inside again. His fourth 3-2 pitch to Johnson was a slider on the inside corner of the plate, and it took a good Johnson swing to fight it off and foul it back. This was the pitch Martinez and Varitek had been setting up with the fastballs away. They had taken their best shot at Johnson, and he was still standing up there, chewing his gum and looking much too comfortable and composed. Martinez was half-tempted to throw one behind his head and load the bases, and he just might have done that, too, if he was anywhere near full strength. Instead, he was sure this was the game right here.

Martinez's fifth 3-2 pitch to Johnson was right back on the outside part of the plate, and there was nothing surprising or even challenging about it. Johnson swung and flipped a soft liner to left field for a base hit, but his swing was almost an afterthought. He had won the battle the pitch before when Martinez had come up with a good enough pitch to end the standoff. Martinez was a gunslinger who had run out of bullets. Johnson and anyone else paying attention knew it, too.

"There you go kid, there you go kid," first-base coach Lee Mazzilli called softly as the ball carried over Bill Mueller's head and landed on the outfield grass and Karim Garcia came in to score and give the Yankees their first lead of the game.

"Nice hitting, kid," Mazzilli shouted, louder now. "Way to go, Nicky! Nice job, kid. That was a great at-bat. Way to battle him."

Theo Epstein tried to stay calm.

"You have to give your ace a chance to work through his issues and find himself," he said. "It'll help him in his next start. You can't just yank your starter. You have to look at the bigger picture."

Joe Torre was shaking his head and smiling.

"To me, that at-bat was incredible," he said.

John Henry had trouble believing Pedro Martinez could let the game get so out of hand. His ace kept stepping around the mound uneasily, taking deep breaths to try to buck himself up. Henry stared out at the left-field scoreboard sadly.

"Nine hits," he said. "Pedro has been sighing a lot."

Henry checked the flags again to see how hard the wind was blowing.

"Dangerous wind, especially with left-handed hitters," he said.

He had reason to worry, too. Jason Giambi had not looked good at the plate at all, swinging through two Martinez fastballs. But Giambi was strong enough to take a bad swing and still hit a home run, and he almost did that. His top hand flew off as he threw the bat at a low, inside pitch and hit a fly ball to right, getting under it a little too much. Jeter tagged and went to third once Trot Nixon gloved the lazy fly. The wind that John Henry had noticed gave Nixon some trouble, and he was drifting back when he made the catch. Otherwise, with his strong throwing arm, he would have had a good chance of throwing Jeter out at third.

It didn't matter anyway. Bernie Williams grounded to Kevin Millar at first to end the inning. Martinez walked off the mound slowly, proud as ever but struggling to understand how his day could have unraveled on him so thoroughly.

BOTTOM OF THE FOURTH

	1	2	3	4	5	6	7	8	9	R
NYY	0	0	2	*3*						5
BOSTON	3	0	1							4

Now the Red Sox really missed Manny Ramirez. They had won the night before without him, and they had taken a big early lead against Andy Pettitte that day without him. But the big early lead had been erased, and now they were paying a price for not having their best hitter in the lineup. The half-inning after a lead change was always critical, and that was true even if baseball old-timers tended to go overboard in stressing its importance—and by overdoing it, the baseball geezers encouraged the notion that they knew less than they thought they did about what actually wins baseball games. After all, from a mathematical point of view, it obviously does not matter when a team scores its runs. Five runs in the first and nothing the rest of the way, single runs in the first, third, fifth, seventh, and ninth—or three here, two there. It's all the same, right? Or is it?

The question cuts to the heart of a basic difference in perspective. Is a baseball game as tidy as a mathematical formula? Figure out the values of each player, using statistical tools, plug them in the right spots, and on any given night they will create a predetermined number of runs? Or is a baseball game a story, an unpredictable mix of character and plot that takes on a life of its own? Can a game be followed as a story so closely and with such attention to detail that someone with years of firsthand observation develops a knack for sensing twists and turns ahead of time? In short, do old men who have spent their lifetimes on dugout benches have access to secrets and insights that are beyond the brightest young minds coming out of Harvard or MIT?

There is undeniably a thrill for some in imagining that decades of experience do not really make baseball men any more knowledgeable about the game. What better salve could there be for all those years of being picked last and getting stuck out in right field? Maybe the authors of the revolution sweeping baseball have it right, and anyone who resists their message is a fool clinging to yesterday's ways of thinking. Or maybe baseball's quixotic relationship to time, its aversion to easy summation, really is a wellspring of its appeal and vitality, not just a sentimental notion that helps fuel all manner of damp iconography. Maybe it's worth wondering why the more time people spent around baseball, the more they expected to be surprised. Ralph Avila was making that point just then down in Santo Domingo.

"I'm seventy-four years old and I've been involved in baseball for seventy-five years, because my mother would go to the stadium to see my dad play when she was pregnant," he said. "And all I know is no one really knows baseball."

Who was Pedro Martinez? *What* was Pedro Martinez? How you answered depended on your view of baseball. To one way of thinking, Pedro Martinez was best summed up this way: three-time Cy Young Award winner. Or by 19-7, 23-4, 18-6, 7-3, and 20-4—his impressive win-loss records starting in 1998, his first season in Boston, up until 2002. Or 2.89, 2.07, 1.74, 2.39, and 2.26—his earned-run average for each of those five seasons. Numbers like that did not lie. They told you a pitcher had physical gifts and competitiveness and other intangible qualities that mixed together to make him something very unusual.

But what of the person who wanted to tell you that if you looked in Pedro Martinez's eyes, even that day in Boston, you could still see traces of the little boy who woke up afraid in the middle of the night because his parents were yelling, and worried it was all his fault because he had done something wrong to set off his father? And that he had resolved then and there to do big things out there in the world, and told himself that doing big things would somehow take away his private pain, only in the end he found out it didn't work out that way? Or what if someone wanted to explain that it ate at Pedro Martinez that back home in the Dominican Republic, the biggest baseball star was Sammy Sosa, and he, Pedro Martinez, was second-best? Or that he was tired, sick and tired, of people in Boston showing disrespect toward his country and his passion for his country? None of these glimpses of emotional truth could tell you who Pedro Martinez was. None offered more than a hint. But together, they might at least point toward the one important fact about Pedro Martinez as he sat in the dugout just after pitching four innings against the Yankees, and pitching poorly: He knew that he didn't know what was happening to his greatness. He knew he didn't know what to expect next. He knew he could not throw as hard as he had as a younger man, but he did not know how much more power he would lose, or how fast.

Pedro Martinez was, in short, a man on the brink, and his teammates all knew it. Martinez played with fury. He was indomitable. But he was also fragile. Sometimes he needed their help to shrug off the signs that his greatness was slipping. That was what being a teammate and having teammates was all about. So when Martinez sat back down in the dugout that day, every Red Sox player on the bench was thinking that if they could only get one run back right then and there, they would be picking up their ace. That was the expression: picking him up. It said a lot.

But instead of Manny Ramirez, the first Red Sox hitter in the bottom of the fourth was the man substituting for him that day, muscle-bound Gabe Kapler, a Triple-A hitter with enough guts not to mind that it took his World Wrestling Federation body and an almost Zen acceptance of his own limitations for him to somehow make a go of being a big-leaguer. Kapler had put up numbers at times. He hit better than .300 over most of a season with the Texas Rangers in 2000, and one season later, finished with seventy-two runs batted in. Those were solid accomplishments, and worthy of respect. But ballplayers had a way of sizing each other up that went beyond numbers, and so far at least, Kapler was a long way from inspiring fear.

"This place is dead," Rich Maloney said out in the Green Monster, truly not understanding why the Fenway crowd was not making more noise.

It had been a long time since Andy Pettitte threw any pitches. The Yankees had kept Pedro Martinez out on the mound for a full twenty-two minutes, giving Pettitte so much time on his hands, he could have headed out to Yawkey Way for a jumbo-sized Italian sausage and still had time to kill before he was back on the mound. Pettitte was a different pitcher now. He had a lead, even after his misadventures in the first, and there was nothing like wriggling off the hook that way to give a pitcher an instinct for the other team's jugular. He looked so relaxed against Gabe Kapler, he almost seemed to be fighting back a smile at times. You could see it in his forehead and around the eyes. Pettitte did not do anything fancy against Kapler, simply moving his fastball in and out, and working away with big, sweeping curves before finally striking him out on a cut fastball in near Kapler's hands.

Trot Nixon was a different story. Pettitte knew Nixon was just the kind of player to ignore the drift of events and step up there and drill a home run to tie it. Kapler could have done that, too, of course. It was conceivable. After all, he homered every once in a while. But the difference was in how each player affected the imagination. Kapler was the perfect candidate to hit a solo shot in a meaningless situation when a pitcher had a big lead and did not really mind getting beat with a homer anyway. It took real work to conjure an image of him cranking a homer against a revitalized Andy Pettitte in that situation. The opposite was true with Nixon—he was what Andy Pettitte would be if he were a slugging outfielder instead of a pitcher. Nixon had an ornery unwillingness to face facts. He was going to do what he was going to do, and outside events did not have much to do with that. That was why images of him stepping up and tying the game with one swing were so easy to picture. Pettitte pushed the idea out of his mind, but he could feel it there, lurking.

Pettitte dropped a crisp breaking ball over the outside corner and had Nixon looking down, angry at himself. Nixon lifted a hand to rub his nose and kicked around the dirt in the batter's box to rearrange it a little and rearrange his perspective, too. It didn't help. Pettitte came back with the same pitch in the same spot and Nixon watched it go by and looked down and kicked at the dirt some more. Pettitte did not waste any time. He had toyed with Nixon's head with the two breaking balls and now came back with a high fastball, ninety-one miles an hour. Nixon swung right through it. Strike three.

Now Pettitte was on a roll. Pitchers had a hard time putting into words what happened on the mound when they found their way back to that higher level of concentration where the ball did just what they wanted it to do, but you could see it in their eyes when they got there. Compared to earlier in the game, Pettitte looked so relaxed and comfortable, he almost seemed a little bored. Ho-hum. Who was up next? Ah, Lou Merloni? Let's get this over with so I can get back into the dugout and one inning closer to a win.

"Andy Pettitte is one of the best pitchers in the American League," Senator Mitchell said. "I think he has been consistently underrated because of the other more high-profile pitchers on the Yankees."

Pettitte started Merloni off with a big curve in on the hands for strike one, and then threw a cut fastball out over the plate that Merloni hit solidly to right field, almost to the Red Sox bullpen. What happened next was comical. Karim Garcia broke back on the ball, running in his crablike way, and almost fell down as he made the catch.

"Later in his career, when he was asked the secret of his success, Lefty Gomez would say 'Clean living and a fast outfield,' " Bob Adair said.

No one would ever describe Karim Garcia as fast, but Adair's point was well taken. It had been a good catch. What mattered was making the grab, not looking good. But still, it was funny. This would be replayed on television over and over and widely referred to as a great catch, but it was no such thing. Garcia caught the ball five full strides shy of the warning track. If he were not so slow, he could have caught up to the ball and made it look easy. Instead, he did his version of a running stagger and carried on after the catch as if he was pretty sure they would have to amend that highest of compliments and instead of saying someone "looked like Clemente" out in right field they would have to say he "looked like Clemente—or Karim Garcia."

Ballplayer vanity always makes for good comic relief, but the

Garcia catch also offered a glimpse of a basic divide in baseball between how most fans and most players saw the game. Very few people really watch games closely, the way most players do. As a result they see less. That's just how it is. Players see the difference between a great outfielder making a tough catch look easy, and a so-so outfielder making a good catch look like a great one. It grates on the nerves of the best players to watch softball-league stuff trumpeted as if it was top-caliber play.

Yet if anything, fans are in danger of growing more out of touch. Even serious fans spend less and less time actually watching baseball games. Out at the ballpark, it has become harder and harder to concentrate. Oh, you can catch the major details just fine, but if you are busy plugging your ears against the canned music or grimacing at the sight of some giant marching orders from the scoreboard, telling you to MAKE SOME NOISE, it inevitably cuts down on your enjoyment of the finer points, like watching an outfielder take a few steps in or a few steps to the side when a pitcher has two strikes on the batter. That's true even of the basics, like watching every movement of an outfielder's route toward a ball and noting the smooth geometry of it all. Who has time for that when you're busy answering your cell phone, or checking to make sure you've turned off your cell phone, or glaring at the guy next to you who has not stopped talking on his cell phone since the second inning, and keeps saying things like, "Nothing much, just sitting here at the game, what about you?"

Baseball is entertainment, right? That's what the marketing experts all say. So if music videos and computer-generated action movies have conditioned people to prefer fragmentary entertainment, ripped clean of a lot of distracting context, it's inevitable that watching baseball would change, too. If something valuable has been lost, who is even going to notice? Leave it to the geezers and the so-called baseball poets to fret over how people used to take the time to educate themselves to always notice more about a baseball game, since if you try, you always can, like someone closing his eyes in a forest and trying to identify as many sounds as possible. Forget that. Put on the Walkman, crank up the volume, and open your eyes just in time to see Karim Garcia stagger-stepping toward the warning track and swaggering all the way back to the dugout.

As soon as Garcia made the catch, a message went up on the big outfield scoreboard: "JANE, THEO HAS A QUESTION FOR YOU: WILL YOU MARRY ME?"

Theo Epstein was not a big scoreboard-watcher. ("I get scores on my phone," he said. "I don't watch the scoreboard because it's brutally slow.") But he was looking out there now.

"Look at the board!" he said, smiling, his mask of indifference dropping away for a moment.

"That's not me, though," Theo Epstein added, just in case anyone wondered.

Rich Maloney was in no mood to watch a Yankee fan do anything, let alone propose right there in the heart of Red Sox Nation.

"That marriage will last maybe to the end of this homestand," he grumbled.

Bob Adair was not much more upbeat.

"Ah, romance rears its ugly head," he said.

Jane Baxter was beaming. She actually preferred the seats down behind third base, but she and Theo Gordon were having fun hanging out on the Green Monster. It was like the rare great cocktail party up there, the kind where you could drop by for half an hour and talk to a few people and actually have fun. One nice woman sitting in the front row had joked, "Hey, maybe we should throw some Yankee fans over onto the field." A fan in a red shirt, sitting just in front of them, asked them to take a picture of him with Fenway Park as the backdrop. Baxter had chatted with several other people, too. Now they were all staring at her, waiting to see if she would say yes.

Did she have a choice, in front of so many people? She told Gordon yes, and then up on the big screen, a much larger version of Baxter also told Gordon yes.

"He's a Yankee fan!" someone complained from nearby in the Green Monster seats.

But the mood was upbeat and cheerful. The Red Sox fans cut Gordon some slack. Baxter pulled off the friendship ring Gordon had given her, and he slipped on the engagement ring. They hugged and kissed and giggled, and then hugged some more and kissed some more and giggled some more. Gordon couldn't wait to tell the whole story of the lies he had to cook up so he could surprise her up there on the Green Monster. There would be time for that later on the train ride back to New Hampshire to have dinner with her parents.

"I've fulfilled my dream," Gordon said.

"I always wanted to be up on that screen," Baxter said. "I always used to ask my dad what you had to do to get up on the screen. That was great."

The woman who had been saying it was time to throw some Yankee fans onto the field turned out to be Stacey Lucchino, Larry Lucchino's wife. She bought Gordon and Baxter a couple of beers to congratulate them. The fan in the red shirt now turned his camera on them, and gave them his card and promised to e-mail them the picture. The novelty of letting a Yankee fan carry on right there at Fenway Park, and on the big screen, too, had everyone feeling pleased with their broad-mindedness. One tall, skinny young fan in a Red Sox jersey stopped by to give Gordon a hard time about being a Yankee fan, but it was all in good fun.

"How will it feel to lose again to the Yanks and when we win the World Series?" Gordon asked.

"Yeah, well, we've lost before," the Red Sox fan said. "We know what it feels like. How will *you* feel when the tables turn and all of a sudden the Red Sox knock you down?"

TOP OF THE FIFTH

	1	2	3	4	5	6	7	8	9	R
NYY	0	0	2	3						5
BOSTON	3	0	1	*0*						4

Someone came out to the mound in a Red Sox uniform before the fifth inning, but it was not Pedro Martinez. Instead, the one-run game would be entrusted to someone named Bronson Arroyo. Other than being named for the actor Charles Bronson, and having a straight-knee leg kick that looked like it was modeled on Dennis Eckersley's, Bronson Arroyo had done a pretty good job of flying under the radar screen. He had pulled off a perfect game on August 10, pitching for Pawtucket, the Red Sox International League Triple-A affiliate, and five days ago he had recorded his first major-league save by holding the Seattle Mariners to two hits over three innings.

Down in Santo Domingo, Ralph Avila was hoping Martinez would put the disappointing outing behind him.

"This wasn't his day," Avila said. "Nobody likes to be taken out, but he has to accept it. Pedro is arrogant and that leads him to be on the defensive. He always sees the negative side. I'm sure Pedro is unsatisfied with his game. We taught him to never be satisfied with his work because there is always room for improvement. Pedro wasn't in his best shape. He's probably asking right now what he did wrong. If he asked me, I'd tell him his pitches were too high. He wasn't in command and his changes weren't working."

Arroyo started out all over the place and walked leadoff hitter Hideki Matsui on five pitches.

"Well that's a great start," Bob Adair said. "You walk the first man, he's got a fifty percent chance of scoring."

But Matsui had never looked comfortable against Arroyo, who had good movement on his pitches, and put them where he wanted, too. He did not look so much nervous as surprised to be out there. He was not the only one. Seeing anyone besides Pedro Martinez out on the mound for the Red Sox in the fifth inning was enough to make any fan at the game do a double take.

David Mellor, the groundskeeper, was sweating it out. The latest weather bulletins had been bad, and all you had to do was look overhead to see the cloud cover thickening. Mellor made the call early in the fifth inning to remove the tarp cover, and the Marriott ad along with it. He wanted to be ready, just in case.

Next up for the Yankees was Jorge Posada, who already had

one no-doubt-about-it homer to his credit. Posada reached down to grab some dirt for his hands and took his time before squeezing his helmet lower on his head and stepping into the batter's box. Arroyo's first pitch started out inside but veered out over the plate and Posada turned on it. He ripped a hard line drive, only it was hit right at second baseman Lou Merloni, who leaped to catch the ball, planted his feet, and threw to first base for a double play. Matsui had done everything right. He broadened his lead off the bag as the pitch was thrown, took two quick steps after the ball was hit, and turned and did his best to dive back to the bag. He was just an instant too late, but he did have some very nice dirt stains on his uniform front to show for his efforts.

"That's Lou!" John Henry called out loudly, and pumped his fist.

A few fans sitting nearby turned to look, surprised to see the low-key Red Sox owner shouting so fervently in public. Everywhere in the stands, fans got up to applaud the double play. But behind home plate, Theo Epstein remained seated, arms folded.

Bob Adair shook his head and smiled.

"You see?" he laughed. "Success in baseball: You throw a fat pitch, the guy hits it squarely, you get a line drive straight to second."

Arroyo, feeling lucky now, went right after Aaron Boone. He jumped ahead 0-2 with two straight breaking balls, both of which had Boone fooled, then left a fastball way high. Even watching the high fastball go by, Boone looked uneasy and uncertain. He leaned awkwardly and after the pitch went by him, took a couple of small steps toward the Red Sox dugout and then kicked his front foot up in the air as if it would somehow explain why he was so off-balance. Arroyo went right back to the breaking ball and struck him out, making it look ridiculously easy. Boone was hitting all of .202, and looked about as harmless as a big-league hitter could look.

BOTTOM OF THE FIFTH

	1	2	3	4	5	6	7	8	9	R
NYY	0	0	2	3	*0*					5
BOSTON	3	0	1	0						4

Johnny Damon was still woozy. He was not sure which had been worse, taking Gabe Kapler's glove to his face or slamming into the Green Monster, but he knew it was a one-two punch he would be feeling for a while. The bruises were already starting to form. Maybe he would feel worse later on and have to miss a game or two, but he was not coming out of the lineup that day. No way. This was too big a game, and the team needed him. Damon took one look at Andy Pettitte warming up before the bottom of the fifth and it was clear Pettitte had breathed a sigh of relief to have Martinez out of the game. Pettitte had struck out three of the last four batters he had faced and not given up a hit since David Ortiz blasted that home run with one out in the third. Pettitte missed twice to Damon, outside and then inside, but with the count full, made a tough pitch inside that Damon lifted into right field for an easy out.

John Henry had noticed the thickening cloud cover, and decided it was time to head back up to his private box. He smiled and shook hands with Peter Farrelly, and said so long to Bob and the other two boys. As Henry walked up the aisle and climbed through the grandstand, fans pointed and called out to him. They were not always original, but their shouts of affection seemed heartfelt.

"I love you, man!" yelled one fan.

Another offered a more practical assurance.

"We'll get even in the eighth, John," he predicted.

Henry kept his faint smile in place and waved at anyone who spoke to him, but he also kept moving.

Bill Mueller was having a tough day. He had scored in the first inning after reaching base on a ground ball, but he was still hitless. Pettitte was a riddle. Mueller was sure he could get a hit off him, but the left-hander seemed to be getting stronger out there. There was nothing much to do with his first pitch, a breaking ball on the inside corner, or the second pitch, a fastball away that Mueller fouled back. Pettitte wasted a fastball way high, and Mueller looked for a low curve and got it. But it was a tough pitch. Even looking for it, all Mueller could do was get a sliver or two of his bat on it, just enough to stay alive. Pettitte got the ball back and took a little more time, tugging on his cap not once but twice and kicking at the dirt around the rubber in a casual, distracted way. He looked more carefree than nervous, the way he had in the first. His pitch, when it finally came, was a chest-high fastball. He had set Mueller up just right. He swung through the ball and headed back to the dugout.

"I don't like this game now," Rich Maloney said out in the Green Monster, speaking for every Red Sox fan.

Nomar Garciaparra was up next, and Pettitte approached him like a man putting together a how-to video he could hawk on late-night television. First he hit the outside corner with a low fastball, then put another low fastball on the inside corner for another called strike, and then went back outside with another fastball. This one was belt-high, not low, and Garciaparra fouled it back. He fouled off another pitch, a high breaking ball, and then went down and got a low breaking ball, lining it to left for a single.

Pettitte slapped at his glove with his pitching hand, and for good reason, too. He had done everything right against Garciaparra, but sometimes that didn't matter. A hitter could make you look bad even when you threw just the pitch you wanted. Garciaparra's single was the first hit Pettitte had given up since Ortiz's homer, and now Ortiz was up again. Pettitte tried playing with his head a little. Ortiz's home run had come on a low, inside pitch that he turned on, so Pettitte started him off with another low, inside pitch, only this was even lower. Ortiz swung and missed and flashed a quick glare at Pettitte. He stepped out of the box and took his time readjusting his batting gloves and generally trying to annoy Pettitte out on the mound.

Pettitte waited until Ortiz stepped back into the box, and then threw over to first base. Even with Pettitte's great move, this was a token toss, his way of killing time and letting Ortiz know that two could play at that game. Pettitte's next pitch was a very hittable breaking ball, inside, and Ortiz took a big rip at it, but fouled it down the first-base line. The tough part was not thinking too much about what he should have done to the ball on the earlier pitch. He had to let it go. Pettitte helped him out by missing outside with a fastball, giving Ortiz more time to collect himself, and when Pettitte came in again with a low cut fastball running away from the outside corner, Ortiz stayed back and went with the pitch, using his wrists to stroke a solid single to left field.

Once again, Pettitte was looking twitchy. This was nothing like the first inning, but to both Garciaparra and Ortiz he had made just the pitch he wanted to make and it had not mattered. That had a way of disconcerting a pitcher. Pettitte was back to taking deep breaths to calm himself, but he looked composed, even after he bounced his first pitch to Kevin Millar, dropping a curveball into the hard-packed red clay a good foot in front of home plate. Posada went down to get it, squaring himself, and the ball wedged into the gap under his chest protector. (That was one way to make a stop.) Pettitte came right back with another breaking ball, a good one, and then left a belt-high fastball right out there where Millar could extend his bat and drive it.

Millar fouled it back, and couldn't believe it. He jerked his bat back, clutched it in his left hand, and then sank down and dug his foot into the red clay in front of home plate, dragging it forward and kicking up a small cloud of clay dust. David Mellor, already grimacing to see Millar let such a good opportunity get by him, grimaced again to see his field being manhandled. One batter earlier, Ortiz had been able to stop thinking about a mistake pitch he should have ripped. Now Millar faced the same challenge. Pettitte, tight-lipped and ashen after making the mistake, came back with a fastball on the inside corner that froze Millar. All he could do was stand there staring out at the mound as if it had somehow been unfair for Pettitte to throw a fastball.

"That can't happen!" Rich Maloney shouted.

His assistant, Garrett Tingle, angrily slammed the inside of the Wall.

Back in the visiting team clubhouse, Mariano Rivera decided after watching Millar strike out that it was time to leave the clubhouse, where he had watched all of the game, and come out to the Yankee dugout and then on to the bullpen.

Between innings, Colleen Reilly came out with her broom. She had changed into her *League of Their Own* dress since escorting Theo Gordon and Jane Baxter up onto the Green Monster. She was all smiles and bouncy charm as she danced around the basepaths, sweeping here and there, but mostly she looked like someone who was having a lot of fun. Theo Epstein squirmed noticeably.

"Don't ask," he said. "It's a long story. It's brutal. It wasn't my idea."

TOP OF THE SIXTH

	1	2	3	4	5	6	7	8	9	R
NYY	0	0	2	3	0					5
BOSTON	3	0	1	0	*0*					4

It still looked odd to see Bronson Arroyo on the mound, but he was doing a good impression of someone who felt like he belonged out there. He missed badly with his first pitch to Karim Garcia, leading off the inning, then threw two quick strikes and got Garcia to swing at an inside breaking ball and send a lazy fly ball to right field. Trot Nixon caught it a good ten feet in front of the Pesky Pole, where lazy fly balls have been known to turn into home runs.

Larry Lucchino had a good look at Garcia's ball from where he was standing. He had gone out to join his wife and stepson out on top of the Green Monster. They had a few seats in the front row, where you could sit on what looked like bar stools and peer out over the edge. It was, without a doubt, one of the best views in baseball.

"I make a trip out here every game," Lucchino said as he made the short walk from his private box out to the Monster seats.

He was greeted warmly most everywhere he went out on the Monster. A lot of Red Sox fans had clearly taken to the new ownership group, even though they were outsiders. Lucchino basked in their enthusiasm, but he also wore it lightly. He knew it could evaporate quickly if things went bad.

"We say around here that the highs are higher in Boston and the lows are lower in Boston," Lucchino said. "We were perceived to be handicapped because we were not born and raised here, our ownership group. But it was also an advantage because we had experience in other places and other markets and had a perspective that was different than the traditional Boston perspective. We recognize that there is a lot we have to learn or absorb by osmosis."

Ask people in baseball about Lucchino, and they will tell you he can be an egomaniac. They will tell you dark stories about him berating not just his peers and close associates, but also the occasional hapless receptionist who was in the wrong place at the wrong time. Lucchino would volunteer some of the stories himself, and talk about how he has tried to change.

"I try to reduce the anxiety you might expect to be feeling by keeping it in perspective," he said, standing a foot or two away from the foul pole in left.

Arroyo missed outside to Enrique Wilson and came back with a hard breaking ball that caught the inside corner and a changeup on the outside corner. Wilson stepped out of the box to stare out at Arroyo, squinting and all but asking, "Who *is* this guy?" Back in the box, Wilson glared out at the mound, and now he was all but adding, "This ain't the Inter-*na*-tional League, young fella." Arroyo threw an eye-high fastball right over the plate, just to get Wilson's attention, and then jammed him with an inside fastball. Wilson got a good swing on it and lifted the ball to deep right, but Nixon caught this one, too, back against the fence. Wilson threw his bat down just after he hit the ball, frustrated he had missed it, and Nixon drifted back in a relaxed way that showed he had a bead on the ball the whole time.

"Uh-oh," Lucchino said, good-naturedly, as Nixon made the catch.

Lucchino was trying to prove his point about not worrying as much as he did when he was younger. He bowed his head and shook it quickly, trying to convince himself of something.

"As I've gotten older, I've been able to control my emotions better," he continued. "I'm still not very good, but I'm better than I was. It's still an effort to control your emotions. We're all fans. Everybody in the organization."

His wife, Stacey, drifted over and half-listened as he spoke.

"In the old days, a couple of chairs got knocked over," Lucchino said. "That was in my volatile youth."

Stacey smiled. She had big, alert eyes and a friendly, open manner, and she was not shy either about adoring her husband or knocking him down a notch or two if given an opportunity. These popped up fairly often, it appeared.

"Is he talking about chairs?" she asked lightly.

Lucchino looked at her sideways, still trying to follow the game.

"He's more mellow than he was," Stacey allowed.

She said it in a friendly way that was not without a note of warning.

The night before, Lucchino had to plead with her to let him check the late scores from the West Coast. She reminded him of the pledge he made over the radio to stop his compulsive scoreboard-watching.

"Well, wait, it's different!" he had told her. "I'm not scoreboard-watching during the game."

"No!" she had told him.

"I just want to see Seattle and Oakland," he had said. "I'm not going to obsess."

Lucchino had checked the scores. But at least now he was out in the Green Monster seats, away from his responsibilities, which as it turned out fit in with another pledge he had made to himself—and to Stacey.

"I make an effort now to try to watch more of the game and enjoy more of the game," he said.

The Yankees were back to the top of their order, but Derek Jeter did not have a chance to do anything against Arroyo. The first pitch he saw ran inside and grazed him just above the belt. There was some grumbling on the Yankee bench. Joe Torre looked down, scratched hard at the side of his face near his temple, and pulled off his cap in frustration.

Up on the Monster, Lucchino admitted he was passionate about games in ways other people might find nutty.

"It's the same mentality as a fan," he said. "I sometimes think where I stand influences the outcome, as preposterous as that is. I have hunches all the time. Don't ask me about them now, though."

Lucchino was staring down as he spoke, watching Derek Jeter take his lead off of first base. Nick Johnson was in the batter's box now and Lucchino was well aware that the Red Sox had not been able to get him out. Johnson had three hits, one to each field, and his long battle with Pedro in the fourth inning was looking like the key to the game so far. No wonder Lucchino did not want to talk out loud about his hunches.

Arroyo started Johnson out with a slow curve for a strike and came back with another breaking ball on the inside part of the plate that Johnson nubbed foul, stepping out and muttering to himself. He knew he had a good chance to come through again, and turn this into a performance to remember. Making a name for himself as a Red Sox beater could help his future with the Yankees. He stepped back in and watched another breaking ball dart low for a ball. Arroyo came back with another breaking ball, only this one was high. Johnson tried to do what David Ortiz had done earlier and push the ball the other way, but the pitch was not outside, making that hard. Bill Mueller ranged two steps to his left and scooped up Johnson's weak grounder in time to throw him out at first to end the inning. Varitek popped up and ran toward the dugout with Arroyo, slapping him on the back and congratulating him for another solid inning of work.

BOTTOM OF THE SIXTH

	1	2	3	4	5	6	7	8	9	R
NYY	0	0	2	3	0	0				5
BOSTON	3	0	1	0	0					4

Varitek was not happy with his first two at-bats. His timing had been off, but he could feel it slowly coming together. He had been watching Andy Pettitte all day, and he was sure he could get the better of him now, leading off the sixth. He fouled one ball off to the left and fouled another ball off to the right. Pettitte's third pitch was a low breaking ball, out over the plate, and Varitek hit a high fly ball that sent Karim Garcia drifting back toward the Red Sox bullpen in right field, where he made the catch several feet in from the warning track.

Gabe Kapler watched two pitches miss for balls and then sent another lazy fly out to Garcia in right. There were times when a pitcher had a team mesmerized, and this was one of those times.

The psychological edge Pettitte had over the Red Sox hitters was all the more potent given his earlier struggles. He had taken a negative, his early troubles, and turned it into more than a positive. It was, for lack of a better word, embarrassing to be a Red Sox hitter right then. They'd had Pettitte just where they wanted him. But he had popped back to life and here he was, making it look easy to pitch to them long after Pedro Martinez had taken his shower and gotten dressed.

"It seriously feels like it's 10–4," Rich Maloney said out in the Green Monster.

No one embodied the way Pettitte had gotten to them better than Trot Nixon. He had struck out last time up, and struck out looking bad. Now Pettitte started him off with a fastball just inside, and Nixon watched it go by for ball one. He fouled off the next pitch, another fastball, and then tried to check his swing on a letter-high fastball, but could not do it. Pettitte missed outside with a low fastball, and came right back with another high fastball, and once again, Nixon tried to check his swing but could not. Mark Carlson stood up to call strike three with an emphatic gesture, as if his hands were pulling apart bread. Pettitte was up to six strikeouts.

Theo Epstein was glum. It was bad enough sitting through a game that seemed designed to make a general manager miserable. Now a fan in a Kevin Millar jersey had walked down so he could stand just in front of Epstein's seats. A big, dumb grin was plastered on his face, and he had his cell phone out.

"Can you see me?" he was asking loudly.

Just another TV whore, ready to be rude, act stupid, make a

fool of himself, whatever it took to be on television for a few seconds. It happened all too often, and Epstein always hated it. Poise and dignity were important to him. He had trouble understanding people who valued neither. But an excuse presented itself for Epstein to get away. An assistant showed up to get the Patterson twins, who had been sitting with Epstein for the last four innings. He was a little embarrassed, worried the parents might be disturbed about missing their children so long. He hopped up and made another dash, this time back to the elevator and on up to his private box.

TOP OF THE SEVENTH

	1	2	3	4	5	6	7	8	9	R
NYY	0	0	2	3	0	0				5
BOSTON	3	0	1	0	0	0				4

David Mellor was sure he had made the right decision to pull off the tarp cover in the fifth inning. He would make the same call again, if given the choice. It was just bad luck that the Marriott CEO happened to be at the ballpark that day. It was more bad luck that he happened to notice when they pulled off the tarp cover and the Marriott ad that went with it. The complaints they raised were all very civil and professional, of course. Why wouldn't they be? But the Marriott CEO had made inquiries, and now Mellor had a corporate-relations person asking him a lot of questions about what he had done and why. Mellor patiently reminded him that from the beginning, the agreement had been very clear that at times they would have to remove the cover if rain was threatening. This was starting to get frustrating.

"It's cool, man, it's groovy," the corporate-relations person told Mellor. "But I've gotta have something to say to these guys upstairs, you know."

Mellor stared back at him.

"I mean, I love your work," the corporate-relations person continued. "I would never interfere with the professionalism. But . . ."

The air at Fenway smelled like rain now. It was almost like the feeling just after getting out of the shower, when the whole place is all steamed up, the air was so heavy with moisture. Mellor did not know when the rain would come, but rain was coming.

"Work with me on this," the corporate-relations person said. "What percentage chance do you think there is that it will rain?"

Mellor did not have a percentage. Nor did he need one. He pointed over to the radar loop sweeping over his computer screen, which made it clear rain was likely.

"I go by the radar," Mellor said, getting the last word.

Bronson Arroyo had pulled off quite a feat. Not only was he back out there to start the seventh, even with Alan Embree warmed up out in the bullpen, but by now it almost felt right to see him out there. The Yankee hitters seemed to think so, anyway. They were giving him all kinds of respect. Jason Giambi came up to lead off and swung at Arroyo's first pitch and lofted it to center for an easy out. Bernie Williams, up next, did his deep-knee-bend thing and watched a low breaking ball catch the outside corner for strike one. He stared at where the ball had just darted past as if a small purple rabbit had hopped out of the Red Sox dugout and offered him a cigar. Williams moved only his knees, unbending them in slow motion as he stared down blankly, then stared out at the mound and then at the ground some more.

Williams was very much a Yankee, as in, the late-nineties Yankees teams that won the World Series four times in five years. To some, those teams seemed too corporate, too businesslike, too polished; they were easy to respect, and hard to like. But they were also very dedicated to playing hard, all the time. Paul O'Neill was different from the others in that his intensity was obvious to anyone; Jeter and Williams and Rivera were just as intense, but their intensity was not so easy to glimpse. It came through more in what you did not see than in what you actually saw. You did not see Jeter or Williams or Rivera make a wrong move. Or if you did see it, you knew right away that it was such a rare glimpse, all it did was remind you of how long you'd had to wait to see anything out of place in their games.

Playing baseball well was mostly about finding a way to maintain unflagging concentration and imagination. Even the muscled-up ones, like Barry Bonds or Mark McGwire, would tell you that. Back in the days before Pac Bell Park opened in 2000 and freed him from the dreary confines of left field at Candlestick Park, Bonds once stood a few steps down the hall from the visiting clubhouse at the Oakland Coliseum and talked at length with a reporter about how difficult it was to maintain the same level of intensity at all times during a game. This was a private, vulnerable Bonds not often glimpsed by the public. He had spoken to the same reporter the week his friend Tupac Shakur had been killed in Las Vegas, and talked with open emotion about his feeling of loss and how he had just phoned Tupac a week before his death and told him, "Violence isn't the answer, man."

Now Bonds was talking in a low voice, almost a whisper. He was talking about how sometimes he was just plain bored out there in left field. It was hard to keep himself interested. Part of it was his frustration with how little people noticed. If he kept himself so into the game, he was thinking ahead, like a Wayne Gretzky or a Larry Bird, and quickly anticipated the flight of the ball and made a great break and ran all out and then, at the last second, eased up and coasted and made the catch look easy, people yawned and said, "Routine play."

If someone else who was not thinking along with the game reacted slowly and ran the wrong route and finally caught up to the ball and grabbed it and tumbled to the ground, it would be on *SportsCenter*. That was how it was. Bonds accepted that. But it made him mad. And that anger was sometimes distracting. In fact, it distracted him so much that once he got started talking about it that day before the Giants played an exhibition game with the Oakland A's, he couldn't stop. It was half an hour before game time and he kept talking. Twenty minutes before game time and he kept talking. Ten minutes before game time and still he was talking. Finally, the reporter he was talking to suggested maybe they ought to break it up.

McGwire used to make reporters laugh when he talked about how the key to hitting home runs was his "mental strength." They laughed quietly. No one stupid enough to laugh in the face of a man staring back with those squinting green dinosaur eyes and huge, hulking physique would survive long on the baseball beat. But laugh they did. How could this be taken seriously? This lumberjack character wanted people to believe hitting was mostly mental? But there was something to what he said. McGwire's fifth full year in the big leagues was miserable. He was going through a tough divorce, and knew it was his fault. That year, he hit only twenty-two homers and barely batted .200. It was a pathetic performance. His head was all messed up and it showed.

Years of therapy later, he felt as if he had a handle on his own emotions and his own powers of concentration and focus in a way he never had. He would stand with a reporter in some visiting clubhouse somewhere and talk about this at length. As a young player, he never studied videotape of other pitchers. Later he did so compulsively. He got into visualization exercises. No doubt McGwire preferred a positive subject to questions about just what Jose Canseco had taught him about how to get so muscular, and just what the Bash Brothers used to do together before games in the men's room at the Coliseum, but the point was: McGwire always knew that even with his comic-book-superhero body, he had to approach every game and every at-bat with complete intensity if he was going to live up to the promise he showed as a skinny rookie hitting forty-nine homers.

Derek Jeter and Bernie Williams and Mariano Rivera never went through inner struggles about how to maintain their intensity during baseball games. Torre set a tone that helped them channel years of Yankee history and the background hum of playing for a team where the owner's mood swings and outbursts were followed so closely and steadily by talk radio and the *Post* and the *News,* it was reality TV before there was reality TV.

The Joe Torre Yankees had more pressure on them than any other team in baseball, year after year after year, and chose the defense of a bland exterior. It worked. Jeter made magazine covers and Sexiest Man Alive lists, but the joke of the television commercials showing him and Steinbrenner talking about his night life was as much on him as it was on the Boss. Jeter and Steinbrenner really had gotten into it over Jeter's nightlife, but that did not change the fact that as a personality and a public figure, Jeter was dull. John McEnroe he was not; Michael Jordan he was not. That dullness worked for Jeter. It worked for Williams and Rivera, too.

Grady Little's decision to leave the kid Arroyo out there so long, even with Embree warmed up and ready to go, sitting on the bullpen bench in his red warmup jacket, was almost an affront to the Yankees. It was, at the very least, a challenge. Don Zimmer and Joe Torre had talked before the game about how a one-run lead at Fenway was almost no lead at all. They needed another run here, which meant Bernie Williams needed to get on base. After watching that first-pitch breaking ball for a strike, Williams looked as cool and unbothered as ever, but you could almost hear the intensity of his focus crackling in the air like a high-tension wire.

It was clear that if Arroyo came back with another breaking ball, Williams was going to take a rip at it. Arroyo did, inside this time, and Williams did. His deep fly to right had home-run distance but not home-run direction. Williams crooked his neck to the right and watched the ball drop harmlessly into the stands down the first-base line. Foul ball. Arroyo came back with a fastball off the outside corner and another one belt-high and on the hands, so that when Williams swung, the ball hit in on the thin part of the bat. Lou Merloni took four quick steps to his right to loud cries of "Lou," sounding a lot like booing, and tossed the ball to first for the out.

Arroyo had a boyish look out there, like a kid still trying to decide whether he could ask for autographs later and wondering if he could fill his pockets with candy bars at the snack table in the clubhouse. What he did not show was any fear. He started Hideki Matsui out with the same pitch he threw first to Bernie Williams, a low breaking ball tailing away from him and over the outside corner. Matsui nodded quickly, almost imperceptibly, and stared down at his feet, lifting one and then the other, one and then the other.

He wasted little time moving back into his upright batting stance, bat poking straight up, hands close to the chest. But when Arroyo came back with a changeup right down the middle, Matsui watched it go for strike two and stared hard at the pitch. He jerked his head upward, as if to say, "Oh man!" (in Japanese). He twisted his body and lifted one leg, looking like a kid who had to go, stepped out of the batter's box to stare out at Arroyo, and used both hands to fiddle with his belt, all while holding his bat. Arroyo waited for Matsui to step back in and came back with another low off-speed pitch, and Matsui hit it hard to the right side. Kevin Millar had no trouble fielding the heavy-topspin grounder to end the inning.

BOTTOM OF THE SEVENTH

	1	2	3	4	5	6	7	8	9	R
NYY	0	0	2	3	0	0	*0*			5
BOSTON	3	0	1	0	0	0				4

John Henry was back in his private box behind home plate, and he prepared himself a plate of chicken diavalo and carried it to his favorite spot in the front left corner. He knew the Red Sox were running out of time. Jeff Nelson was up in the Yankee bullpen now, and more than anything, seeing him out there offered a reminder that soon enough it would be Mariano Rivera time. The Red Sox probably had two more innings without facing him, but you never knew. Torre might bring Rivera out in the eighth in a game like this. The only certainty was that Rivera was not coming out in the seventh. This was the time for the Red Sox to get something going.

"Come on, Lou, get us started," John Henry said, pushing his chair back and standing up, arms folded, to rock back and forth from one foot to the other.

Lou Merloni had made solid contact his last time up, driving that ball almost to the wall and giving Karim Garcia the opportunity to do his stagger-step thing, and he was feeling more comfortable at the plate. He watched Pettitte's first pitch catch the outside corner, and then swung through a big, sweeping curve. Pettitte tried to catch the outside corner again and just missed, then left a curve low. One thing Merloni had was a good eye for the strike zone. Pettitte tried to hit the outside corner with a fastball one more time and Merloni had no problem at all laying off to make it a full count. Another outside fastball was close enough to merit a swing, and Merloni fouled it off, but Pettitte had set up another breaking ball, and this one was sharp and down in the zone. Pettitte had his seventh strikeout of the day.

It was strange. Nelson was throwing in the bullpen and Pettitte had to be running out of gas. He had by then thrown 117 pitches. (Pedro Martinez could have been out on Cape Cod, it had been so long since he left the game.) But the Red Sox hitters looked almost docile against Pettitte. The crowd felt it, too, and just sat there inertly. Some people actually started hitting a beach ball around, something that one had a right to hope and expect would never happen at Fenway Park.

"That's what they do when they are bored," Debi Little said.

Johnny Damon, up next, squared half-around, as if he were going to try to bunt for a base hit, and watched Pettitte's first pitch bounce in front of the plate for ball one. The next pitch was a belt-high fastball that jammed him, and he popped it up. Second baseman Enrique Wilson took six steps back onto the outfield grass to make the catch. Bill Mueller watched a couple of pitches, one a fastball just outside, the other a good breaking ball, and then grounded out to Derek Jeter. Pettitte, so demonstrative early in the game, had a poker face as he walked off the mound and back to the dugout for what was sure to be the last time that day. Pitching coach Mel Stottlemyre stood up and came over to meet him, his clenched hand extended to knock fists and congratulate Pettitte for his day's work.

TOP OF THE EIGHTH

	1	2	3	4	5	6	7	8	9	R
NYY	0	0	2	3	0	0	0			5
BOSTON	3	0	1	0	0	0	*0*			4

There was almost a *Twilight Zone* cast to this game now. Bronson Arroyo was still out there. He just would not go away. Jorge Posada came out to lead off the Yankee eighth, and there young Arroyo still was on the mound, looking fresh and eager. What Joe Torre had noticed earlier in the game about Pedro Martinez was not so much that his throwing motion was off or anything in particular about the actual flight of his pitches. What Torre noticed was his hitters were not fooled by Martinez's pitches. Watching now, he saw that his hitters were still having a hard time getting a handle on Arroyo.

Posada had turned on an inside pitch his last time up against Arroyo and hit the ball hard, but lined into a double play. Arroyo started him off this time with a breaking ball over the outside corner, the way he had started off so many Yankee hitters, and Posada let it go by for strike one. Arroyo came right back with a similar pitch, and Posada watched that one for a strike, too. Even with two strikes on him, Posada still looked in no mood to get the bat off his shoulder. Arroyo tried hitting the outside corner again with a breaking ball and missed, but not by much. The count was 1-2. Arroyo peered in for the sign, fresh-faced and wide-eyed but still somehow calm, and came back inside with another breaking ball. Posada swung and missed. He had not even come close.

Grady Little was staring out at the mound deep in thought. He would be making his moves soon enough, but first he was going to watch Arroyo go to work against Aaron Boone. The kid had done a great job for him, coming out of the pen and giving them everything they could ask for. He had kept them in the game and they had pitchers out in the bullpen who earned their living working the eighth and ninth innings, and earned a good living at that.

Little had not been a player for thirty years, but somehow he remembered his time in the minor leagues almost as if it was more recent than the years of managing. His heart was always in the game of baseball. He stuck around six or seven years in the minor leagues, but never had much of a chance to play. "I knew I stunk," he said. He knew he would have an opportunity to manage once he gave up on being a player, and sure enough, that same year he was released in spring training, he got an offer to consider managing the Yankees' rookie-league team starting that June. So he went home, figuring he would be managing within a couple months, but George Steinbrenner had bought the team and replaced the fellow who had offered Little the job. So Steinbrenner had in a backhanded sort of way been responsible for firing Grady Little as manager, before Little had ever managed a single game.

"So probably I was the first manager he ever fired and he didn't even know it," Little said, laughing at the craziness of it all.

Little moved to Texas after that and leased some land. He had liked cotton farming. It was hard work, but it was honest work, and no one was ever looking over his shoulder. He did everything himself except the irrigation. Little had 660 acres by his last year, but the economics of farming were brutal. It was hard to say which was harder to predict, the weather or the fluctuating market for cotton.

"It was pleasurable," he said. "But you put in a lot of hard work, and you'd like to get paid for it. You're talking about Mother Nature. You're talking about people changing the price. Here's an indication of how tough it was: I sold some cotton in 1977 for more than they're selling it for now, twenty-six years later."

The best part about it had been making all his own decisions and living with the results. He had a cab on his tractor with heating and air-conditioning and all kinds of music, mostly country music. He'd work through the night sometimes, twenty-four hours straight in that cab, or thirty hours straight, if that was what it took to get something done before the rains came.

A part of him would always be uncomfortable knowing that when you managed a big-league ball club, especially the Red Sox, you could do your part and more, but it didn't always matter. What mattered, too much of the time, was what others did. Little could only keep on doing the job his way, and try not to let it get him down. That was a lot easier when he was faced with agreeable surprises, like this kid Arroyo pitching so well for them against the Yankees.

Aaron Boone had looked bad striking out the last time up, and came up this time determined not to swing. Arroyo had struck him out with his best pitch, a slow breaking ball that ducked away right as it was reaching the plate. He started Boone off this time with a fastball toward the outside corner. It missed just low. He tried coming inside with the dipping breaking ball again, and Varitek caught it and held his big catcher's mitt frozen in place to give Mark Carlson a long look, but they did not get the call.

"Don't let this guy hurt you!" Rich Maloney pleaded from behind the Green Monster.

Frustrated, Arroyo tried a similar pitch, only this time it did not do much and was not over either corner but out over the heart of the plate. Boone lined it off the Green Monster for a double.

"They should bring in Embree, but they're not," said Theo Epstein, now back in his private box.

Karim Garcia stepped up to the plate, mouth stuffed with a fresh load of tobacco, and looked in to the Red Sox dugout to see if that was all for Arroyo. It was. Pitching coach Dave Wallace reached over Grady Little's head in the Red Sox dugout to pick up the phone and call out to Euclides Rojas to ask if Embree was ready. Little made the slow walk out to the mound and talked with Varitek.

"OK, good," Epstein said, sounding relieved. "Here he comes."

Spike Lee was not a big fan of Grady Little.

"Go back to your cotton farm in Texas," he thought as Little stood out on the mound. "It seems to me like the Red Sox have a history with these southern ballplayers. It seemed like they always had these rednecks from the South."

Arroyo stood right next to Little and Varitek, staring off into space and wishing he could have that one pitch back, but he was already gone. Neither Little nor Varitek talked to him. Mark Carlson headed out to the mound to break it up, and that meant it was time for Arroyo to leave. Some fans started booing, apparently upset that they would not be seeing more of Arroyo.

"What are they booing for?" John Henry asked from the front row of his private box.

"The manager!" answered Debi Little from her seat near the Red Sox dugout.

She had just been asked the same question about the boos by a friend sitting next to her.

Cheers soon overwhelmed the booing. Arroyo trotted to the dugout with the Fenway sound system blasting "Stray Cat Strut" by the Stray Cats. Todd Walker bounced out of the dugout and onto the field to lead the fans in a round of applause. All around the ballpark, people stood to give the young pitcher a hand. John Burkett stepped out to shake Arroyo's hand (none of this fist-bumping stuff), and Walker slapped him on the back.

Henry liked Arroyo and was pleased at the fuss they were making.

"He's a great guy," he said.

For a young pitcher with only limited success over parts of

three seasons with the Pittsburgh Pirates, a young pitcher claimed off waivers that off-season by the Red Sox, Arroyo had held up well under the pressure of a big game against the Yankees. He had earned himself more chances down the line. Now he had to watch and hope the hard-throwing left-hander Embree could take care of business and keep Boone from scoring.

Karim Garcia walked back toward the Yankee dugout as soon as Grady Little came to the mound. Garcia's replacement turned out to be Ruben Sierra, the switch-hitting slugger. Torre liked the idea of pinch-hitting Sierra, who had come through with some big hits for him and was an experienced veteran. But there was a downside, too, given Sierra's defensive limitations. Torre would really be burning two players, since he would have to send Juan Rivera out to play right field. Torre turned to Don Zimmer, sitting next to him in the dugout, to get his opinion.

"What do you think of this?" Torre asked.

Zimmer had done his time at Fenway. He managed the Red Sox from the middle of the 1976 season until October 1, 1980. He had a winning record each of those seasons, but never finished better than second—even in 1978, the year the Sox won sixty-two of their first ninety games, but only thirty-seven the rest of the way. They fell one game short on October 2 when the ninth batter in the Yankee lineup, Bucky Dent, lofted that famous fly ball to left that somehow ended up carrying for a three-run homer. Torre relied on Don Zimmer to keep Fenway in perspective for him. He relied on the round-faced, goggle-eyed baseball lifer to tell him how tough it could be on managers. If Don Zimmer told you no lead was safe at Fenway, you listened, and you rolled the dice and sent out your pinch-hitter and hoped for more runs.

Sierra was an interesting case. He was thirty-seven years old and had lived about five lifetimes in baseball. Growing up in Puerto Rico, he was friends with Luis Clemente, middle son of the great Roberto Clemente. Sierra made his major-league debut for the Texas Rangers at age twenty, and in some corners was dubbed the next Clemente. Sierra could never live up to that. Who could? Clemente was not only an amazing baseball player (he hit .317 over eighteen seasons with the Pittsburgh Pirates and roamed right field and threw out baserunners as few outfielders ever have), Clemente was also a saint, or he was remembered as one, anyway. It was a tragedy for every Puerto Rican when the plane carrying Clemente and the load of food and clothes and medicine he had organized for victims of the Nicaragua earthquake went down in the Caribbean on New Year's Eve 1972.

Sierra was probably the best player in the American League in 1989, and he was only twenty-three. He was sleek and fast and played hard. It was a pleasure to watch him go into the right-field corner to scoop up a potential double and spin and throw to second to nail a runner who thought he could coast. Sierra hit .306 that year and led the league in runs batted in (with 119) and slugging percentage and extra-base hits. That was well before the Juiced Era (the balls, we're talking about the balls—*they* were juiced), and Sierra collected a respectable twenty-nine homers, seven shy of Fred McGriff's league-leading total. Sierra came in second that year in voting for the league's Most Valuable Player.

He was on pace for greatness. One week into his seventh season, he already had one thousand hits and he was all of twenty-six.

But Sierra let success go to his head, and turned himself into a cartoon character. He liked to make a spectacle of himself, but mostly with his clothes, mustard-yellow suits, complete with a matching mustard-yellow bowler hat, and yes, a plum-colored suit with a matching plum-colored bowler hat. It had to be seen to be believed. Sierra ballooned up to ridiculous proportions, and ballooned was the word: He looked overinflated, and could hardly throw the ball anymore. Soon he was kicking around from team to team, seven in seven years, and was so limited by injuries, he sat out all of 1999 and played only a handful of games from 1997 to 2000. Sierra spent part of 1996 with the Yankees, and Joe Torre remembered not liking what he saw. Sierra was the toughest challenge and worst listener of any player Torre had ever managed. Sierra did not like Torre, either. He made headlines by calling him a liar.

But the Ruben Sierra who had rejoined the Yankees earlier that summer was a man who had learned from his mistakes. He had grasped how foolish he had been to fritter away so much and fall so far short of what he could have been. This Sierra was modest and team-oriented. He sat back and watched, eyes wide open, even if it hurt to see young players who reminded him of what he had been when he was a young player and what he could have been. Sierra was also sleeker now than the old ballooned-up character. Torre was glad to have him back on the team.

"He was very hard to reach," Cashman said. "He's completely different now."

Embree completed his warmup tosses, and Sierra walked up to the edge of the batter's box. He kept kicking at the packed red clay with his right foot, looking like a cat in a litter box, and finally achieved whatever it was he was hoping to achieve and stepped out again. Embree was ready, but Sierra was not about to rush. He raised the bat with his flexed forearms and did a slow-motion pantomime of a swing, keeping his eye on Embree the whole time, sizing him up. Sierra stepped back in, made the sign of the cross and kissed his fingertips, and watched a low Embree fastball catch the outside corner for strike one.

Embree came back with another fastball, this one high, and Boone broke with the pitch, trying to steal third base to put himself in position to score on a sacrifice fly. Boone got a great jump. Like many hard throwers, Embree took a lot of time to get rid of a pitch, even working from the stretch, and Boone was off and running well before Embree released the high fastball. This was a pitch Sierra could drive. Instead, he hit a foul pop-up behind first base.

Third baseman Bill Mueller, seeing Boone break for third base, had already taken six steps in toward the bag to be ready to take a throw from Varitek. When Mueller saw Sierra pop up the ball, he got an idea. He made a show of keeping his eyes straight ahead and crouched down, glove to the dirt, pretending to field a ground ball. Even if Boone thought maybe Mueller was faking him out, he could not be sure. He had no choice but to slide.

Alertness and a certain craftiness had always come naturally to Mueller on the baseball field. He was the type of player who knew when to let a breaking ball graze his arm, and he was always going to think one step ahead on the base paths or at third base. It ended up not mattering this time. The pop-up landed in the stands. But if Kevin Millar had been able to catch it, there was at least a chance he could have thrown down to second base before Boone could get back up on his feet and run ninety feet back to the bag. That would have been a great way to erase the baserunner. Even if Boone had made it back safely, it would have been fun to watch him have to work so hard to avoid being doubled off.

Embree peered back in at Sierra, ahead 0-2, and gave him another high fastball. This was up out of the zone, but as the saying went, you did not walk off the island. Sierra went ahead and swung anyway and fouled this one off, too. Embree was throwing the ball ninety-four miles per hour, and at that speed, it was even harder to judge how high a pitch would be. As Bob Adair had calculated, it took a player 150 milliseconds to swing the bat, and at least that long to process enough information about the flight of the ball for his brain to make the decision whether or not to swing the bat. A fastball traveling at around that speed made it to home plate in 400 milliseconds, so Sierra had at most 100 milliseconds—that is, one-tenth of a second—to decide if he was going to swing. He stepped out to scold himself for swinging at a ball, and held his right hand out flat, pushing it down, his way of reminding himself to stay down and not let Embree dictate to him.

Boone had Embree's attention, and he was not about to stop playing with his head. He took a lead off second base, widened it a little, danced back toward the bag, then away again. Embree craned his neck back and stared at him, more annoyed by the moment. Finally he wheeled around and faked a throw to force Boone to go stand on the bag for a moment, not sure if Merloni would be breaking over to take a throw. Boone quickly took a decent lead again and stood there leaning over, hands on his thighs, waiting to annoy Embree some more. This was an art form, getting under the skin of a pitcher, and while Aaron Boone was not exactly in the category of a Rickey Henderson, say, he was getting somewhere with Embree. Once again, he went into his stretch and started his delivery and then wheeled off the mound and faked a throw to second. Boone was having fun now. He went over and touched the bag, playing along, and then took his lead again and stood there, hands on hips, a clear challenge.

Embree stared in and Varitek went through his hand signals, pointing fingers down to the plate, and reached up and patted his left forearm near the red sweatband. He did it again, this time patting twice, but Embree did not seem to understand the signal. Varitek called for time and headed out to the mound for a quick conference. He did all the talking and Embree stood listening, head bowed, nodding now and then. Back behind home plate, Varitek did not even give a sign. They had that worked out already. Embree ignored Boone this time, and Boone ignored him, too, as if he knew his game had run its course. Embree came in with another fastball, this one low, and Sierra reached down and lifted it to center for a routine fly ball, not even deep enough to advance Boone to third.

Up came Enrique Wilson. He had started that day because he had Pedro Martinez's number, and always seemed to get a hit off him. Martinez was long gone, but a veteran like Wilson was always more dangerous when he already had two hits for the day. Embree started him off with a fastball way outside, and then made his best

pitch so far, a ninety-five-mile-an-hour fastball on the outside corner. Wilson knew it was a good pitch, and stepped out to collect
himself. Embree was still ignoring Boone, but continued to take
his time between pitches. Finally he came in with another fastball
away and this one was also low, but it caught the outside corner.
Wilson twisted around quickly to ask Mark Carlson about the
pitch, and took a step toward him to try to seem more friendly and
less confrontational.

"This place had better get up now," Rich Maloney demanded
out in the Green Monster.

Wilson fouled off Embree's next pitch, a fastball that was a
notch less fast than the others, and Varitek flipped off his mask,
ready to run it down if it stayed fair, and quickly saw it would not.
Mark Carlson handed him a fresh ball and he threw it out to Embree. Sure enough, the crowd that had been so oddly subdued
through much of the game was into it now. They chanted "Let's go
Red Sox," in that sing-song way of fans, and cheered for Embree to
strike out Wilson.

There was no great mystery to what was coming next. Embree
was throwing nothing but fastballs, and he was working Wilson
away. Embree glanced at Boone, just for kicks, rubbed his face
against the shoulder of his uniform, and then came back with another fastball away. Jason Varitek wanted it high, and actually
stood up even before Embree went into his motion and released
the ball, the way he sometimes did. But Embree's pitch was not
high. It came in at thigh level, just where Wilson was looking for
it, and he took a quick, compact swing and poked it down the

first-base line. Kevin Millar made a flying leap toward the line, extending his body parallel to the ground, but could not get over in time. It was a base hit, and the Yankee lead was up to two runs. Trot Nixon backhanded the ball a foot shy of the foul line and threw in to second in a hurry to hold Wilson to a single. Embree had jogged toward home plate, ready to back up, and walked back to the mound shaking his head slowly.

Out in the Green Monster, Rich Maloney slumped forward, unable to speak. Garrett Tingle punched the Wall, hard enough to break something, and then got up and lifted a yellow "1" into place to record the Yankee run.

"We can't get that guy," Theo Epstein said. "He's killing us."

The game was turning, and so was Epstein's mood. He admitted he did not like Varitek's habit of standing up behind home plate when he wanted a high fastball.

"How is the ump gonna call a strike when Varitek stands up?" he asked.

Embree had been unable to get the better of the ninth hitter, Wilson. Now he had to face Derek Jeter. He went into his stretch and stared over at Wilson at first base, even though he was taking a small lead. Embree threw over there once, mostly to give himself time to regain his concentration. His first pitch to Jeter was a low fastball, fouled into the stands down the first-base line.

Spike Lee turned to his son, Jackson, to make sure he was checking out Jeter's at-bat. Lee loved watching Jeter. His favorite Jeter moment was everybody's favorite Jeter moment, that time out in Oakland during the 2001 playoffs when Jeter came all the way over from shortstop to grab that ball in foul territory and flip to home in time to get lumbering Jeremy Giambi, who did not have the sense to slide. That was no coincidence that Jeter happened to be there. He knew what was going to happen, and because he did, the Yankees won that game and came back to win that playoff series.

All great athletes, no matter what their sport, were visionaries. Spike Lee figured that anybody who achieved greatness had to have vision, but that could mean different things. In sports the visionaries were the people who saw stuff before it happened. Willie Mays, Ali, DiMaggio, Magic, Jackie—they all had that ability. You could work at it, but basically that was God given, like being an artist. Ali was a Michelangelo. Michael Jordan was an Ellington or a Van Gogh. Lee was sorry if people did not want to hear that kind of talk, but he had to tell it like he saw it. To him, Willie and Jackie were just as much artists as Hemingway and Baldwin. No one could convince him that because they played a sport, that demeaned what they did. Jeter was not quite in the neighborhood of Mays, Ali, DiMaggio, and Jackie; not many were. But Jeter was already great.

Torre was still going back and forth with Zimmer in the Yankee dugout, looking ahead to the possibility of bringing Rivera in for the eighth inning.

Embree made another meaningless toss over to first base, and then missed just outside with a good fastball, and, inanely, threw over to first base again. So far Embree had thrown nothing but fastballs, but next he tried something different. He came in with an eighty-four-mile-an-hour slider out over the edge of the plate and Jeter let fly with an all-out swing, driving the ball to right. It sailed over Trot Nixon's head and bounced once, just in front of the wall, and then caromed up and off of the hands of a Red Sox fan in the front row.

"Jeter will only get a double," Theo Epstein said quickly before anyone else sorted out what had happened. "That's a break right there. The runner will have to be held at third."

First-base umpire Paul Nauert had run down the line for a better view and raised both his fists in the air over his head, the signal for fan interference. Joe Torre hustled out of the Yankee dugout and met up with Nauert near first base for an extended discussion. If the umpires ruled the ball bounced into the stands, that was an automatic ground-rule double. Wilson would only advance two bases from first and would not score. But a fan interference call was more complicated. The umpires had the job of ruling on whether Wilson would have scored if there had not been fan interference. Torre thought he would have.

"Did the ball bounce off the fence?" Torre asked. "I saw it go down."

"No," Nauert said. "The fan knocked the ball straight down."

They talked some more.

"If they reverse it, it's a bad call because that ball hit the ground, hit the fence, and came up quickly and hit the guy in the chest," Theo Epstein said. "It's a double. Or it should be."

Larry Lucchino had just arrived in John Henry's private box in time to see Jeter's drive to right.

"Torre's got no beef," he said. "The view from the dugout is one of the worst. It's four hundred feet away and he thinks he can see it?"

Bob Adair was thinking of how technology could help the umpires.

"We should have instant replay, like in football," he said, half-joking.

Out in the Green Monster, Rich Maloney was screaming mad.

"That ball was going in the stands," he shouted, voice hoarse again. "Ground-rule double. That's the rule."

He was just sure that the umpires would cave and give the Yankees their way. If that happened, the Red Sox manager had better go ballistic.

"Grady better get kicked out," Maloney said darkly.

Torre was a long way from giving up.

"You had a better look at it than I did," he acknowledged to Nauert.

But he went on to make the case that he thought Wilson would have scored if there had been no fan interference.

"Wilson was just about getting to third base when the ball was touched," Nauert said.

"OK, fine, but they still have to pick the ball up and throw it four hundred feet while he runs a hundred feet," Torre said.

Over near the Yankee dugout, Spike Lee was enjoying the chance to watch Torre operate. He could see that Torre had a washed-out look to him that day, and the strain of the job was getting to him. But the beauty of Joe Torre was that he was going to go out and handle himself just the same, no matter what else was going on. For Lee, Torre's leadership was a huge factor in all those recent World Series championships.

"He's a great manager," Lee said. "He has a whole lot of personality and he's able to keep everybody on the same page. He's a winner."

Torre thought he had a good argument with the umpires, and continued to press his case. He preferred to think of it as a discussion, not an argument. He wanted to get the rest of the crew involved. Soon he was standing near home plate talking with all four umpires, but especially Mark Carlson and Ed Rapuano.

"The runner would not have scored if the fan interference had not occurred," Carlson told him.

The longer the argument went on, the more the Red Sox players worried about how it would turn out. Veteran pitcher John Burkett stood on the first step of the Boston dugout to yell out at the umpires in his Texas accent.

"What are you doing, trying to change history?" he shouted.

All the fans had stood up in the sections near the Red Sox dugout, trying to figure out what was happening. That went for Peter Farrelly, too.

"Daddy, when are you going to sit down?" Bob asked him.

The umpires actually liked these sessions. To fans at the game, or watching on TV, it looked contentious. True, Torre was shaking his head and looking a little red-faced when he finally headed back to the dugout. But it was understood among umpires that Torre was the kind of manager who always wanted to understand just how the crew had arrived at their decision. And in a way that was a sign of respect.

Torre had learned from past mistakes. Early in his managing career, he was less sure of himself and let the pressure get to him. It wasn't until his sixth season as a manager that he had a winning season. That was with the Atlanta Braves, where he moved after five seasons as New York Mets manager. Back in those first years managing, Torre sometimes did things because he felt he was supposed to do them, like arguing with umpires, for example. Those days were gone. He knew that a lot of times, if you argued balls and strikes with an umpire, or even if you had your players do that, you were giving players an excuse for making an out. That idea did not sit well with Torre. Somewhere a long ways back he had decided to do his best not to worry about the things that happened on a baseball field that were out of his control.

Torre kept two things in mind talking to umpires. He liked to hear an umpire explain his thinking, and he liked to make sure they were in the right position at the right time to pay close attention and make a call. Umpires were human, and if they missed a call now and then, that was OK with Torre, so long as they were prepared. That was what Torre would preach to them when he went out for a discussion, or most of the time, anyway. Now and then, if he objected to a call on a bang-bang play at a key time in the game, he might get emotional and scream at someone. But that was the exception. Most of the time, Torre went back to the dugout feeling good about having his say.

"That was a waste of five minutes," Rich Maloney grumbled out in the Green Monster.

Torre also knew that it never hurt to let a struggling pitcher stand out there on the mound and think about getting knocked around. It was like the old college-basketball move of calling a time out near the end of a game before letting a kid shoot his free throws. Give him more time, and let his stomach churn. Now Alan Embree had to go after Nick Johnson. Not only was Johnson a good fastball hitter, he already had three hits, and each of those hits had been important in the game. Johnson was hot. Embree started him off with a fastball that missed low, and took his time out on the mound before his next offering.

"We need Alan to get this . . ." John Henry began, trailing off when Embree came in with a belt-high fastball right down the middle.

It was hard to imagine Nick Johnson failing to pounce on a pitch like that, given the kind of day he was having. Sure enough, he smacked a hard line drive to center for a single. Wilson and Jeter both scored. So much for the Red Sox being helped by the fan interference call.

"Oh, Jesus," John Henry said. "Oh, Jesus."

"Oh my, oh my," Larry Lucchino said. "Nick Johnson killed us today."

The crowd booed heartily.

"He's the toughest out," Theo Epstein said. "Now they're crushing Embree."

"It's the old reverse luck," John Henry said. "Pedro goes, and they get eight runs."

Jeter and Wilson high-fived at home plate and scampered back to the Yankee dugout. Nick Johnson stood on first base, mouthpiece wedged sideways in his front teeth, and calmly peeled off his batting gloves, doing his best to make it look as if, to him, four-hit games were no big deal. Jason Giambi stepped in next, blinking, and squinted hard out at Embree as if that eye infection that had been plaguing him that summer was still making itself felt.

Lucchino and Henry were discussing Grady Little's managing decisions.

"Did you think about Jeter batting against a lefty as opposed to someone else?" Lucchino asked.

Henry looked down at the stat sheet in front of him and scanned for the right information.

"Jeter's hitting .308 against righties, .358 against lefties," he said, letting the facts sit out there in the still air of the suite.

Embree picked up one strike with a big, sweeping curve, only the third breaking ball he had thrown. He went back to his fastball, putting one letter-high, and Giambi fouled it off. Both did some stalling after that. Giambi stepped out, lifting his arms above his head like someone stretching in the morning, and adjusted the pad above his right elbow. Embree tossed over to first base just to give himself something to do other than pitching, and finally came in with his 0-2 pitch, a high fastball that hit ninety-four miles an hour. Giambi could not catch up to it. The Yankee inning was finally over.

Marty Martin and his brother Dean decided it was time to get going. They had been watching the game out in front of Gate B, where Fenway security had taken them after kicking Martin out for throwing Jorge Posada's home-run ball back on the field. Martin had taken it all in stride. He was actually having fun. Never in his life had so many people come up to him. They all seemed to think of him as some kind of hero. Martin just smiled and talked to them all. But he had finally had enough. He and his brother went to look for the bus that would take them back to Bristol. It would feel good to lean back and take a load off.

BOTTOM OF THE EIGHTH

	1	2	3	4	5	6	7	8	9	R
NYY	0	0	2	3	0	0	0	*3*		8
BOSTON	3	0	1	0	0	0	0			4

It was time for the Rally Karaoke Guy Video. (Or maybe it was not time, but they were going to roll it anyway.) The big screen out beyond the outfield filled with a blue background and big white letters asked, "What did Kevin Millar do for fun as a teen?" A tinny soundtrack kicked in with the opening strains of "Born in the USA." The blue background stayed, but new letters popped up: "We found out. And now, so will you. Are you ready?" The scene cut to grainy images showing a rear view of a young man standing in what looked like some kind of strip mall office or garage, bending his left knee forward more or less in time to the music, and shaking his butt and pumping his right fist straight up in the air, also more or less in time to the beat. What Millar's left hand was doing, in front of him, was not altogether clear.

The vocals kicked in and as Bruce Springsteen's familiar straining voice sang about being born down in a dead man's town, the figure on the screen spun around and made a playful attempt to lip-sync along with the Boss. What a surprise: There was a time when Kevin Millar did not have a gut. Was that some actual definition showing through that tight white T-shirt? Ooh, and what was he *thinking* with that poofy, frosted hair? The young Millar on the screen grinned awkwardly, like a teenager who had never had his picture taken, and kept pumping his right fist in the air in some sort of rhythm. He moved his lips less and less in time as Springsteen sang about ending up like a dog that's been beaten too much.

The shit-eating grin and the cute-boy, look-at-me raised eyebrows could not have been more incongruous a match with the music, but the point was, Millar was having a great time. The chorus kicked in, and Millar did not have to work so hard to remember the words, or pretend to remember them. He bobbed his head all over the place repeating "Born in the USA," pointing like a Vegas lounge act, and ducked his head down so he could concentrate on shaking his hips, Elvis-style. The music kept playing, and the scene cut to footage obviously shot a short time later.

Now Millar was wearing some sort of white golf hat and a blank-to-the-world expression suggesting many hours of studious attention to his beer bong. His hip-grinding looked more like an audition for a porno movie, but fortunately, he redeemed the sequence with a don't-ask-me-my-name-I'm-not-sure-I-can-remember open-mouthed stare, and danced an odd little jig at the end. Presumably, as soon as the song ended and the camera stopped recording, he ran down the hall and hurled.

Putting the Millar video up onto the big screen at Fenway in a bid to trigger a Red Sox rally had become a sort of tradition in Boston. It was, of course, a fake tradition, artificially implanted, like the so-called Rally Monkey that Anaheim fans cheered the year the Angels won the World Series. As insipid as the Rally Monkey video was, the fans never failed to make a fuss over the images of a monkey jumping up and down. That sort of thing might have seemed more likely to go over in good-time Southern California, but Boston fans, too, had taken a gleeful pleasure in the stupid fun of looking to an old, cheesy-beyond-words video for inspiration. Now it was playing up on the big screen, even though the Red Sox were down four runs and did not even have a baserunner yet.

"Jeez, wait till we start a rally or something," Theo Epstein said over in his private box. "It's stupid to do it now."

He glanced up at the big screen, where the youthful Millar was jerking his hips like an aerobics instructor, and looked down at the mound, where Yankee reliever Jeff Nelson was making a show of warming up.

"I reserve the right to take that back if we mount a miraculous rally," Epstein added.

John Henry was not exactly thrilled to see the video, either. He glanced up at the screen quickly and slumped back in his chair, like a small child who did not even want to hope.

"Oh, man," he began, "I'd be very . . ."

He did not finish the thought.

Out on the mound, Jeff Nelson was calling attention to himself, as he always did. He looked weird out there. Nelson did his best to knee himself in the chest every time he threw the ball. It was a funky, herky-jerky delivery a step beyond syncopation, and it brought to mind someone wrestling to push a sack of potatoes over a low fence.

Up on the screen, Millar had reached his glaze-eyed conclusion, but the crowd remained unconvinced it was time to get excited.

"The fans don't seem to be responding," John Henry told Lucchino.

Henry decided that they could have had more fun with the video. Instead of giving the setup at the beginning, they should have just started playing it, and let people try to guess what it was.

"I think it would be so cool if they didn't know what it was," the owner said.

Jeff Nelson had finished warming up and stood off the rubber to reach down and adjust his cup, then tugged at his cap, and leaned over to pick up the resin bag and let it drop immediately, as if he had been startled to discover it was piping hot. Nomar Garciaparra stepped into the batter's box and started wagging the bat again and again, the way he did every time up, holding it so it poked straight up, and twisting his body and sliding his wrists through the hitting zone at half-speed every second or so, again and again and again, and dragging one foot and then the other back through the dirt, again and again and again.

It was a mesmerizing performance, and Nelson looked entranced. He was staring in for the sign from Posada, but just kept staring, obviously confused. Finally he stepped off the rubber and took a few steps toward the plate. Posada ran out for a quick conference, steering Nelson back toward the mound to go over the signs. This was pathetic. Nelson had not thrown a pitch yet, but he was sending a message of not being ready. He might still make great pitches—you never knew—but he was already looking shaky, like an attorney who tripped and dumped the entire contents of his briefcase on the floor in front of a jury just before his closing argument.

"Four runs is a lot in the eighth inning, but you know the team isn't out of it," John Henry told Lucchino.

Over in the Yankee dugout, Joe Torre arched his back and leaned against the rear wall of the dugout, looking like a man ready to start hitting the Tums hard. Nelson finally made a pitch, and it was an inside breaking ball for a strike. Garciaparra left his right foot where it was and stepped out of the batter's box with his left foot so he could readjust his batting gloves seventeen times, or whatever it was, and then step in again. Nelson's next breaking ball was away and Garciaparra fouled it back. Now Torre had his left hand up to his face, thumb to one side, index finger just to the other side of his nose, as if he was trying to hold in the bad thoughts. His eyes went from Nelson to Garciaparra, Nelson to Garciaparra, back and forth and back and forth. Nelson missed outside with another breaking ball, forcing Posada to lunge just to catch the ball and giving Garciaparra a chance to step out and readjust his batting gloves seventeen more times. The next pitch was another slider, and this one was down in the zone but right over the plate. Garciaparra nailed it, hitting the ball right on the sweet spot and sending a huge, towering fly to left field.

"See ya!" Rich Maloney called out happily in the Green Monster. All those years of watching games from out there gave him an impeccable sense of when a ball was gone. This ball was gone.

Hideki Matsui thought so, too. He drifted back and then stopped on the edge of the warning track, staring up and all but raising his hands at his sides to show how perplexed he was. He expected the ball to land up in the new Green Monster seats for a home run. Hard to be sure, though. He had practiced fielding balls off the Monster and he felt comfortable with most of them. High fly balls were the exception. They were very difficult to handle. To him, staring up, it looked as if someone had dropped the ball from the sky. It was a big struggle to guess where the ball might land. But this time, Matsui was fortunate and the ball caromed high off the wall, hitting eight feet below the top, and came almost straight down.

"Damn! I thought that was out!" Lucchino said to John Henry.

Matsui watched it bounce once on the warning track and kick up high in the air again, and waited for it to come back down. He had to twist awkwardly but he used both hands to collect it and toss back to the infield.

"How did that ball not get out?" Rich Maloney asked, voice cracking, he was so surprised to hear the loud *"ping"* of the ball striking high on the Wall.

Peter Farrelly was not worried.

"I've got a very good feeling about this game!" he shouted over the roar of the crowd.

The Red Sox needed four runs to tie, and if Garciaparra trotted around the bases or scored later, it was all the same. Either way, a lot more was going to have to happen for the Red Sox if they had any chance at making it close. Mariano Rivera had just stood up in the Yankee bullpen and was limbering up, ready to throw his first warmup tosses. It was not going to be easy.

"The designated hitter, Number 34, David Ortiz!" Fenway PA announcer Carl Beane called out, and now the crowd was buzzing with excitement. They may have been rooting for something to root for, as much as anything, but they were rooting hard.

Brian Cashman found himself having a disagreeable flashback. One month earlier, the Yankees were at Fenway trying to pull out a win in a game in which they had trailed four-zip and then rallied to tie. David Ortiz came up in the ninth as a pinch-hitter that day against reliever Armando Benitez and ripped a drive off the Green Monster to score Jeremy Giambi from second and win the game.

Nelson's first pitch to Ortiz was a big, sweeping breaking ball that missed way inside. He came back with a low breaking ball that started outside and broke late, back toward the plate, catching the outside corner, the way Mark Carlson saw it.

"That's a horseshit call!" Theo Epstein said sharply, more animated now that the game was on the line.

Ortiz stepped out of the box, tapped at his feet with his bat, and then watched Nelson miss way outside with another curve. But when he came back with another breaking ball near the outside corner, Ortiz swung and missed. He had no choice but to swing. If Mark Carlson had called the earlier close pitch a strike, he might call this one, too. Nelson tried to hit the outside corner with another breaking ball, but this one missed way outside. Now with a full count, the crowd was loud and insistent. Kevin Millar, standing in the on-deck circle, looked down and kicked at the ground expectantly. Ortiz stepped out, almost smiling he was enjoying the pressure so much.

Nelson took his time and finally came in with another breaking ball out over the outside corner. Ortiz fouled it off and stepped out quickly, mad at himself. He grabbed the bat out of the air with his left hand, angry that he had not driven the ball over the Green Monster.

Joe Torre paced back and forth in the Yankee dugout, tipping back a bottle of spring water to drain the last of it. Grady Little stood near the front of the Red Sox dugout, arms folded over his chest.

Brian Cashman, sitting behind home plate, was staring out at Nelson thinking: Throw a strike. Don't walk him. It's a four-run game, so challenge him. Don't put people on base, especially in this ballpark with that short left field and that short corner down in right, the Pesky Pole.

Nelson looked in for the sign, and shook off Posada. He wanted to throw a fastball, and tried to catch the corner, but missed inside for ball four. Ortiz flipped his bat over to the batboy and hurried down the line to first.

"All right, and we have a mean customer on deck, too," John Henry said to Lucchino.

Theo Epstein was not as happy to see Kevin Millar coming up now.

"This is not a good matchup for us," he said. "Nelson can drop down and throw that Frisbee slider. Kevin is more of a fastball hitter."

Epstein thought that over, worried he sounded too negative.

"If he hangs one, we'll be in good shape," he added.

Nelson, red-faced now, pulled off his Yankee cap and wiped his head and face, trying to calm down. Mel Stottlemyre ran out to the mound for a quick talk. Out in the Yankee bullpen, Rivera paused between warmup tosses to peer in toward the infield. It was not time for him yet.

"Yankees suck! Yankees suck!" fans chanted in the stands behind home plate.

Nelson glared at Garciaparra at second and turned and missed low and outside to Millar with a fastball. Relieved cheers surged through the crowd like a waterfall.

"Boy, it would be great to force Torre to bring in Mariano this early," John Henry said.

He was looking around the ballpark, taking in the details. He spotted Jason Varitek in the on-deck circle, getting himself ready, and then noticed a small bird that had hopped over and was standing in the on-deck circle with him.

"See the bird?" he asked, smiling shyly.

Nelson's next pitch was a cut fastball out over the plate, and Millar tried to pull it to left and instead hit a slow bouncer. Derek Jeter hurried to his right to grab it and make a quick toss down to second to force out big David Ortiz. There was no chance at a double play. The only suspense was watching Ortiz rumble into second; watching him slide was never dull. That put runners on first and third for Jason Varitek, who did not have any hits that day.

All pitchers knew their numbers against hitters, especially hitters who struggled against them, and Nelson knew that Varitek was hitless against him in their six previous meetings. That gave Nelson extra confidence, and he went right after Varitek. His first pitch was a fastball toward the outside part of the plate. Varitek seemed surprised. He did not swing, and stepped out and looked out at Nelson with a confused look. Nelson missed low and then came back with a good, low breaking ball that Varitek foul-tipped to make the count 1-2.

By this time Senator Mitchell had arrived at Logan Airport, and he and his friends were driving around in circles. It was frustrating. The signal cut out just as Nelson was making his third pitch to Varitek, and they had to wait for a few precious seconds before it came back. Once it did, they still needed a few tense seconds to piece together what had happened.

Garciaparra did not like the way this was looking. He stood down near third base, hands on hips, and sized up Nelson. It looked like he had Varitek right where he wanted him. He had set him up with that tough breaking ball he foul-tipped into the dirt, and now Nelson came back with a fastball. Only one problem: It was two feet inside, and hit Varitek right in the ass. The bases were loaded.

"That's the way to go," Bob Adair called out cheerfully. "Everybody get hit! Everybody get hit!"

"That's a break," Theo Epstein said. "Varitek has not been swinging well today. You bring the tying run to the plate. That's all you can ask for."

The managing was kicking into high gear on both sides. Gabe Kapler was due up next, but he was called back to the dugout. Todd Walker came out and started swinging a bat in the on-deck circle, getting ready to pinch-hit.

"What's he doing?" Rich Maloney asked out in the Green Monster. "Nelson is out of gas. Why give Torre an excuse to yank him?"

Torre had both Rivera and left-hander Gabe White ready to go in the bullpen. Once Walker was announced as the pinch-hitter, Torre walked out to the mound and signaled to the bullpen with his left arm, indicating he wanted Gabe White.

"He's letting Torre make all the decisions for him!" Rich Maloney groused, now in full rant mode.

John Henry did not like the way this was shaping up.

"Does he have a right-hander he's going to pinch-hit for Walker?" he asked Lucchino. "I'd have pinch-hit Mirabelli."

Back in the dugout after making the change, Torre was feeling uneasy. He was not going to look over at the Red Sox dugout. That was just not something he would do, as much as he might have wanted to. Ever since Kirk Gibson limped up to home plate in the 1988 World Series, nobody could ever convince Torre that someone was unavailable in a game. You never knew. He sat there expecting any minute to hear one of his players tell him, "Manny is coming out to hit." He waited, and he waited, and when he did not hear anything, and Todd Walker stepped into the batter's box and got ready for the first pitch from Gabe White, Torre felt a little better.

John Henry could not sit still for this. He stood up and sighed loudly, almost dramatically.

"I don't understand," he said.

He threw his hands up in the air, horrified.

"You never want to have a lefty-lefty matchup," he added, sighing again and starting to pace.

Grady Little and Jerry Narron, his bench coach, liked sending Walker out there against White.

"He had only hit a couple of times against him in his life but one time he had hit a home run," Little said.

Narron had walked over to David McCarty, a journeyman the Red Sox had claimed off waivers earlier that month when the A's designated him for assignment to clear a roster spot for Jose Guillen.

"Hey, are you ready to pinch-hit?" Narron asked him.

McCarty said he had done all his stretching and the rest of his routine a few innings earlier and could not have been readier.

Little came over to talk to him next.

"How do you feel about facing Mariano?" he asked.

"I've faced him before," he told his manager. "You just have to be ready for that good cutter away."

"Well, you're going to be going up and hitting," Little told him.

White checked the runners and caught the outside corner with a fastball. It wasn't much, not even hitting ninety miles an hour on the gun, but it was well placed and Walker did not swing.

"White and Walker were either traded for each other or they were with each other," Theo Epstein said. "I think they were team-mates. They should know each other pretty well."

In fact, the Yankees had picked up White in a trade with the Reds less than a month earlier. Todd Walker had been with the Reds the year before, too.

White, having worked the outside corner, now came in with a changeup. It was toward the inside of the plate, but belt-high. Walker swung and sent a foul pop-up into the stands.

"Aw, that was a good pitch to hit!" Theo Epstein said.

White did not throw hard, but he got rid of the ball in a hurry, and his pitches could be hard to pick up. He tried another changeup and put it way outside and almost in the dirt.

David McCarty stepped into the on-deck circle. Originally drafted by Minnesota, which picked him third overall in 1991, he had kicked around and played for seven teams in his nine years in the big leagues. This was McCarty's first Red Sox–Yankee series, and he had not been disappointed. It was always more fun to get into a game in a tense situation like that when every-body was paying close attention and everything was on the line. He swung once in the on-deck circle, then slid the doughnut off the bat and glanced over at White, getting ready to deal to Walker.

White came in with a high fastball, up out of the strike zone. It was all of eighty-eight miles an hour and Walker got under it, sending a little pop-up that Derek Jeter gloved on the infield grass.

"Dad, we can't score!" a young fan sitting near Bob and Eleanor Adair said in a loud whine.

"Arghgh!" Theo Epstein said. "They'll probably bring in Rivera now to face McCarty. McCarty doesn't have a hit against a right-handed pitcher this year."

"He's due!" one of Epstein's assistants said, earning a laugh from the boss.

Joe Torre stood up in the Yankee dugout and walked over to the steps and paused, holding his left hand up against the dugout ceiling. He was holding on until McCarty was officially announced as the pinch-hitter. Once he was, the die was cast. Grady Little could not pull him back. Manny Ramirez could not somehow materialize.

"Attention, please, ladies and gentlemen . . ." Carl Beane said over the loudspeakers and Torre stepped out onto the field and walked to the mound.

". . . pinch-hitting for Nixon, Number 10, David McCarty."

Torre gestured with his right hand and summoned Mariano Rivera, who threw two more pitches out in the bullpen, and then started the walk in from the outfield.

"We get to see them all," Eleanor Adair said, laughing.

Brian Cashman was shaking his head. He couldn't believe it. All year long he had been working to get this damn bullpen together so it would do its job and Rivera could take care of the ninth inning, and never have to come out in the eighth, but they were obviously still not there.

"So the two most crucial at-bats, we have their matchups, not ours," John Henry said.

This was the most frustrated he had been all day.

"It's tough to be short-handed in a game like this," Theo

Epstein said, letting himself wish for Manny Ramirez's bat in there against Rivera.

Grady Little did not let himself think about how much better it would have been to have Ramirez up there. His job was to go through all the possibilities and consider every possible matchup. He knew what Torre was going to do, so he had to line his hitters up as best as he could to be ready. Sometimes you did all the right thinking and it didn't work out. Little had known that this inning was going to come down to David McCarty against Mariano Rivera. Generally speaking, he liked having a right-handed batter out there against Rivera. The numbers told you that was a good thing.

The Patterson twins had been enjoying the game, and enjoying listening to Epstein's thoughts. Now they were so intent on what would happen next, they were leaning as far forward as they could, practically falling out of the box. They were both wearing Red Sox caps and shirts, but one was in a red shirt and red hat and the other was in a blue shirt and a blue hat with a red bill.

"They're the same age as I was in 1986," Epstein said, watching them. "They remind me of myself."

Rivera reared back and left his first pitch to McCarty up high for ball one. It was a cut fastball that registered at ninety-three miles per hour. Rivera shook off Posada and came back with another cutter, and this one caught the outside corner, though not everyone thought so. There was grumbling in the stands, and a few boos rang out.

"We just need a *hit* here, and Grady'll look great," John Henry said. "Then we have Merloni."

"Come on, McCarty!" Garrett Tingle said out in the Green Monster. "Become a friggin' legend."

Rivera's next cutter hit ninety-four miles an hour, but was just outside. Rivera's cutter was so explosive, it didn't matter if a hitter knew it was coming, and he came back with another one and put it just where he wanted, low and on the outside corner. McCarty had to work just to get a piece of it to stay alive. He stepped out afterward, reached a hand down to readjust himself, and winced. He took a couple of choppy practice swings and they did not look like much. Rivera came back with his best cutter so far, ninety-five miles an hour and out on the outside corner. McCarty took a good defensive cut and slashed it foul. The ball shot past Lou Merloni, standing in the on-deck circle, and slammed into the wall, just missing two kids sitting near the Red Sox dugout.

"Thank God that hit the wall," John Henry said. "Jesus."

McCarty was hoping Rivera would leave one of the cutters up and on the plate a little, but he was doing a good job of keeping the ball down and out on the corner. All you could do with pitches like that was shoot the ball to right or right-center. Rivera tried another cut fastball off the outside corner, and again McCarty was able to protect the plate and lift a foul off to the right side. This was turning into a good at-bat for him. Rivera had worked him away, away, away, and now came inside with a cutter, and left it higher than Posada wanted. McCarty was not thinking about driving the ball. He was just hoping to get the barrel of the bat on the ball. He did, and sent a line drive slamming off the Green Monster.

"McCarty!" Theo Epstein exclaimed in amazement, always quicker to react than anyone else.

"Wall! Wall!" Rich Maloney was screaming out in the Green Monster.

McCarty took off running as soon as he made contact. He knew that at Fenway, you had better run hard the whole way when you hit a ball off the Wall, otherwise you might not get to second base.

Hideki Matsui raced back and to his right, and made a clean pickup, wheeled around, and threw a strike to cutoff man Derek Jeter, but McCarty was in with plenty of time. Garciaparra and Millar scored, cutting the Yankee lead to two runs. Varitek moved to third.

John Henry, as promised, gave credit to his manager.

"Oh, baby!" he said. "One! Two! He's a genius!"

McCarty had a moment to enjoy the feeling of getting to Rivera. He called time out and reached down to pull off his shin guard, and then stood on the bag and stared out at the big screen in the outfield showing a replay of Rivera going into the stretch, McCarty holding the bat high, and then lacing the double off the Wall.

Damian Jackson came out to pinch-run, and McCarty loped back to the Red Sox dugout to high-five with everyone in sight. David Ortiz was the last to congratulate him, and shouted his encouragement and then raised his arm to get some extra speed when he swung and whacked him on the butt.

The Fenway crowd had gone wild with cheers, but now they were making a sound like booing: Lou Merloni was up.

Rivera stood out near the mound, holding the ball in his fingertips thoughtfully. He looked as calm and collected as ever, but his first pitch to Merloni missed low for a ball, and missed by enough to make it clear that was not where he wanted it to go. He attacked the outside corner again with a cut fastball, and it was 1-1.

Merloni thought to himself, "You know what this guy has. He's going to throw a cutter."

He tried visualizing something positive.

"OK, this is it," Merloni told himself. "It's your first game back. You have the tying run on second. He's going to hang you a cutter and you're going to hit a double off the wall to drive in two runs."

Merloni told himself that if he saw a cutter that started down the middle of the plate, it would move toward the outside corner, so he should lay off. But if the ball started in and ended up over the middle of the plate, he could pull it. Rivera made his next pitch, and it was a cut fastball away. Merloni held off, thinking it was a ball. Mark Carlson did not see it that way, and held up his right hand for the strike signal.

"No!" Theo Epstein shouted in his private box, his face contorting with anguish. "God, that's brutal. No way!"

John Henry was still pacing.

"Oh, that did not look like a strike," he said.

Rivera got the ball back and stood staring at the ground, collecting himself, before he came back with another cutter. This time Merloni swung and fouled it back to the screen.

"You would think that Manny would have gotten out of bed no matter how sick he was," John Henry said.

Now the place was really getting noisy. Merloni heard the fans looing, but most of the crowd noise he tuned out. He was busy focusing on the ball. The arm angle. The slot.

Rivera's next cutter slipped away from him a little and was far enough outside, Merloni knew it would miss. He was able to check his swing and hold off. That made it two balls and two strikes, and it was an important moment for Merloni. He knew that if he was going to chase a bad pitch, that was the one. He had shown himself he could hold off on the cutter away, and that helped him pick up a little more confidence. Rivera's next cutter missed outside, too.

"Come on," John Henry said, pleading now. "He needs a hit here to get his average to .200. We just need a little dinky single. A dinky winky single. A little Texas blooper."

The count was full and the crowd pretty much had to stand up, which they did and let loose with another hearty round of looing as Rivera looked in for the sign and prepared himself for the next pitch. It was a good cutter, out over the plate again, but also low and getting lower fast as it approached the plate. Merloni swung and fouled it off to the right and then hopped on his back foot, glad to have been able to get to the ball.

Joe Torre was staring at his feet. Rivera came back with a high cutter and left it up out of the zone. The bases were loaded.

"Oh, yeah!" John Henry said.

Merloni flipped the bat away and ran down to first base. Rivera took the throw back from Posada and spun quickly around, his back to home plate, and took a few of his graceful strides away from the rubber, needing to do something to distance himself from what had just happened.

Joe Torre was swallowing hard, almost as if he was on the verge of tossing his cookies.

Grady Little always looked worried, but in this situation he had an odd calm about him. The truth was, this was his favorite part of the job. It was so challenging. Sometimes you got rewarded for all the moves you made and sometimes you didn't, it was as simple as that. Either way, you got over it and went on and got ready to manage the next game.

Johnny Damon stepped up to bat and the cheering of the crowd had a giddy, gleeful sound to it, oddly high-pitched for a Red Sox–Yankees game. They were standing all the time now and had declared this a party.

"Look at this," John Henry said. "Everyone's on their feet."

Rivera's first pitch to Damon missed high, and now there was no mistaking it: He was wobbly. The great Mariano Rivera was wobbly.

Rivera had been on the disabled list three times the year before and missed a month that season because of a groin injury in spring training. He had gone through a stretch from late July to early August where he converted only two of the six opportunities he had for a save. That was unheard-of for Rivera, but Bob Adair said even so, it was important not to forget how inevitable ups and downs were to the game.

"Chance plays an awful role in these things," Adair said. "A guy is lucky for a while, and then he's not so lucky. You do a statistical analysis and you find out that chance is a big factor."

Rivera took his time, and came back with a good cutter that looked like it was going to catch the inside corner. Damon cocked his arms and started his swing, but at the last possible second, he decided no, and checked his swing. His wrists moved out over the plate, but he halted their forward motion just before they got to the black strip marking the front of the plate. The pitch missed inside. Mark Carlson called it a ball, and Posada asked for a second opinion on whether Damon had been able to check his swing. Carlson gestured down to Ed Rapuano at third, and he ruled that Damon did not go around. It was two balls and no strikes with the bases loaded.

"These two teams are like heavyweight fighters," John Henry said. "Every time you think one has the other knocked out, he hits back."

Senator Mitchell's car had stopped in front of the airport terminal, and he and his friends were waiting to hear what happened to Damon before Mitchell ran in to catch his flight.

Rivera came back with a good, live cutter for a strike, and then another cut fastball inside. Damon swung and fouled it off and it rolled all the way down to ballgirl Kasey Lindsey, past the outstretched hands of three different fans who were leaning out over the tarp (minus its Marriott ad). She quickly grabbed it and gave it to the kid she'd picked out a moment earlier.

The battle between Rivera and Damon was getting really interesting. Damon had an extra gleam in his eyes, and bobbed the head of his bat back and forth in the air with a little extra intensity, ready to protect the plate with a short, chopping swing, if that was what it took. But Rivera missed way high with his next pitch. Full count. All three runners would be running on the pitch.

Rivera moved his hands slowly downward in front of him, the

way he did with every pitch, and then started his motion. Varitek broke from third base, Damian Jackson broke from second base, and Merloni broke from first base. It was another cutter, low and inside. Damon was just able to foul it off to keep the at-bat going. The ball was borderline, and might have been ball four, but Damon was not about to put the game in the hands of Mark Carlson. No, he would force Rivera to pitch to him and get a hit, or let him walk him on a pitch he was sure about, if that was how it was going to go.

Damon stepped out of the box and stared up into the crowd, licking his lips. It looked to him as if Rivera was throwing better than he had against the Red Sox all year. He was just having trouble throwing strikes, because his ball was moving too much. But sometimes you could be effectively wild.

Rivera shook Posada off once. He did not want to throw the straight fastball. Again, he moved his hands slowly down in front of him and corkscrewed his body for the pitch, and Varitek, Jackson, and Merloni all started running. There was motion around Rivera in every direction. He wanted to challenge Damon with a high cutter, and strike him out and head back to the dugout with the Yankees still ahead 8–6.

But Rivera's pitch was no challenge. It was way too high, not even close. Damon watched it go for ball four, and the Red Sox were within one run.

"We've got a chance!" Senator Mitchell told his friends just before hurrying in through the entrance to the departures terminal.

John Henry covered his eyes, showing how relieved he was, and turned to look through the glass partition and into the .406

Club next door. He lifted his arms up and urged everyone inside to stand up and cheer.

"Has Rivera ever walked in a run before?" Theo Epstein wondered aloud.

Down in the Yankee dugout, the color had drained out of Joe Torre's face. He looked waxier than he had even just a few minutes earlier. His eyes were pointed out toward the field, but his stare seemed directed miles away. He slowly reached up a hand and started scratching his ear in slow motion.

Posada was not happy. He headed out to the mound for a talk with Rivera, and his expression was angry.

"We have to get this out!" he told Rivera sharply, staring into his eyes to emphasize how serious he was. "Just calm down and concentrate."

All season long, Rivera had only walked seven batters. Now in one day he had walked two in the same inning. The last time he had done that was more than a year earlier. What was going on?

"The league's leading hitter comes up," John Henry said, doing his sportscaster voice. "The stretch, the hesitation, the pitch."

Rivera started Bill Mueller off with a good, hard cutter for a strike, right over the heart of the plate. He was throwing with everything he had now. His next pitch was another cutter, but this one was up and in. Mueller hung in there as long as he could, and then ducked out of the way at the last second, jerking away so suddenly he lost his balance and almost fell backward. He took one step, two, three—soon he had taken six quick steps and backed up all the way out of the dirt hitting circle and had one foot on the grass. He stood there a moment, collecting himself and trying to act as if it was the most normal thing in the world to end up there.

Grady Little turned to his bench coach, Jerry Narron, sitting right next to him in the Red Sox dugout as he always did at key moments in the game, so he could be ready to discuss any fine points of strategy or matchups that Little might be kicking around in his head.

"Jerry," Little said. "Is there anybody else on the ballclub you'd rather have up here right now?"

Narron's answer was immediate.

"No," he said.

"Me, either," Little said.

Posada glared out at Rivera and punched his mitt once hard, real hard, and then again more softly. He put down the signal for a cutter, and Rivera delivered it thigh-high and out over the plate. Mueller fouled it off to make it 1-2.

"Oooh!" Theo Epstein called out, as if he had been hit in the stomach. "Great pitch to hit right down the middle."

The next time, Rivera shook off Posada and came in with a letter-high cutter that Mueller fouled off. He looked at his bat to make sure it had not cracked, twisted it this way and that, just to be sure, and then just kept staring, as if he was wondering if someone had slipped him a different piece of lumber.

Rivera reared and let loose with another high, inside cutter up out of the zone. This was ninety-five miles an hour and up around Mueller's neck. But it did not look like it was going to be that high as it came out of Rivera's hand. Mueller was ready to swing at a high cutter, and hit a high cutter. This one just happened to be higher than he expected. It moved side to side, too, which made it harder to locate. He swung and made contact, too, just getting a piece of it. He immediately turned to see if Posada had been able to hang on to the ball. He had, and that was it. Inning over. Mueller had struck out.

"Ohh, ohhh, the Evil Empire!" John Henry said to Lucchino.

He clasped his hands together, not sure what to do or say or even what to think next.

"He's still got to pitch the ninth," John Henry said finally. "Or maybe not."

TOP OF THE NINTH

	1	2	3	4	5	6	7	8	9	R
NYY	0	0	2	3	0	0	0	3		8
BOSTON	3	0	1	0	0	0	0	*3*		7

The Red Sox were a team with more than their share of quirky personalities: Garciaparra with his elaborate routines, before and during a game, actually watching the clock to time just when he would put on his jock strap over his Calvins; Manny Ramirez, the slugger lost in his own world much of the time, and still so unwilling ever to worry what a pitcher might throw him; Pedro Martinez, the pitching genius, whose mercurial talent had taken him so far but somehow had done nothing to change his dark worldview. But of all the diverse personalities who came together in the Red Sox clubhouse, the one least understood by his teammates, the coaching staff and front office, and, quite possibly, himself, was the submarining pitcher Byung-Hyun Kim.

No one questioned his talent. He had a great slider, and when he was putting the ball where he wanted, he could be devastating. But a major-leaguer was in part the sum of his past experiences in big games, and few histories were as lurid as Kim's. There was Kim in a Diamondbacks uniform, one out away from closing out the Yankees, giving up that two-run, game-tying homer to Tino Martinez in Game Four of the 2001 World Series. There was Kim in that same memorable game at Yankee Stadium, setting down the first two Yankee batters in the tenth and watching Derek Jeter foul off three two-strike pitches before Jeter hit a game-winning, opposite-field home run just after midnight. And there, of course, was Kim back at Yankee Stadium less than twenty-four hours later, again trying to protect a two-run lead, but instead giving up another two-run, game-tying homer, this time to Scott Brosius with two outs in the ninth, prompting Joe Torre to say, "It's *Groundhog Day.*" Kim watched the ball go and squatted down on the mound, legs trembling, face contorted, fighting back tears.

All that prime-time trauma had left Kim with a complex, but it was not an easy one to sort out. He struck many as childlike in the extreme, but not in the happy-child style of Manny Ramirez. Out in the bullpen, he sometimes liked to kid around, but he never quite seemed to connect with his teammates. His pride in his ability too often came across as aloofness. He swung between extremes, sometimes too confident, other times too morose. All that was clear was that where Kim was concerned, just as where Pedro Martinez was concerned, it was necessary to travel far away from Boston to gain any insight.

Kim had problems, but he also had heart. That might not have been obvious to his Red Sox teammates, but it was to his high-school coach, Heo Sae-hwan. Coach Heo always knew Kim had a big future in baseball. Just how big became clear Kim's last game at Kwangju Jeil High. Kim already had seventeen strikeouts when coach Heo went out to the mound to offer to take him out of the game. Kim said no way, thank you very much. He was determined to finish his last game. He did, and wound up striking out nineteen that day. Kim was always sure of his own abilities, but he was also quiet and shy. If he was not out on the baseball field, he liked to spend his time sitting in a corner by himself listening to music on his Walkman. Coach Heo knew that Kim was still very shy and sometimes he worried about him. It was hard to be a foreigner pitching in the big leagues. There could be misunderstandings.

Back home in South Korea, they called Kim the Nuclear Submarine and followed his every move. (As the nickname made clear, South Koreans were not nearly as jumpy over North Korea's nuclear weapons program as many Americans seemed to be.) If one of Kim's games was on South Korean TV, people everywhere would watch. They would gather at bus stops and train stations to watch TVs hastily set up for the game. Stockbrokers would use one of their transaction screens to tune in to the game.

Kim was actually embarrassed when he came home to South Korea after the Diamondbacks won the 2001 World Series, and so many people made such a fuss over him. He felt the most comfortable when he went back to Kwangju Jeil High School and played soccer with the baseball team.

"Going to the show is all about fighting one's self," Kim told the youngsters.

Given the eleven-hour time difference between the Korean peninsula and the East Coast of the United States, a day game in Boston did not start until after 2:00 a.m. Korea time, but that was OK with coach Heo. He didn't mind missing out on some sleep to watch the Red Sox against the Yankees.

Heo played amateur baseball and went to work in 1992 as baseball coach at Kwangju Jeil High School, where he had earlier graduated. Kwangju was a major industrial city near the southern tip of the Korean peninsula, and had a population of more than 1.4 million. Over his first seven seasons, coach Heo's teams won three national championships. That success led to a job at a different school for a few years. Now he was back at Kwangju Jeil High, which had fielded a baseball team since 1923, just five years after the school was founded.

Coach Heo had coached some very good players at Kwangju Jeil High, including Hee Seop Choi, who was with the Chicago Cubs. Jae Weong Seo was having a good season with the New York Mets. Coach Heo was not a man who bragged. He only talked about his success if someone pushed him with specific questions. But for Koreans, prestige and status in the workplace were closely tied to alumni connections. A *seonbae,* someone who had graduated from a school earlier, was honor bound to take extra care of a *hubae,* someone who had graduated from the school later. Coach Heo took great pride in having gone to two of the same schools as Kim—Mudeung Middle School, and Kwangju Jeil High School.

Coach Heo did not think Kim would make it into that Saturday's game between the Yankees and Red Sox. The game had been wild and back and forth, so you never knew, but it looked like the

Yankees were in control. Coach Heo thought several times about turning off the TV in his small room at the Kwangju Jeil High training facility and getting some sleep. He had a simple room with a desk and a bed and not much else, up on the second floor, and the players lived all around him. That was typical for Korea. Especially before an important game or tournament, the coach and all the players lived together, right next to the field, so they could stay focused on baseball all the time.

Coach Heo was disappointed Pedro Martinez had lasted only four innings—he considered his pitching an art form. He was also fascinated by David Ortiz and his combination of bulk and a smooth, compact swing.

"If Korean players were big like him, we would have more playing in the majors," he said, sitting in front of his TV.

When the Yankees took their four-run lead in the eighth, coach Heo told himself it had been a mistake to stay up so late to watch the game. Kim definitely wouldn't be pitching that day. But he had watched so much of the game, and it was the Yankees and the Red Sox. Then Boston came right back to make it a one-run game. Now there was a chance Kim would pitch. The Korean broadcast came back from a commercial break and there was Kim on the mound to start the top of the ninth inning. Coach Heo was very proud.

Not every Red Sox fan was happy to see Kim out on the mound now against the Yankees, though. There was no telling what the Red Sox could do against Rivera, and it was important to hold the deficit to just one run and see what happened. Pulling off a win now, after everything, would make this a great game and a great win. It would cost Mariano Rivera something that might not be so easy to get back. But Theo Epstein, for one, liked the move.

"Your best reliever should be used in the highest-leverage situations," Epstein said. "This is it."

Spike Lee was ecstatic to see Kim out there.

"Bring him in!" he was calling out, even before Kim came to the mound. "Bring Kim in! He's the worst. I love when they bring him in."

One of the sillier old saws in baseball was that any time someone went out late in the game to take over in the infield, the ball found him. Funny how many old baseball men believed in that sort of thing. Kim looked in for the sign and dropped down for his pitch to Bernie Williams, and threw him a slider that broke sharply over the outside corner of the plate. Williams swung and grounded it to Todd Walker, who had just taken over at second base after pinch-hitting for Gabe Kapler. One down, two to go.

"That's my boy," coach Heo said in Kwangju. "I knew he would be like that."

That brought up Hideki Matsui. Kim needed to work on his mound presence. He was small, which made it difficult to look imposing, so instead he went for an impish look out there. He stood, hip cocked, head ducking to the side, and went into his odd motion, dropping down and flinging the ball toward the plate from an awkward angle. His first pitch to Matsui was a fastball low and away. Matsui fouled it off. Kim came right back with a changeup on the outside corner.

Matsui thought it might have missed low, but when Mark Carlson gave the signal that it was a strike, Matsui did not complain. Instead, he practically whistled, pursing his lips for several seconds and replaying the pitch in his mind. If Kim had his changeup working like that, he was going to be difficult to hit. Matsui knew how important it was to get on base and start some kind of rally. The Red Sox had already wiped out three-quarters of the Yankee lead of an inning earlier, and Rivera had thrown a lot of pitches and had also had trouble finding the strike zone at times. They needed to put at least one more run on the board.

Kim came back with the same pitch in the same place and Matsui was waiting for it. He reached out and tried to hit it up the middle and into center field, but did not make good contact. The ball bounced past Kim and slowly up the middle. Walker had the best play on it, but for some reason he moved sideways instead of aggressively cutting the ball off. He was too late to have a shot at Matsui at first by the time he gloved it.

"If Merloni's at second, that's an out!" shouted a fan sitting behind Eleanor and Bob Adair.

Matsui, standing at first now, agreed. He considered it a lucky hit. Nothing wrong with that. Everyone needed a little luck now and then. Maybe the *katsu* had come through for him after all.

"This is not good," coach Heo said in Kwangju, 6,798 miles away from Fenway Park.

The crowd was quiet as Jorge Posada readied himself near the batter's box. Coach Heo shook his head.

"BK is in trouble," he said. "Catchers know how to win the ball count."

Kim went into his stretch and threw over to first base, even though Matsui had only tried to steal second base twice all year.

Then he dropped down low for his first pitch to Posada, and missed outside with a low changeup. Kim's next pitch was a slider over the inside part of the plate, and Posada seemed surprised to see it, letting it go for strike one. Kim came back with what looked like the same changeup he had thrown Matsui for a strike. Mark Carlson thought it just missed. Here and there fans who were not already exhausted from an afternoon of yelling let loose with a few deep-in-the-gut boos.

"That's right where Nelson's was!" Theo Epstein cried out.

Epstein was visibly tense now in a way that he usually tried hard to avoid. He pulled his keys out of his pocket and fiddled with them, and folded his right hand under his left arm, as if he was worried it might keep wandering around on its own. Not having gotten the call on the outside corner, Kim came back with a belt-high fastball in on the hands. Posada fouled it back to make it 2-2.

This time, Matsui was going. Torre had called for a hit-and-run. Kim's delivery was another low changeup out over the edge of the plate, and Posada fouled it back to stay alive. Another changeup away dipped way low to make it three balls and two strikes. Matsui would definitely be breaking with the pitch, and might be able to score on a double. Kim glanced over at him and looked in for the sign. He didn't like what he saw, and shook Varitek off. Kim came back with another slider, trying to hit the corner again, but did not get the ball out far enough or down low enough. Posada had been waiting for Kim to leave a slider up. He crushed it.

"That's outta here," Theo Epstein said immediately after Posada made contact.

Johnny Damon also knew right away that it was gone, and

watched it land beyond the Wall. Posada had his second homer of the day and the Yankees had a three-run lead.

"He should not have gone to a full count," coach Heo said sadly. "He's going to get a lot of heat for that one. Red Sox fans are tough."

Theo Epstein was standing shaking his head.

"He just hung a slider," Epstein said. "He's had trouble with it the last couple weeks."

John Henry watched the ball carry well over Damon's head and bounce around until it ended up with a fan. Henry wanted to see the fan throw it back onto the field, just as Marty Martin had done a few minutes before he was escorted from the premises by a security detail. Henry got what he wanted, and more.

"Did you see that?" he asked. "They threw the ball back and Damon got the ball and threw it over the Green Monster?"

Out in the outfield, the crowd was revved up by the small act of defiance. The feeling passed quickly, though. The Adairs looked around and noticed how deflated the fans suddenly seemed.

"I'm afraid it's going to end in a whimper," Eleanor Adair said.

Spike Lee was just glad he had been there to see how this one had turned out. You just never knew with these two teams.

"That's the thing I love about sports," he said. "I mean, in movies the outcome is dictated."

Even outside the ballpark, the disappointed roar of the crowd was unmistakable. Marty Martin and his brother had found their way back to the bus, and were standing in front following the game on the radio. Martin wished he had been inside to have a chance at catching Posada's second homer, too.

"That guy's good," he said to his brother.

Larry Lucchino was still sitting in his director's chair in Henry's box. He looked down at the stat sheet he had been poring over.

"John, you see the matchup?" Lucchino asked Henry. "Posada was 0-for-4 lifetime against Kim."

Henry cocked his head slightly, the way he often did, one of his eyes suddenly looking more alert. It was a way he had both of listening more closely and also gently challenging a listener.

"You think that's statistically significant?" Henry asked.

"It was to the manager," Lucchino said.

Coach Heo waited for the TV to show Kim going to work on the next batter, and waited and waited. Korean television had cut away from the game after Posada's homer. It was not coming back.

BOTTOM OF THE NINTH

	1	2	3	4	5	6	7	8	9	R
NYY	0	0	2	3	0	0	0	3	*2*	10
BOSTON	3	0	1	0	0	0	0	3		7

The Red Sox had the ideal batter coming up to lead off the bottom of the ninth. Nomar Garciaparra already had three hits and had drilled that ball to left that everyone thought was a home run. Against Mariano Rivera, Garciaparra was an incredible six for twelve. Rivera's first pitch was a cutter in on the hands and Garciaparra jumped on it, but got under it. Matsui drifted over to catch the fly ball for the first out.

David Ortiz always enjoyed himself, no matter what was going on in the game, and he bounced out to the beat of some dance music and blew a big bubble just before Rivera wound and made his first pitch. It was a fastball that caught the outside corner for strike one. Ortiz stared out at the mound, blowing a smaller bubble this time. He fouled off an inside cutter, and then Rivera uncorked a fastball that flew over everyone's heads and back to the screen behind home plate. Mark Carlson and Jorge Posada both spun around to watch it fly. There was a strange fascination to watching a ball thrown that hard just keep buzzing past the batter and hit the netting on the fly.

Ortiz stepped out and readjusted his wristbands and tried not to think too much about what Rivera's wildness could mean for him. He stepped back in and foul-tipped a cutter in on his hands and up, and Posada could not quite hold on, so Ortiz was still alive. He stood and waited, blowing no bubbles now, and seemed surprised to see an inside cutter. He fought it off and singled to center to give the fans something to murmur about.

Kevin Millar fouled off the first pitch he saw, a good cutter over the inside part of the plate, and then jerked his neck away from the ball and swung at a pitch well outside. Rivera was cruising now. He just wanted to get through this, the sooner the better. He came back with a cut fastball on the outside part of the plate. Millar dropped the head of the bat on the ball and sent a deep fly down the first-base line toward the Pesky Pole. Ortiz lumbered down toward second, trying to get in position to make it to third, and waited to see if Juan Rivera would be able to get to the ball. He could not. It bounced a few inches to the right of the foul line.

Rivera had kept the ball in the strike zone on his first 0-2 pitch, but now he knew Millar would swing at anything close, so he took advantage. He put another cutter off the plate a few inches and Millar strained to reach his bat out to make contact. He hit a little nubber to the right side of the infield and Nick Johnson hardly had to move. He stood still, leaned to the right, and took five quick steps over to first base to record the out unassisted.

This was not Los Angeles. No one was leaving early. Then again, no one was fully there anymore, either. They had checked out, chalked this one up as yet another painful loss, and now they were just waiting to take care of a few stray details in the stories they could tell themselves and other people about how the Red Sox would always find a way to lose the big games, no matter how good they were, no matter how much they deserved to win.

Varitek came up next. He had four hits in ten chances against Rivera, but was not quite right at the plate that day, as Theo Epstein had noted earlier.

"Jason Varitek is in a slump," John Henry said. "But every once in a while he hits a home run."

Rivera called Posada out for a brief exchange and then quickly set himself and delivered, throwing a cutter down the middle that missed high for ball one. Rivera came back with another cutter, this one lower and more inside. Varitek made good contact, but Nick Johnson gloved it without much trouble and flipped to Rivera, running over to cover first base. The ballgame was over.

The flow of fans streaming out of Fenway was lethargic. People took small steps and looked down a lot. They traded familiar wisecracks and complaints about life as a Red Sox fan. Most of these people had long résumés of tough Sox losses they had been there to see. This would crack the list, but there was plenty of time to mull over just how high to rank it.

Peter Farrelly thought the game was a great introduction for Bob. It offered a full supply of everything that being a Sox fan had represented to Farrelly his whole life. There were ups and downs. There was huge excitement. There was a ton of hitting and lackluster pitching. It all came down to the last pitch, where the Sox always, inevitably, sadly, lost. The game offered a microcosm of Farrelly's whole career as a Red Sox fan, and that was as it should be. No matter how painful it had been, and it had been painful, being a Sox fan had brought him much more joy than pain.

Farrelly had friends who went so far as to warn their kids off the Sox.

"Don't root for them," kids all over Red Sox Nation were told. "They'll kill you. They killed my father. So pick another team."

That was not how Farrelly felt. He was glad to be passing the Sox along to Bob. He was glad his four-year-old son was tuning in to what it felt like to be a Sox fan.

"Dad, why do the Yankees always win?" Bob asked as they were leaving Fenway.

Farrelly's first thought was to tell his son that there were more people in New York City and they prayed harder. But that would inspire a lot more questions.

"They have more money, Bob," he said.

"What do you mean?"

"Just accept that they have more money. That will help you feel better."

POSTSCRIPT: MANNY AT THE RITZ, LATER THAT NIGHT

Joe Torre had suffered through an eighth inning that felt to him like torture. The biggest question in his mind was whether Manny Ramirez would come out to pinch-hit. Torre's baseball imagination summoned images of Ramirez hobbling out like Kirk Gibson and one-handing a homer that would turn the game around and send the crowd into giddy convulsions. John Henry, too, had sat in his private box behind home plate and quietly noted that you would have thought that no matter how sick he was, Manny Ramirez could have gotten out of bed and showed up at Fenway just to pinch-hit. Theo Epstein had clung to a similar hope that no matter what his medical people said, Ramirez would come back to

Fenway and step up to the plate one time and make the difference for the Red Sox.

It did not happen. Ramirez never appeared in the game. That night, he felt well enough to socialize with a Yankee player, Enrique Wilson, at the Ritz Carlton. Word leaked out to the press, and Boston was scandalized. Ramirez did not seem to care about winning. He did not seem to burn with passion to beat the hated Yankees. He skipped a doctor's appointment the morning after hanging out with Wilson, and sat out the entire three-game series against the Yankees. He made things worse when he rejoined the Red Sox the next day for a makeup game in Philadelphia but announced he was unavailable even for pinch-hitting duty because he felt weak.

The furor over Ramirez's Saturday night Ritz appearance soon threatened to ruin the season. Teammates were upset. Club officials seethed. Fans wondered whether Ramirez was just scheming for a trade to the Yankees. It was an ugly situation and threatened to turn uglier. That was when Grady Little did something that surprised everyone. Even when Ramirez was finally ready to play when the team moved on to Chicago for a series against the White Sox, Little told him: Thanks, but no thanks. Little told him, in so many words: We would rather lose without you today than win with you, that's how disgusted we all are with you.

Ramirez could not believe it. But to the rest of the Red Sox, Little's show of toughness was the defining moment of the season. Little was not managing scared. He was going to do what he had to do, no matter the consequences. There were certain things he just could not tolerate, and that was true whether the offender was making twenty million a year, or ninety-five grand.

Fans and the media spent a lot of time the rest of the season celebrating the way the Red Sox had come together. They talked a lot about Kevin Millar and his good-natured "Cowboy Up" shtick. They talked a lot about a clubhouse full of players working together to keep something going, no matter how bleak a particular game might look. That fun-loving, fight-back-no-matter-what style was no mere media creation, and it showed when the Red Sox found themselves one game away from dropping the American League Divisional Series to the Oakland A's. They came back to win three straight games, pulling off unforgettable victories against the odds.

The dynamic at play the last six weeks of the Red Sox season called to mind the sort of thing that Barry Bonds had once talked about. The fans and the media tend to focus on the snapshot at the end, the outcome, and not see or not look for the events that set up that outcome. This was probably inevitable. But now and then, it was possible to identify the deeper explanation.

Ramirez's Ritz gaffe and the fallout it generated gave Grady Little an opportunity to make a strong statement, and his willingness to do that altered the dynamic of the season. As much fun as fans had second-guessing a manager's moves during a game, there was no question that the job of managing a big-league ballclub had mostly to do with what you did behind closed doors between games. A fan had every right to follow along with a manager's moves and pipe up if he disagreed. That was part of the fun of being a fan. But it was a good idea to keep in mind that the fan was not always privy to all that a manager had to consider.

"I've been a broadcaster, and there are a lot of things that come to mind that you question," Joe Torre said. "But you know what? The manager is the only one to know the temperature of his own team. There is never one clear-cut move to make. There are always options. And a lot of times when it seems like the clear-cut thing to do and it doesn't work, it doesn't mean it was the wrong thing to do."

The job of managing a big-league team gets more aggravating every year as players make more and more money. Simply put, riches breed selfishness. Different managers find different ways to influence high-priced stars notoriously difficult to influence. Some posture and rant. Some keep their private talks private. How they manage the personalities they need behind them remains a mystery not only to fans and media but also in many cases to the players themselves.

If a manager does not keep them guessing, he has probably lost their respect, and a manager who loses his team soon loses his job, too. Grady Little showed in his handling of Ramirez that he was a tough old goat, and his players respected that. He showed he could be unpredictable. He showed that his most important decision in 2003 was not, as Red Sox lore demanded it be remembered, raising his right hand or raising his left hand to bring in a reliever in place of Pedro Martinez, but rather his choice to, in effect, raise his middle finger to Manny Ramirez.

BEYOND AARON BOONE

I'm not a religious person, but spiritual. That was a religious experience, that Game Seven. When that Aaron Boone homer went out, I don't care who you were, you were hugging your fellow Yankee soulmate. I was like in a trance. I was cursing up a storm. They all looked at me like I was crazy. The cops looked at me like I was crazy. I was foaming at the mouth. I wasn't talking to anyone in particular, just screaming at the top of my lungs about how the Red Sox were never going to win.

—SPIKE LEE

No one who set foot in the Red Sox clubhouse just after Aaron Boone's Game Seven, eleventh-inning homer at Yankee Stadium will ever forget what it was like to be there. It almost hurt to be in the room with the Red Sox. It almost hurt to step into the line of sight of hunched-over players staring galaxies away. They all sat around morosely, replaying the mental pictures of that Tim Wakefield knuckler that did not knuckle, the crack of Aaron Boone's bat, and the instant certainty that the ball would land in a throng of bouncing, grinning Yankee fans.

All around the close quarters of the room, men who were paid millions of dollars to play a boy's game looked as lost as children. They had no idea just how bad the disappointment would be when it kicked in with full force that they had lost Game Seven of the American League Championship Series to the Yankees, and lost it in a way no one in baseball would ever forget.

Their millions could not help them. Call it their dirty little secret: Almost all of them cared far more about winning and losing than they let on. Even for spoiled, pampered, big-league players, a loss like this stung and stung deeply. None of the players moved. Neither did any of the reporters ushered into the room fifteen minutes after the game. It seemed indecent to probe these psyches. It already felt redundant to voice the obvious questions that would reverberate in New England throughout the long, long winter.

Only one man was moving. He went from player to player, and to some he gave hugs, to others a slap on the back. To all of them he offered words of gratitude, delivered with the understated conviction of a man who had accomplished enough in life to save his thanks for special occasions. John Henry did not join some of his players in shedding tears. He had cried joyfully back at Fenway Park when a David Ortiz deep fly fell behind Oakland right fielder Jermaine Dye, sending that playoff series back to Oakland for a deciding Game Five. But for Henry, this was no time for tears; this was a time for duty. He hugged infielder Lou Merloni, red-eyed and disoriented, and drifted toward the clubhouse door, moving like a sleepwalker.

Outside, Henry did not know what to do with himself. He took a few steps toward the dark tunnel leading to the visitors' dugout, and suddenly stopped. He turned back toward the clubhouse, and thought better of that, too. I approached Henry and asked in a low voice about his circuit around the room. He started to move his jaw, ready to form words, but none came.

Henry and I had spoken often that memorable fall, and I sat with Henry in his private box during the early innings of that wild Game Three with the Yankees, the infamous game where Pedro Martinez stiff-armed Don Zimmer to the ground and all hell broke loose. But now Henry was staring right through me. He was staring right through the concrete walls behind me, like a man who just wanted to know when this sudden dizziness and disorientation would let up enough for him to feel his feet touching the ground again.

The answer, of course, is that it might never. Henry was five outs away from taking the Red Sox to the World Series and having a great shot at becoming the man who killed the Curse. It was a Red Sox owner, Harry Frazee, who sold Babe Ruth to the Yankees on January 5, 1920, offering an intoxicating story line to stitch together more than eight decades of Red Sox teams finding colorful ways to fall short of winning the Series. The idea that the Red Sox have been cursed ever since is a romantic notion, a story that gets told and retold until the retelling is the whole idea. To argue over whether the Curse exists is to miss the point: It exists if enough people feel that it does. It exists if Aaron Boone of all people can hit that homer to put the Yankees back in the World Series and talk afterward about the importance of ghosts.

John Henry thinks he is a man of fate. He has believed ever since he bought the Red Sox in early 2002 that it was up to him to end the Curse. He has known that the only way to do that is to win a World Series. Once Grady Little stuck with Pedro Martinez in Game Seven and it all unraveled for the Red Sox, a prevailing view took hold in New England that 2003 was in the end mostly about adding a fresh entry in the long, long roster of disappointments to pull out and work like worry stones. That is how Red Sox fans have been brought up to react, and how they will always react, until their team finally wins another World Series.

Peter Farrelly was probably not alone among Red Sox fans when he said that, six months after the Game Seven disaster, he could not even recall where he was that day, even though he can describe in detail each of the Five Most Painful Sporting Events of his life. "I swear I can't remember where I was when Grady Little left Pedro in too long," he said. "I may have been in L.A., maybe Massachusetts, possibly Texas, maybe at a bar, or a hotel room, or home. I really can't recall. And that's good. Because it means I've learned to block this shit out. I did watch the game. Somewhere. But this is all I recall: I remember never thinking for a moment that they were going to win. I remember being proud that I wasn't getting sucked in, feeling grown up."

Farrelly actually picked up the phone late in the game to call one of the nephews he had brought to the August 30 game at Fenway.

"Tommy, protect your heart," he said.

"They're gonna win," his nephew told him.

"Thomas," Farrelly said. "Protect your heart."

"They're gonna win!" Tommy said, louder now.

"Tom—they're not," Farrelly said.

"Shut up!" Tommy said. "They are too!"

Farrelly gave it one more try.

"I'm not breaking your balls here," he said. "I'm doing this for your own good. I've been hurt real bad by these guys before, real bad, and I promised myself that they would never, ever again hurt me and or anyone I loved, so I'm telling you, protect your heart."

Tommy was not persuaded.

"They're gonna win!" he screamed, and then hung up and went back to sit through a last few minutes of pleasure and hope before Aaron Boone dashed them all with that home run.

John Henry may never take Sox fans closer than they were that night, five outs away from the World Series. The topsy-turvy Game Seven with Pedro Martinez on the mound might have been his one and only shot. But I don't think so. Based on what I saw during the several months of the 2003 season I spent studying the John Henry Red Sox from up close, and helped in the preparation of this book by unprecedented access, I believe the Henry ownership group is really going to do it. That is just a guess. But one thing I picked up in nine years covering professional sports for the *San Francisco Chronicle* was a conviction that when you have a hunch about a team, or an organization, you're right often enough to trust your hunches. Bostonians would be unwise ever to go on record with such a prediction, but as an outsider, a Californian of all things, I'm willing to say it here in black and white: The Red Sox will win a World Series on Henry's watch. It may be this October. It may be next October. It may take several more years. But it will happen.

It will happen because the Henry group, led by fiery Larry Lucchino, has shown an inspired understanding of what the

George Steinbrenner–era Yankees are all about. Lucchino came right out and called the Yankees the "Evil Empire," and people around the country know what he means. The Yankees are not just a rich organization with the delusion of the rich that the things they buy are all about character. The Yankees are an organization very comfortable using any and every advantage to rub out real competition. One of these advantages is influence over how events on and off the field are presented in the national media.

Flash back to that crazy Game Three at Fenway Park. Pedro Martinez had lost it out there on the mound and thrown at Karim Garcia's head in a situation that made it way too obvious just what he was doing and why. Don Zimmer had lost it and gone after Martinez, throwing a wide, wobbly left hook before Martinez stiff-armed him and sent him toppling like a pillow in a pillow fight, as Harvey Araton memorably put it in the *Times*. A group of Yankees, probably including Jeff Nelson and Garcia, had lost it and beat up an overzealous member of the Boston grounds crew. A Yankee executive named Randy Levine had lost it, and made the mistake of venting his frustration to reporters without first checking his facts.

"There's an attitude of lawlessness that's permeating everything and it needs to be corrected," Levine said. "The events of the entire day were disgraceful and shameful and if it happened at our ballpark, we would apologize, and that's what the Red Sox should do here."

This was pure gamesmanship. The Yankees had taken a lead in the series, and they wanted a lead in public opinion, too. They saw a way to deflect some of the attention and sympathy the Red Sox get as the lovable losers everyone wants to see knock off the big, bad Yankees. They knew it would be to their benefit to position themselves as victims. They fully expected the national press to bury the Red Sox, and in the avalanche of negative stories, Red Sox players would have even more trouble shaking off a difficult loss and making a series out of it. The Yankees have won so often before, they use inevitability as a weapon.

That was where Henry, Lucchino, and Werner rolled the dice. Baseball's commissioner, Bud Selig, had issued a gag order directing teams not to comment on the mess that Game Three became. Henry, Lucchino, and Werner ignored him. They took the podium for a press conference and fired right back at Levine's charges. Henry, a man with a dry sense of humor, good-naturedly mocked the Yankees. "I spoke with Randy yesterday," he said. "I didn't feel it was necessary for him to apologize for his remarks or for the attack. . . . I essentially asked him to retract his statements—statements that I thought were irresponsible and probably made in the heat of the moment—and he declined to do so."

Most papers played the owners' press conference as a fiasco. The general sentiment was: How dare they? But the calculated bold move was one of the most important developments in the series. People are supposed to be afraid of George Steinbrenner, and many are. Many let themselves be influenced and intimidated by his whims in ways they barely notice. But John Henry showed he had no fear. He served notice that under his leadership, the Red Sox are proud and fierce and, most important of all, undaunted. Teams have ups and downs, and the skeptics might have been right when they said it would take the organization years to dig out from the psychic wreckage of the great disappointment of 2003.

But John Henry and Larry Lucchino didn't see it that way, and they just might have been in a position to know. They went out in the off-season and upgraded their team by adding bulldog starter Curt Schilling and closer Keith Foulke, and when they fell short in their bid to acquire Alex Rodriguez, George Steinbrenner took great glee in rubbing it in later, once Aaron Boone's pickup basketball injury prompted the Yankees to swoop in and add Rodriguez as their new third baseman. Henry had once been a part-owner of the Yankees and a friend of Steinbrenner's. Henry was known for being low-key and mild-mannered. But he released a statement reading in part, "Baseball doesn't have an answer for the Yankees. . . . Although I have never previously been an advocate of a salary cap in baseball out of respect for the players, there is really no other fair way to deal with a team that has gone insanely far beyond the resources of all other teams."

This from a billionaire owner of a team with baseball's second-highest payroll behind the Yankees. Steinbrenner fired back immediately and unforgettably.

"We understand that John Henry must be embarrassed, frustrated, and disappointed by his failure in this transaction," Steinbrenner said. "Unlike the Yankees, he chose not to go the extra distance for his fans in Boston. It is understandable, but wrong that he would try to deflect the accountability for his mistakes onto others and to a system for which he voted in favor. It is time to get on with life and forget the sour grapes."

This was, in effect, a knee to the groin. Talk about a tabloid headline waiting to happen! But if anything, the exchange confirmed that the Red Sox were setting the tone. They were turning this into a street brawl against the best street brawler around. They were trying to out-Yankee the Yankees, even if it meant turning off a lot of people in baseball, who could stomach one Steinbrenner but not these new Steinbrenneresque upstarts in Boston thumbing their noses at everyone else. The strategy might have struck some as foolhardy, but it reaped instant benefits: Interest has never been higher in the rivalry between the Red Sox and the Yankees.

Brian Cashman, watching the off-season theatrics with fascination, and from one of the best seats in the house, preferred to think of the Henry outburst as mere emotion, rather than part of an "Evil Empire" strategy.

"I wouldn't turn up the heat," Cashman said. "You mess with a beehive, you're going to get stung."

He let the words sink in.

"I think they are too smart for that," Cashman added. "The great thing about the fans of Boston is they now have fans running that team, real passionate fans that are smart. But on the short-term stuff, the negative reactions toward things that we might do with an emotional response, that just gets us more emotional. That's not healthy for everybody else. This is like Russia and the United States—we're being the United States, they are Russia—it's the two big superpowers, and now it's like: How many missiles do we need? We're going to increase our missiles, and you're going to increase your missiles. Oh, you got another one? We're going to increase ours now."

It's easy enough to see why Cashman does not like the drift of events. Who can blame him? But his vision of mutually assured destruction, baseball style, makes a lot of sense. That is just what the Henry group wants. John Henry may once have been a shy and awkward boy too timid to come out and ask the neighbor kids if he could play in a ballgame in his own yard, but he's not making that mistake again. He could not be more involved in this rivalry, and he's willing to roll up his sleeves and get a little dirty if that's what it takes. He's putting himself on the line in just about every way imaginable. If Steinbrenner challenged him to go at it mano a mano, right there between home plate and the pitcher's mound, John Henry just might surprise people and take him up on it. Imagine the ratings *that* would get.

Henry and Lucchino know that the old story line of perpetual disappointment had a potency and power that could always find a way to snatch success away from them at the last possible moment. They believe in the power of story. They believe in a narrative's ability to keep moving itself forward, even when it seems to have spent its force. So they have assembled a baseball club with great pitching and great hitting, and yet they know that the battle cannot be only on the diamond. Their verbal sparring and their Steinbrenner-like spending have helped turn this rivalry into something it never was before: a national happening. Fans in other markets may get tired of the unfairness of it all, but everyone senses that this is building toward a fascinating conclusion. The twists and turns in the rivalry have an off-the-map feel to them, and anything seems possible. As with any media spectacle, people are simultaneously annoyed to have their attention grabbed so aggressively and curious to discover whether the events themselves will live up to the hype.

"That's what sells our game," Cashman said. "Now that reality TV is so successful, people are like: Turn on a baseball game, *that's* reality TV."

The off-the-charts intensity and fan interest give the Red Sox just what they have been craving for decades: a fresh context. So the crazier this gets, the happier they are. After all, they know they are the ones willing to steer this rivalry off the road and go smashing through windows and shopping malls like Jake and Elwood Blues. The added intensity pays dividends for the Red Sox. Among other things, it guarantees that if the high-priced Yankee lineup falters against the Red Sox, a Steinbrenner back-page tongue-lashing will never be long in coming. Steinbrenner got the better of Henry in the "Sour grapes!" exchange, but sometimes losing is winning and winning is losing. The "Evil Empire" strategy of throwing everything toward the goal of beating the Yankees might or might not pay off for the Henry ownership, but they are having one hell of a time playing their hand as if they are sure they're going to get the last laugh on Steinbrenner.

Red Sox fans who talk about the decades of pain and disappointment they have suffered are really talking about something else. They are talking about the luxury of caring about something deeply. Nowhere has a deep and abiding attachment to a team been passed from generation to generation the way it has been in Boston. Most sports fans aren't so lucky. Passion like that has become rare in American life, where allegiances tend to last weeks or months. People move from state to state, picking up new teams and new loyalties and leaving others behind. Fans outfit themselves head to toe in the loud colors of their new team and scream their lungs out—on cue—in state-of-the-art stadiums and arenas. They celebrate their new teams' victories like a personal entitlement. But do they really know anything about passion without living through bleak times that test their loyalty? New England fans do, oh how they do.

NOTE ON SOURCES

The kaleidoscope effect of being in different places at the same time was achieved by having reporters in most of those places: Brian McGrory, metro columnist for the *Boston Globe* and the author of three novels, including *Dead Line,* joined Red Sox owner John Henry at his house on the morning of August 30, and followed him throughout the day. Samantha Power, a lecturer at Harvard's John F. Kennedy School of Government and author of the Pulitzer Prize–winning *"A Problem from Hell": America and the Age of Genocide,* followed Theo Epstein for the day.

Mitchell Zuckoff, an award-winning *Boston Globe* reporter and author of the forthcoming *Ponzi: The Man and His Legendary Scheme,* spent the game inside the Green Monster with Rich Maloney and the boys. John Plotz, an English professor at Brandeis, arrived at Fenway Park before sunrise and spent the day with David Mellor and the ground crew, and also was there when Theo Gordon proposed to Jane Baxter. Sean McCann, an author and Wesleyan English professor, joined Bob and Eleanor Adair at Thornton Wilder's old house in New Haven, and spent the rest of the day with the Adairs. Sarah Ringler, formerly a reporter in Berlin, Germany, spent the day with Debi Little, Grady Little's wife.

Sankei Sports Yankee correspondent Gaku Tashiro, the first Japanese sportswriter ever to be accepted as a member of the Baseball Writers Association of America, performed detailed reporting on Hideki Matsui. Andres Cala, formerly Dominican Republic correspondent for the Associated Press, spent the day with Rafael Avila in Santo Domingo. Brian Lee, a reporter for South Korea's English-language *JoongAng Daily,* spent a late night in Kwangju watching the game with Heo Sae-Hwan, Byung-Hyun Kim's coach at Kwangju Jeil High School in South Korea.

Jorge Arangure, now a baseball writer for the *Washington Post,* conducted detailed interviews with Mariano Rivera, Jorge Posada, unlucky fan Marty Martin, and many others. Amy K. Nelson, a reporter for Sports Ticker, the Associated Press, and MLB.com, rode to the game with Lou Merloni, and also talked at length with Mark Carlson and Ed Rapuano, the umpires, and Jason Varitek and Peter Farrelly. Pete Danko, formerly a *New York Times* copy clerk and *Riverside Press-Enterprise* sports columnist, also interviewed the umpires. Veteran baseball writers Pedro Gomez (now of ESPN) and Tom Keegan (now of ESPN Radio) both contributed background reporting.

Steve Kettmann organized the other reporters and spent most of August 30 with Larry Lucchino, the Red Sox CEO, and also watched portions of the game with former Senate majority leader George Mitchell, and later discussed the game in detail with Joe Torre, Brian Cashman, George Mitchell, Peter Farrelly, Marty Martin, Spike Lee, Euclides Rojas, Bill Mueller, Mark Carlson, and Grady Little.

ACKNOWLEDGMENTS

Luke Dempsey, my inspired editor at Atria, came up with the idea for this book one night at Shea, and has my unending gratitude. As a sportswriter, I often cursed agents, but Richard Abate of ICM has shifted my perspective. Thanks to Richard and his talented assistant, Kate Lee, for being so generous of their time and imagination—and fighting for this book at every turn.

I want to thank Major League Baseball, the Red Sox, and the Yankees for supporting this project. In particular, Sandy Alderson at MLB, Charles Steinberg of the Red Sox, and Rick Cerrone of the Yankees went out of their way to help; this book would not exist if not for the spirit of cooperation I encountered at every turn. My gratitude, too, to Spike Lee, Peter Farrelly, George Mitchell, Joe Torre, Brian Cashman, Larry Lucchino, and John Henry for their openness, and to Tony Massarotti, Jeff Horrigan, Gordon Edes, Tyler Kepner, and all the sportswriters who answered my endless questions. Special thanks to Pedro Gomez, David Davis, T. J. Quinn, Jason La Canfora, and Kim Komenich for reading all or parts of the manuscript and helping it considerably, and to Julian Rubinstein and Lisa Hyman for their help—and, of course, to Jill Fromm for hers.

Thanks, also, to my parents; my brother Dave, and his wife, Heather; my sister, Jan; my brother Greg and my brother Jeff—we loved baseball as a family. Finally, to Ed Beitiks: You helped me every day on this book. *Und Sarah Lisa, mein Schatz: Habe ich heute gesagt . . . ?*